Baby Rhyming Time

Linda L. Ernst

Neal-Schuman Publishers, Inc.

New York   *London*

Published by Neal-Schuman Publishers, Inc.
100 William St., Suite 2004
New York, NY 10038

Printed and bound in the United States of America.

The paper used in this publication meets the minimum requirements of American National Standard for Information Sciences—Permanence of Paper for Printed Library Materials, ANSI Z39.48-1992.

Library of Congress Cataloging-in-Publication Data

Ernst, Linda L.
　　Baby rhyming time / Linda L. Ernst.
　　　　p. cm.
　　Includes bibliographical references and indexes.
　　ISBN 978-1-55570-540-4 (alk. paper)
　1. Children's libraries—Activity programs—United States. 2. Libraries and infants—United States. 3. Libraries and toddlers—United States. 4. Libraries and caregivers—United States. 5. Early childhood education—Activity programs—United States. I. Title.

Z718.3.E76 2008
027.62'5—dc22

2007043246

Contents

Preface

It is never too early to start creating learning experiences for children. This long-known truism is now a scientifically documented fact. Continuing scientific and medical research demonstrates how important very early childhood—birth to 24 months—can be. Those who work with children now know that it is important to help children develop early literacy skills before they can learn how to read and write. Exposure to activities like rhymes, actions, and simple stories during these crucial months can have a significant positive impact on how easily a child ventures into the world of reading.

Short interactive story times for young children and their caregivers are one of the best ways to promote early literacy. In these programs the traditional rules of story time are relaxed for those who do not yet understand "proper" story time behavior, such as sitting still. Materials reflect the shorter attention spans of the participants, leaning more towards action rhymes, brief stories, and songs that allow for repetition. The programs in *Baby Rhyming Time* focus on infants (newborn to 12 months) and young toddlers (12 to 24 months). The term "caregiver" here refers to the adult accompanying the child at the program.

Baby Rhyming Time provides both a conceptual framework and proven effective, fun programming activities and resources. It is also designed to familiarize librarians with resources, concepts, and terminology important for understanding early literacy development. Readers will learn about current research data on brain development and language acquisition, how to work effectively and sensitively with young children and their families, and how to support early literacy throughout the library. Also covered are topics that have attracted great interest in recent years, such as using manual signing to communicate with the preverbal child, using movement to assist brain development, and the importance of play in young children's lives.

Throughout the book, examples show how the ideas discussed really work. The section on how to relate to caregivers offers specific suggested phrases. The chapter on books includes tips on how to use the books and ideas for themes that might be considered. Programming for infants and toddlers should be both practical and solidly based in knowledge and research about how children learn and how best to serve their needs. The ultimate goal is always to help the baby and the adult caregiver successfully explore the world of language together. The books, rhymes, games, music, and activities highlighted here also facilitate mutually satisfying literacy experiences for the adult and child at home. Everyday life and routines are the first environments where learning takes place.

As fields of study concerning the very young child increasingly overlap and converge, librarians and educators must expand their knowledge beyond the traditional boundaries of their own professions. Librarians may be called upon to teach parents and caregivers, educators may need to develop more in-depth knowledge of biological development, and parents want to know it all. The more knowledgeable those who work with children become about child development, the greater the potential for productive networking, grant sharing, partnerships, and data collection among different agencies and organizations—all to the benefit of the very young.

Organization

Part I, "Baby Rhyming Time Basics," lays out the fundamentals behind programming for infants and toddlers. Chapter 1, "Understanding How Baby Learns," introduces the reader to information on child development and how the brain works, especially in the first 24 months. Chapter 2, "Meeting the Cast," discusses the unique needs of different types of families and outlines the presenter's role. Chapter 3, "Setting the Stage," looks at how the library as a whole can support early literacy, examining topics like facilities, collections, staffing, partnerships, and seeking additional funding. Chapter 4, "Finding Answers: Baby Rhyming Time FAQ," addresses fundamental questions about how to undertake programming for young children. Chapter 5, "Creating Successful Story Times," delves deeper into the specifics of a baby rhyming time program from beginning to end, including how to strike a balance between energetic and quieter activities and how to avoid overstimulating the audience.

Part II, "Baby Rhyming Time Programs," offers ideas and resources for infant and toddler story times as well as full-fledged programs. Chapter 6, "Books That Work," offers up an annotated selection of books that both entertain and educate young children. Chapter 7, "Rhymes and More Rhymes," details suggested actions and finger plays for both classic and less familiar rhymes. Chapter 8, "Music That Works," emphasizes the importance of sound and rhythm for young children and lists excellent recordings, music books, and other music resources. Chapter 9, "Great Programming Enhancement Ideas," covers many other elements that could be incorporated into a successful program for infants and toddlers: games, puppets, balls, flannel boards, bubbles, and more. Chapter 10, "A Dozen Ready-to-Go Programs," contains a dozen full scripts for programs and a dozen detailed outlines that can be adapted to fit a particular situation. Chapter 11, "More Programming Ideas," provides a jumping off point for brainstorming by listing books by topic and rhymes by type (tickling, stretching, etc.). Chapter 12, "Handouts, Displays, and Signs," guides the reader in creating effective and eye-catching visuals.

The accompanying CD-ROM features audio recordings of most of the rhymes included in the book—look for the 🆑 icon next to the titles mentioned in the text. It also includes a selection of handouts and signs that can be reproduced as is or edited to fit particular needs.

In addition to the positive benefits for the child, offering early childhood programming can help create a relationship between the family and the library from the start. A caregiver who comes to the library for a Baby Rhyming Time program has an opportunity to learn about the many other services the library has to offer. An infant or toddler who participates in Baby Rhyming Time programs learns to see the library as a fun and educational place to be, an attitude we can hope will persist for a lifetime.

Acknowledgments

A book such as this can only be created with the help of countless people willing to share their knowledge and expertise. All of the children's librarians and early childhood educators around the world who share the stories, rhymes, and songs in the public domain through the oral tradition, along with other adults who have kept these alive for new generations, deserve heartfelt thanks.

Thanks to the Children's Librarians of the King County Library System in Washington who allowed me to observe their programs and examine their collections, and who were more than willing to share their ideas, concerns, handouts, and programs while serving as a sounding board for this text. Extra thanks to Shannon Schinagl for sharing her actual program outlines and handouts and to Jeani Littrel-Quik for her input. To the wonderful staff of the Newport Way Library who supported me in this endeavor, all I can say is thank you.

I am ever so grateful to Nancy Stewart of Friends Street Music for her willingness to share materials from *Plant a Little Seed, Little Songs for Little Me,* and *Baby Rattle & Roll* along with her patience and guidance with my first-time recording experience. Christine Roberts of Nurturing Pathways showed me a different way to use action rhymes and movement and for that I thank her.

My thanks to Jane Cobb of Vancouver, British Columbia, author of *What'll I Do with the Baby-O?,* Tess Prendergast, and Kathryn Lee for their enthusiasm and willingness to exchange ideas across the border.

I also need to extend thanks across the waters and acknowledge the members of the Australian Library and Information Association Children and Youth Services listserv (otherwise known as "aliaCYSS") for their willingness to exchange ideas and resources. An additional thank you goes to the Children's Team at Launceston Library, Tasmania, Australia, for permission to include their program for mixed ages; Zoe Lewis and the Adelaide Hills Council Library Service in South Australia for allowing the *Baby Bounce & Rhyme* booklet Web site to be included; and Narelle Adams and the Parramatta City

Council Information and Library Services in New South Wales, Australia, for use of "Bibs 'n' Books" materials.

Since children's librarians around the world have the same amazing characteristic of exchanging ideas and materials great effort was made to give credit where credit is due. Acknowledgments can also be found in the text for specific contributions. My apologies if any omissions were unintentionally made.

On practical matters, thanks to Carole Woodard whose skill in indexing makes this text more accessible.

Cheryl Hadley, an incredible friend, has my heartfelt thanks for everything, especially her ever-ready red pen.

To all the children and families who attend my programs for the very young, a great big thank you.

My family and friends have my never-ending gratitude and thanks for their constant encouragement, support, and love, for I could not have done this without them.

Finally, this book is dedicated to all those who bring joy into our lives, especially my faithful friend, Buddy.

Introduction

With all there is to do, expanding the traditional role of the library to include infants and the very young child may seem like a low priority, but programs for the very young offer many benefits for all concerned: the child, the caregiver, and the library.

- Since research has shown children begin life already learning, story times provide quality stimulation for brain growth and development.
- Offering infants and very young children a positive experience that they can repeatedly share with their caregivers helps children build a foundation for learning and success in the future.
- By regularly bringing the very young to the library, the adult establishes a pattern of using the public library. As the child grows, the library develops into a place of lifetime learning.
- Reaching out to non-traditional library users through non-traditional library services helps parents prepare their children to succeed.
- By offering programs for the very young, the library becomes a place where families with very young children are accepted and infant, toddler and preschool behavior is understood and tolerated.
- Programs for the very young are another way of showing that the library is a useful and positive place, thereby gaining community support for both the specific programs and the library in general.
- The library shows itself worthy of being "invited to the table," along with early childhood educators, health departments, etc., for discussion and interaction with local, state and federal governments evaluating the importance of programs for early childhood development and education.

In examining the history of library services for children, Virginia Walter sees three elements that have remained constant throughout: (1) the concept of child as reader, (2) outreach to the unserved or underserved, and (3) a renewed commitment to accountability and managerial excellence (Walter, 2001). Story time, originally designed to introduce schoolage children to literature, has broadened to include children under the age of five. The socializing and entertainment elements are no longer enough; education and role modeling have now supplemented them.

Early literacy skill development has become a component of story time, supported by the Public Library Association/Association for Library Services to Children initiative and research that led to the creation of the "Every Child Ready to Read @ Your Library" program. Story time has developed to the point of becoming, as Lynn McKechnie of the University of Western Ontario Information and Media Studies explains, an "information ground" (McKechnie, 2004). McKechnie discovered through observing actual story times, interviewing participants, and examining research in the field, that many things were happening in story times for the very young. Participants informally exchanged a wide variety of information, the presenter and participants read aloud to children, children developed physical and social skills, and early literacy skills were encouraged and developed. Behaviors once deemed disruptive really indicated the children's involvement with the stories, rhymes, and people around them. Story time has become an essential component of library service to children preschool-age and younger.

Becoming a Nation of Readers: The Report of the Commission on Reading states that the "single most important activity for building the knowledge required for eventual success in reading is reading aloud to children" (Anderson, et al., 1985: 23). Research has documented that children's development is impacted by all that is around them from birth (see Chapter 1). Taking time to share a story creates an intimate connection and bond between child and adult. Reading aloud teaches vocabulary, grammar, and dialogue in an enjoyable manner and the lessons can be easily repeated at any time. Being read to can encourage the very young child to become the best that he or she can be.

In today's economy, the budget more than likely is tight. Public money must cover an enormous range of community needs. Private grants and foundations can sometimes help support public library services, but may not be available to everyone. However, time and money spent developing programs and outreach for the very young are well worth it. Such programs bring nontraditional users into the library, make children and their caregivers aware of books and the library, demonstrate that public libraries and their services are free, reach out to those who need library services the most, and help build a supportive clientele for the future.

Sharing Information

Sharing information is one of the things children's librarians do very, very well. Our field has grown to include knowledge of not only children's literature but also

- child development (for example, determining age appropriateness when selecting story time materials),

- brain research (for example, understanding what is happening to an infant's mind when the child is sung to or touched),
- socialization (for example, understanding how sharing nursery rhymes and stories can strengthen the bond between adult and very young child),
- communication (for example, using alternate forms of communication, such as sign language, to help preverbal children communicate).

Encouraging exchange among these various fields of study nurtures the scientific research and data we need to support the importance of our programs, enriches us with information and experiences, and helps build unified support for children's success. Elements of all these fields are included in *Baby Rhyming Time*.

Why story time for the very young? Because it is an early literacy learning experience that just happens to be a lot of fun for everyone!

Resources

Anderson, Richard C., Elfrieda H. Hiebert, Judith A. Scott, and Ian A. G. Wilkinson. 1985. *Becoming a Nation of Readers: The Report of the Commission on Reading*. Urbana–Champaign, IL: Center for the Study of Reading.

Hart, Betty and Todd Risley. 1996. *Meaningful Differences in the Everyday Experience of Young American Children*. Baltimore, MD: Brookes Publishing.

McKechnie, Lynn. 2004. "The Young Child/Adult Caregiver Storytime Program as Information Ground." Paper presented at Library Research Seminar III, Kansas City, MO, October.

Public Library Association/Association for Library Services to Children. 2005. *Every Child Ready to Read @ Your Library*. Chicago: PLA/ALSC. www.ala.org/ala/alsc/ECRR/ECRRHomePage.htm

Trelease, Jim. 2001. *The Read-Aloud Handbook*. New York: Penguin.

Walter, Virginia. 2001. *Children and Libraries: Getting It Right*. Chicago: ALA.

PART I

BABY RHYMING TIME BASICS

1
Understanding How Baby Learns

"Over the last thirty years, we have learned more about what young children know and do than we had known in the preceding 2000 years."—Dr. Alison Gopnick, University of California at Berkeley at the 21st Century Learner Symposium, 2003

"How in the world did I get here?" was the question I asked myself while waiting for the 21st Century Learner Symposium to begin. Held in Washington, DC in 2003, this was a presentation by researchers, neurologists, educators, psychologists, doctors, and other scholastically oriented people. There I sat, a children's librarian. In fact, a large number of those attending were children's librarians. Could the exchange of information among these various disciplines be beneficial? The answer was, and is, yes. What common factor unites us? That is simple—the children we serve.

Those in academia and research have uncovered data, statistics, and facts about brain growth, including how learning takes place. Modern technology using PET scans (positron emission tomography), EEG (electroencephalography) scans, MRI (magnetic resonance imaging) scans, and even special nipples that have sensors to measure the intensity and pattern of an infant's sucking enable researchers to watch a live brain in action. They have medical proof that the brain grows and develops through stimulation of all the senses. Librarians have increasingly become aware of the impact of reading aloud, doing action rhymes, using dialogic reading, and interacting through play on very young children and their caregivers. Children's librarians have observed that reading aloud to children can have a major impact on how well children do in school. Now research supports this.

Armed with facts about the brain, child development, and how learning takes place, we are better able to create age-appropriate literacy programs. We can pass educational bites of information to our community. Educating caregivers helps them ready their children to succeed. Research touting the importance of reading aloud to children reinforces the importance of story times and other library services to children and justifies to the administration and community the need to support these services.

What does the research show is taking place in a child's brain when we create this literacy experience?

How the Brain Works

First, some definitions.

The brain cell, or *neuron*, consists of three basic parts: cell body, receivers (dendrites and spines), and sender (axon and terminals). (See Figure 1.1 on page 5 for diagram of neuron.)

The *cell body* is the part of the neuron where the DNA is located. Nutrients brought by the blood maintain the cell and create the "chemical messengers" or neurotransmitter molecules that enable the neurons to communicate with one another.

Dendrites and *spines* receive messages, information, or stimuli from outside the cell. The dendrites look like thin strings branching out from the cell body. Each dendrite is covered with tiny spines. These spines increase the cell's surface area and thereby enable it to receive more stimuli or messages. The number of dendrites can vary from a few hundred to thousands per cell body. Dendrite branches increase in number through stimulation.

The neuron uses the *axon* and *terminals* to send messages to other cells. Generally, each neuron has one axon extending from it. The length of the axon varies considerably, with some reaching three feet in length. The longest ones extend down the spinal cord. At the end of the axon are the terminals, or transmitters. Brain cells do not touch one another. There is a tiny space between them identified as the synaptic gap. Chemical messages sent through the terminals of one neuron cross the *synaptic gap* to the dendrites of another neuron.

During childhood, the axon develops a protective coating around itself called myelin. This thin, fatty insulation around the axon enables messages between neurons to be sent more efficiently. Myelination develops over time and, in fact, is not complete until sometime in late adolescence. For the brain to develop myelin, a proper diet is important. Development of myelin, or lack of it, has a definite impact on the child's achievement of milestones such as crawling, walking, running, and making the jump from oral to written language. Myelination can be stimulated but not rushed, with each individual following a unique developmental timetable.

Pruning

A neural pathway forms when a message is sent repeatedly from one neuron to another. Over time, this pathway becomes hard-wired and the message is able to speed along an established pathway. The synapses involved become established connections and relatively permanent. Other neurons may

FIGURE 1.1. Brain Cell Parts

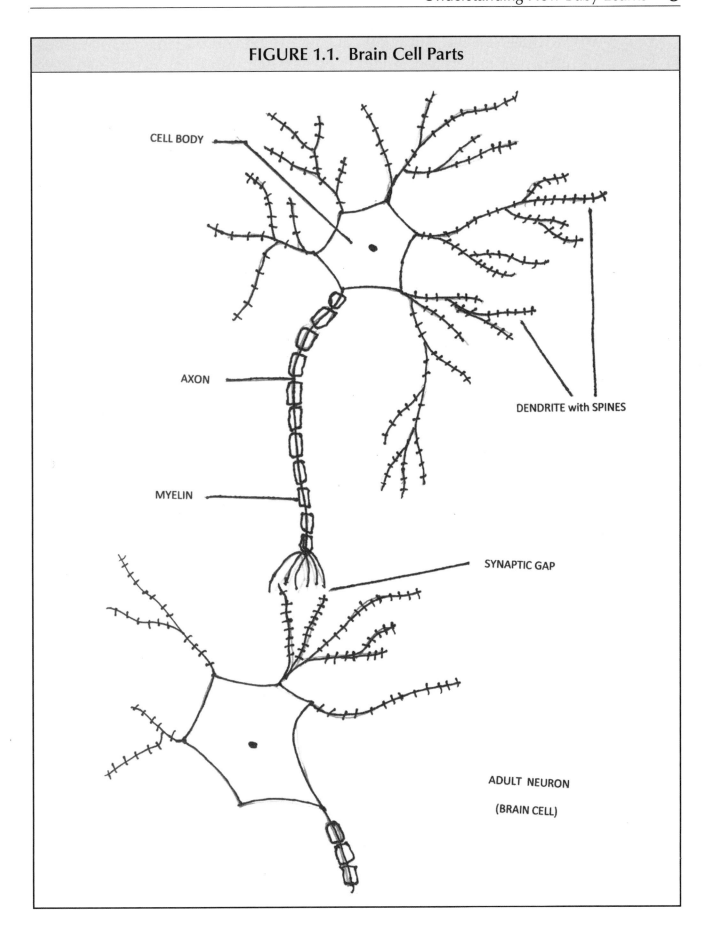

CELL BODY

AXON

MYELIN

DENDRITE with SPINES

SYNAPTIC GAP

ADULT NEURON

(BRAIN CELL)

be left outside the path and thus unused. Pruning is the term used when these extra cells and synapses wither away, ultimately increasing the brain's effectiveness and strength.

Plasticity

The brain is always changing. Some have compared the brain to a super computer, the difference being that the brain has proven it can change its "program" or wiring, whereas in general the computer must rely on someone to create a fixed program for it. Plasticity is the ease by which these changes in the brain take place.

During the first three years of life, the brain has the most plasticity, reshaping itself with each new experience and creating a foundation for skill-building. Between ages three and ten, the brain continues to develop and refine itself at a very brisk rate. The mature brain does have plasticity, but not as much. Challenging and interesting stimuli will still create new synapses in the mature brain, but more repeated stimulation and repetition is required. This reinforces the old adage, "Use it or lose it!" The brain will continue to create neurons and pathways in response to new stimuli and experiences, staying healthy and active well into an individual's senior years.

Neuron Facts:

- At birth, 100 billion brain cells (neurons) are already at work, with 50 trillion connections (synapses) between them.
- In the first months of life, the number of synapses in the brain increases 20 times to more than 1,000 trillion.
- Synapses that are not used are "pruned," a process in which they wither away.
- Neurons grow when stimulated, enabling the brain to process more information efficiently.
- At birth, an individual has 50 trillion connections; at three years of age, she has 1,000 trillion; as an adult, she has 500 trillion.
- A single neuron can fire, if necessary, up to 50,000 times a minute.
- Sensory experiences create new synapses that grow stronger through repetition.
- New synapses form throughout an individual's lifetime.

—Rima Shore. 1997. *Rethinking the Brain: New Insights into Early Development.* New York: Families and Work Institute.

Parts of the Brain

Each part of the brain has its own major purpose and function. The three primary sections are the *brain stem*, the *limbic system,* and the *cortex.* These continue to develop over a lifetime.

The brain stem, called the "survival brain," is the most developed and functioning part of the brain at birth. Located at the base of the brain, the brain stem controls the autonomic nervous system or the "fight or flight" response. Often called the "reptilian brain," it identifies survival needs such as hunger, discomfort, thirst, fear, etc. "Above the brain stem is the *cerebellum*, which is associated with movement. This densely packed area has many connections with the parts of the brain related to abstract thinking and mental focus. When young children do not move and exercise regularly, the connections are weaker than they otherwise would be, and thinking and focus suffer. Vestibular stimulation, such as swinging and spinning, particularly supports one's ability to focus" (Lessen-Firestone, 1998: 1).

The *limbic system* is located directly above the brain stem. It identifies and acts on the emotional needs of the individual. Part of the subconscious mind, it also contains the area of the brain responsible for long-term memory storage.

The *cortex* is the "gray matter" of the brain, or the conscious mind. It is located on top of the limbic system and is the largest part of the brain. It deals with higher-level thinking, attention and concentration, emotional control, intelligence, imagination, and sensory perception. The final area of the brain to develop is the prefrontal lobes of the cortex, located directly behind the forehead. There are two hemispheres to the cortex, a left and a right, each having its areas of specialization. The left side is analytical, language-oriented, and reality based. The right side of the brain is intuitive, holistic, and experience-oriented. The two hemispheres communicate through a band of 200 million fibers called the *corpus callosum*, which acts as a bridge between them.

The basic developmental sequence of the brain is from base to top (brain stem to cortex), back to front (prefrontal lobes last to fully develop), and between left and right brain hemispheres, across the corpus collusum.

Brain Facts:

- At birth the brain weighs about one pound; the mature adult brain weighs about three pounds.
- The brain analyzes and processes information/stimuli faster than the world's fastest computer.
- The brain changes as it learns.
- New (active) experiences cause the brain to grow new connections in response.
- The brain cannot be worn out through use.
- The brain is "hard-wired" by repeated experiences, creating established pathways along which messages can move more efficiently.
- The brain loses neurons throughout life, but new ones can form in response to repeated new and interesting stimuli.

Influences on Brain Development

The brain has environmental as well as physical rules regarding its development.

Nature vs. Nurture

"Brain wiring involves an intricate dance between nature and nurture. Genes direct the growth of axons and dendrites to their correct approximate locations, but once these fibers start linking together and actually functioning, experience takes over, reshaping and refining these crude circuits to customize each child's hardware to his or her unique environment" (Eliot, 1999: 29).

The argument over whether one is simply born with a fixed intelligence, or acquires the greater part of intelligence through experience, is no longer valid. Some now call it a dance between the two, each contributing to development. Each individual has his or her own genetic brain components, chemistry, and physical being or "nature." However, the brain also acts like a sponge, using the senses to soak up experiences in the environment and developing in response to "nurture." The brain craves stimuli through sound, sight, touch, taste, smell, and experience. An impoverished environment causes the brain to diminish its ability to develop. Research has also found that active participation in an experience can trigger a strong emotion and, as a result, the response is "hard-wired" faster. "For good or bad, the emotions your baby experiences in reaction to individual events make an actual physical impression on the brain. Each one leaves a kind of footprint in the form of chemical changes, and the more often a particular emotion is felt in a particular context, the deeper that footprint becomes . . ." (Acredolo, 2005: 20).

Diet

Proper nutrition has a direct impact on brain development. Starving or malnourished cells cannot create neurons/dendrites or respond in the presence of stimuli. Myelination requires an individual's diet to supply the fat that creates the insulation around the axons. "Mylin production is the primary reason why pediatricians recommend a high level of fat (including whole milk) in children's diets until about age two. . . ." (Eliot, 1999: 34). Myelination takes place at a specific rate that is unique to each individual. This affects one's readiness to accomplish certain activities successfully. In fact, trying to force a child with an immature brain network to do something he is not ready to do can not only lead to frustration but also create inefficient networks. Once "hard-wired" into the brain, this kind of negative response is hard to change.

Interaction

Research with Romanian orphans led by Dr. Harry T. Chugani of Children's Hospital of Michigan, Wayne State University School of Medicine, clearly shows the impact that physical, emotional and social deprivation can have on brain development. The orphans received the necessary care but were deprived of consistent interpersonal and physical interaction with their caregivers and their environment. Using PET scans, the lack of brain activity is evident. The lack of movement influenced how the brain cells functioned, and inactivity lead to pruning. (For the full report see "Local Brain Functional Activity Following

Early Deprivation: A Study of Postinstitutionalized Romanian Orphans." 2001. *NeuroImage* 14: 1290–1301.)

Developmental Milestones

Many consider these developmental milestones the "firsts" in a baby's life. It is important to remember that every child is an individual who develops at his own unique pace. Being aware of these milestones makes planning age-appropriate programs possible. If a prolonged delay (two months or more) is evident in any of these areas, a pediatrician or specialist should be consulted.

Birth to Six Months

Physical

- Turns head, examines feet and hands
- Lifts head
- Grasps small objects
- Ability to focus increases from about 10 inches at birth
- Likes to bounce

Emotional and Social

- Enjoys interacting with primary caregiver(s)
- Smiles
- Dependent on caregiver
- Likes to observe the human face

Intellectual

- Likes to investigate surroundings
- Recognizes familiar human faces
- Reacts to changes in routine
- Turns towards familiar voices
- Can track moving objects using eyes
- Learns by using all his senses

Language

- Listens
- Babbles and makes sounds
- Responds to familiar sounds and voices
- Communicates through cooing, crying, and body language

Six Months to Twelve Months

Physical

- Sits unassisted
- Can pull self up to standing position
- Starts to move independently—crawls
- Can transfer items from one hand to the other

Emotional and Social

- Likes to play peek-a-boo
- Comfortable with familiar people
- Laughs

Intellectual

- Likes to "experiment" and will repeat it until satisfied (e.g., dropping a spoon to see if it will fall)
- Explores by putting things in mouth
- Starts to play with toys
- Begins to identify pictures with real objects
- Looks for hidden objects

Language

- Sounds created are purposeful
- Babbles and tries to talk
- Uses gestures to help communicate

Twelve Months to Eighteen Months

Physical

- Able to stand and sit alone
- Walks independently
- Able to bend over and picks things up
- Able to go up and down steps with assistance.
- Gains competence of thumb and forefinger pincer grasp—turns pages of a book but not individually

Emotional and Social

- Separation anxiety apparent when separated from parent or other primary caregiver
- Enjoys being applauded
- Imitates others' actions
- "MINE"—starts to claim own possessions and space
- Plays alone

Intellectual

- Comprehension development ahead of verbalization skills
- Understands simple commands—one-step directions
- Very sensory oriented
- Loves to sort and dump things from containers

Language

- Vocabulary of 10 to 20 understandable words
- Babbles, incorporating real words and sounds

- Starts to identify people and objects verbally—naming
- Scribbles using whole-arm movement

Eighteen Months to 24 Months

Physical

- Starting to run
- Can walk up and down stairs without assistance
- Begins to manipulate objects, such as puzzle pieces, to fit in required spaces
- Good control over large muscles

Emotional and Social

- Will play alongside other children doing the same thing (parallel play)
- Wants everything *NOW!*
- Can get physically aggressive when frustrated
- Difficulty managing feelings and may need help
- Likes to play "pretend" using familiar surroundings and situations
- Starts to show preferences in making choices

Intellectual

- Points to body parts and can identify them
- Can follow two or three simple directions
- Remembers routines and patterns
- Memory still developing
- Likes to take things apart and put them back together

Language

- Vocabulary now up to several hundred words
- Identifies pictures of objects and can name them
- Still inventing words and learning rules of grammar
- Likes to "read" stories, turn pages
- Enjoys listening to longer stories, songs and rhymes

The resources listed at the end of this chapter cover early childhood developmental skills more completely. Your state's Department of Health can also supply information, not only for self-education, but to share with participants.

How Learning Takes Place

Learning happens when the brain makes new connections to what is already known and in place. To learn from an experience, children need to be actively involved and use their senses. This is most often called "play."

Play

In *Einstein Never Used Flash Cards* (Hirsh-Pasek and Golinkoff, 2003), the connection between play and learning is thoroughly examined. In fact, the introduction states quite clearly that:

"PLAY = LEARNING"

To help remember this concept, keep in mind this equation:

"PLAY + LEARNING = PLEARNING!

(Thanks to the unknown creator of this term at the 21st Century Learner Summit in 2003.)

Research has found that "when we are actively engaged in doing something, we learn it much more quickly and grasp its complexities more easily than if we passively experience the same thing" (Acredolo, 2000: 22). Having a caring adult actively participating with an infant and working to create an environment that promotes development has a definite impact on how the child develops. Play encourages development in such areas as problem solving, interacting with others, and creativity—and above all, it is fun! Professor Catherine Garvey (1991), University of Maine, gives five elements of play:

- Pleasurable and enjoyable
- Has no extrinsic goals (in other words not, "I'm playing this in order to learn . . .")
- Spontaneous and voluntary
- Active engagements
- Has an element of make-believe

Movement

"Movement is essential to learning. Movement awakens and activates many of our mental capacities. Movement integrates and anchors new information and experience into our neural networks. And movement is vital to all the actions by which we embody and express our learning, our understanding, and our selves" (Hannaford, 1995: 96).

Movement can increase and maintain the oxygen level in the blood that supplies cells with energy to do their various jobs. It also allows for exploration of the senses: touch, taste, smell, sight, and sound. To express what is learned, the physical body uses speech (vocal or sign language), writing, or moving/doing (dancing, drawing, building, etc.). *Amazing Babies*, by Beverly Stokes, gives essential movements that adults can do with babies through the first year of life for development and bonding. Neurophysiologist and educator Dr. Carla Hannaford's *Smart Moves: Why Learning Is Not All in Your Head*, examines the body's role in learning from infancy through adulthood, supplying scientific evidence that movement is crucial to learning. There are programs that support this concept of using movement to aid brain development, including Brain Gym (www.braingym.org), developed by Dr. Paul Dennison and Gail E. Dennison in the 1970s. Nurturing Pathways (nurturing pathways.com), developed by Christine Roberts, uses creative movement, rhymes, songs, and music to develop the body and mind during the first three years of life.

Language Acquisition and Development

During the first three years of life, the window of opportunity for speech and language development occurs. At birth, infants have the ability to develop speech in any language, but it is through hearing a language consistently that they are able to vocalize it. Babbling is how infants "practice" the sounds that make up the language they hear. Even hearing-impaired infants will babble by using their hands (Golinkoff and Hirsh-Pasek, 1999: 36). By the age of three, the ability to both hear and vocalize sounds not common to the primary language will diminish. By supplying an environment rich with sounds, words, and interactions, the caregiver can provide an infant with the tools necessary to build language skills. Language is best developed through real life interaction rather than through recordings or television. Talking to infants increases not only the opportunity to hear the language in its true context but also develops a vocabulary. Children will develop listening comprehension first before they are able to be fluent in the language.

G-R-O-W

The term *GROW* was coined by Jill Olson, children's librarian for the King County Library System in Washington, and used in its "Ready-to-Read" Early Literacy workshops. These workshops support the King County Library System's Initiative for Early Literacy developed in 2004. The King County Library System provides workshops for parents, childcare educators, caregivers, and other adults interacting with children. This term helps adults remember how children learn and develop. (See handout on p. 202.)

G—Get Active

The early years are a time of incredible growth and development in learning how the world works. Children need to "do" by using real objects in a real environment. They need to experience the world around them by using all their senses and through active play. It is important for an adult to be actively engaged in this experience with them to act as guide, role model, protector, and cheerleader.

R—Relationships Matter

Learning happens best in relationship with a caring adult. Having a responsive, loving adult to guide him in an experience does more than keep the child safe. When the adult creates a safe, confidence-building, and positive emotional environment, the child's brain is able to grow and flourish. Feeling safe and secure enables a baby to have confidence to explore what is around him knowing the caregiver is there to give support. Strong emotions, both positive and negative, influence learning; if a crying baby learns through experience that no one is there to care for his needs, he may learn distrust and feel a sense of abandonment.

O—Over and Over and Over and Over

Repetition allows the brain to become "hard-wired." Neurons strengthen each time an experience is repeated. The sent message moves faster and the pathway becomes more efficient with each repetition. Like a scientist, the child will keep trying out her theory (e.g., "Will the spoon fall if I drop it?"). Until she is satisfied with the result, she will repeat the experiment ("Yes, the spoon always falls to the floor.").

W—Windows of Opportunity

There are certain periods that are the most opportune times for certain types of learning to take place. The "window of opportunity" for language development occurs very early, and the sounds that a baby hears will become his primary language. It is possible, of course, to learn foreign languages later in one's life, but perhaps not as easily, and, more than likely, the secondary languages will be spoken with an accent! The challenge in learning a foreign language comes in vocalizing the sounds of that foreign language without having had previous early exposure to them.

Very few of these "windows" slam shut forever, although the development of vision, or the ability to see, is one such "window of opportunity" that exists during the first six months of life. The area of the brain that deals with vision needs stimulation within this short time after birth in order to fully develop. If this area of the brain does not receive the proper stimulation, the cells will not develop and the child's vision will never be normal (Acredolo, 2000: 12–13).

Print Resources for Further Information

The Brain

Acredolo, Linda and Susan Goodwyn. 2000. *Baby Minds: Brain-Building Games Your Baby Will Love*. New York: Bantam Books.

Eliot, Lisa. 1999. *What's Going on in There? How the Brain and Mind Develop in the First Years of Life*. New York: Bantam Books.

Garvey, Catherine. 1991. *Play*. 2nd rev. ed. London: Fontana

Gopnik, Alison, Andrew Meltzoff, and Patricia Kuhl. 1999. *The Scientist in the Crib: Minds, Brains, and How Children Learn*. New York: William Morrow.

Shonkoff, Jack P. and Deborah A. Phillips, eds. 2001. *From Neurons to Neighborhoods: The Science of Early Childhood Development*. Committee of Integrating the Science of Early Childhood Development. Washington, DC: National Academy Press.

Shore, Rebecca. 2002. *The Baby Teacher: Nurturing Neural Networks from Birth to Age Five*. Lanham, MD: Scarecrow Press.

Sousa, Edward. 2001. *How the Brain Learns*. 2nd ed. Thousand Oaks, CA: Corwin Press.

Development

Acredolo, Linda and Susan Goodwyn. 2005. *Baby Hearts: A Guide to Giving Your Child an Emotional Head Start*. New York: Bantam Books.

Bailey, Becky A. 2000. *I Love You Rituals*. New York: Quill.

Brazelton, T. Berry. 1992. *Touchpoints Birth to 3: Your Child's Emotional and Behavioral Development*. Reading, MA: Perseus Publishing.

Carlson, Frances M. 2006. *Essential Touch: Meeting the Needs of Young Children*. Washington, DC: National Association for the Education of Young Children.

Conkling, Winifred. 2001. *Smart-Wiring Your Baby's Brain: What You Can Do to Stimulate Your Child During the Critical First Three Years*. New York: Quill/HarperCollins.

Conners, C. Keith. 1989. *Feeding the Brain: How Foods Affect Children*. New York: Plenum Press.

Dennison, Paul E. and Gail E. Dennison. 1986. *Brain Gym: Simple Activities for Whole Brain Learning*. Ventura, CA: Edu-Kinesthetics.

Dennison, Paul E. and Gail E. Dennison. 1994. *Brain Gym*. Teacher's edition, revised. Ventura, CA: Edu-Kinesthetics.

Diamond, Marian and Janet Hopson. 1998. *Magic Trees of the Mind: How to Nurture Your Child's Intelligence, Creativity, and Healthy Emotions from Birth through Adolescence*. New York: Dutton.

Go, Joanne, Janet Pozmantier and Laurie Segal Robinson. 2001. *The First Years: A Parent and Caregiver's Guide to Helping Children Learn*. New York: DK Publishing.

Hannaford, Carla. 1995. *Smart Moves: Why Learning Is Not All in Your Head*. Alexander, NC: Great Ocean Publishers.

Hirsh-Pasek, Kathy and Roberta Michnick Golinkoff, with Danie Eyer. 2003. *Einstein Never Used Flash Cards: How Our Children Really Learn—and Why They Need to Play More and Memorize Less*. Emmaus, PA: Rodale.

Lessen-Firestone, Joan. 1998. *Building Children's Brains*, "Ready to Learn Summits." Available: www.mi-aimh.msu.edu/publications/JoanFirestone.pdf

Stokes, Beverly. 2002. *Amazing Babies: Essential Movement for Your Baby in the First Year*. Toronto, ON: Move Alive Media.

Language and Literacy

Acredolo, Linda and Susan Goodwyn, with Doug Abrams. 2002. *Baby Signs: How to Talk With Your Baby Before Your Baby Can Talk*. New York: Contemporary Books.

Apel, Kenn and Julie J. Masterson. 2001. *Beyond Baby Talk: From Sounds to Sentences—A Parent's Complete Guide to Language Development*. Roseville, CA: Prima Publishing.

Fox, Mem. 2001. Reading Magic: *Why Reading Aloud to Our Children Will Change Their Lives Forever*. New York: Harcourt.

Garcia, Joseph. 2001. S*ign With Your Baby: How to Communicate With Infants Before They Can Speak*. Bellingham, WA: Stratton Kehl Publishers.

Golinkoff, Roberta Michnick and Kathy Hirsh-Pasek. 1999. *How Babies Talk: The Magic and Mystery of Language in the First Three Years of Life*. New York: Dutton.

Hart, Betty and Todd R. Risley. 1995. *Meaningful Differences in the Everyday Experience of Young American Children*. Baltimore: Paul H. Brookes Publishing.

McGuinness, Diane. 2004. *Growing a Reader from Birth: Your Child's Path from Language to Literacy*. New York: W.W. Norton.

Schickedanz, Judith A. 1999. *Much More Than the ABCs: The Early Stages of Reading and Writing*. Washington, DC: National Association for the Education of Young Children.

Sousa, Edward. 2005. *How the Brain Learns to Read*. Thousand Oaks, CA: Corwin Press.

Zigler, Edward. 2004. *Children's Play: The Roots of Reading*. Washington, DC: Zero to Three.

Electronic Resources for Further Information

www.brainnet.wa.gov

Washington State Department of Social and Health Services, Department of Child Care and Early Learning

This page supplies information on brain research findings and stages of development.

www.fpg.unc.edu/~ncedl/PAGES/research.cfm

National Center for Early Development & Learning (NCEDL)

Sponsored by the National Center for Early Development and Learning, this site give access to reports from 12 national research and developmental centers on cognitive, social, and emotional development of children birth to age eight.

www.ala.org/ala/pla/plaissues/earlylit/earlyliteracy.htm

Public Library Association: "Every Child Ready to Read @ Your Library"

Joint project of the Public Library Association and the Association for Library Services to Children. Workshop information, handouts, and research on the topic of early literacy.

www.talaris.org

Talaris Research Institute

From homepage: "Talaris is dedicated to advancing knowledge of this early learning and the important role parents play in this development. Our work focuses on translating early brain and behavioral development science into easy-to-understand tools and information for parents and anyone who regularly interacts with parents and their children: parenting educators, childcare workers, health professionals, and the like."

www.cfw.tufts.edu/topic/4/76.htm

Tufts University Child and Family WebGuide

The Child & Family WebGuide describes trustworthy websites on topics of interest to parents and professionals. Graduate students and faculty in child development have systematically evaluated sites listed on the WebGuide.

www.childprofile.org/hpmats/materials.html

Washington State Department of Health—Child Profile

From homepage, click on Information for Parents, click on View each CHILD letter and material, and scroll down to Developmental Chart: Birth to 18 months

zerotothree.org

Zero to Three

A national, nonprofit, multidisciplinary organization that informs, educates, and supports adults who influence the lives of infants and toddlers.

2
Meeting the Cast

In order to provide services and plan programs for the very young child and caregiver, it is helpful to understand the individuals involved: the child, the caregivers (families), the librarian or presenter, and in reality, the entire library staff. All these individuals and groups interact with each other to create a fun learning experience for the very young child.

In this text the term "infant" or "baby" will be used when referring to a child who is newborn to 12 months of age. For the child between 12 months and 24 months, the term "young toddler" or "pre-toddler" will be used. "Caregiver" will be used for the adult with the child.

The Family—Adult and Very Young Child

The very young child does not exist alone in the world but as part of a family. Every child is part of a family. Every family has its own special identity and has a direct impact on how a child develops. Each family also has distinct needs influenced both by the individuals in the family and the family's particular situation. Some of the challenges facing new parents and families are:

- Being pulled in many directions daily
- High stress levels
- Lack of support—due to a more mobile society, parents may have few immediate family members or friends nearby
- Economic responsibilities and challenges
- Having a child is new territory—a child does not come with instructions on how to raise a healthy and happy child
- Limited experiences or role models to call upon
- Internal pressure from the desire to make sure the child gets a good start for success in life

Reading through the descriptions of the various types of families you may realize that in addition to their unique traits, all families have many similarities.

One thing is for certain—families of all kinds benefit from library services and programming for the very young.

Bilingual Families

In most US libraries, programs are offered primarily in English, sometimes with other world language programs available. However, even at English language programs, English may be only one of the languages present in the room. Non-English or bilingual families will sometimes attend storytimes to help their children as well as themselves learn English or reinforce their English skills. Very young children babble the sounds they hear consistently around them. Therefore, if they are living in a home where more than one language is spoken to them, they will grow up hearing the sounds of those languages and "learn words in both languages for the same concept" (Golinkoff and Hirsh-Pasek, 1999: 196). Caregivers can expose their child to the language they feel comfortable speaking and another language present at the program. For example, a caregiver may speak Spanish at home but English outside of it thereby exposing the child to both languages. The pace of infant and very young child programs can be slower to allow time for the child to process what is going on and the necessary repetition helps everyone, even those unfamiliar with the material, learn and master the rhymes, songs, and so on.

Bilingual families also have much to contribute of their own cultural songs, rhymes and finger plays. Giving an opportunity to share a favorite rhyme or song during the class offers a learning experience and an exchange between cultures. It also provides positive reinforcement to the individual sharing and perhaps increases his or her confidence. Families can also expand their circle of acquaintances by meeting others in the class, and the English speakers have an opportunity to gain knowledge of different cultures.

Know the cultures in your community so you can select program materials that will not cause cultural misunderstandings. As an example, using the term "fat" in some cultures is considered an insult and is best replaced with a more acceptable term.

Special Needs Families

The special needs family is just that—special. This family, due to the physical or mental limits of a member, sees itself as not fitting the definition of an "average family." The term "special needs" can cover a wide range, from Down's syndrome to deafness, cerebral palsy to feeding tubes. Special needs families face restrictions and requirements. The caregivers may be hesitant to participate in public programs such as storytimes or feel self-conscious when visiting public places because of their needs. These families need to be made aware that their special needs infant or very young child can benefit by participating in programs that encourage adult/child interaction just as a "normal" child can. Developmental delays generally become more apparent as the child gets older; many are not yet fully identified at birth to one year.

Provide educational information in a brief, informal manner, interspersed with the fun, interactive, literacy components of your program. Help the adults understand how the very young child grows and reinforce the fact that each child is unique and developing at an individual rate. By praising the caregiver bringing the child you can increase the adult's confidence.

It is important that the librarian or presenter be aware of and sensitive to the special needs family. Adapting the space is not always necessary, since infants are usually carried and have limited mobility. Supplying various levels of directions for fingerplays and action rhymes can help everyone feel included.

Understanding what "inclusion" means and the intent of the laws that apply to inclusion is beneficial. The public library can help the special needs family by acting as a source for medical information and government services. Every state has someone who coordinates services for special need families. It is best to first check with the local/county/state department of health for resources. Even the local school district may be able to assist with referrals.

Early intervention can give the child a better start and can cut costs for treatment in later years. For example, speech therapy begun before or by preschool can increase a child's ability to communicate and succeed in school. Having material from special needs agencies available at programs helps families be aware of services open to them. Inform families that prefer to do their own research that websites such as that of the National Early Childhood Technical Assistance Center can get them started in the right direction. Some states have councils or committees that offer grants to further inclusion; for example, New York State's Disabilities Planning Council has supplied grants to public libraries in this area of service.

Day-to-day life can be very stressful for special needs families. What better way to serve them than to provide a fun, supportive, and caring environment and a program in which they can participate? Even if the adult caregiver and child must observe from the back of the room, they are part of the group and can glean things to share at home.

Giving special needs families the opportunity to be part of a "regular" program helps them feel less isolated from the mainstream community. What are some of the ways that a special needs family can fit in? All infants are born with limited vision, relying at first on touch, smell, and sound to explore their world, as a blind child does. Muscle control takes time to develop in all children, and using nursery rhymes to make exercise time fun can be beneficial. Deaf children enjoy being bounced, rocked, or tickled to music and rhymes and can feel the beat by movement or vibration. Using sign language with all preverbal children, not just deaf children, helps the child and adult communicate. Because touch is vital to all children's physical and emotional development, build interactive touch into the nursery rhymes, children's action songs, and lullabies you present. Once learned, these activities can be used wherever and whenever the adult and child desire, strengthening the bond between them. Touch can help family members gain confidence in their ability to connect with the child.

Sign Language

Teaching sign language to very young children gives them the ability to communicate before they are physically able to verbalize. Studies have shown that children who are signed to as infants have "a developmentally appropriate way to communicate before they can talk" (Acredolo, 2000: 14). A deaf child babbles by using his hands. Early exposure to sign language increases a deaf child's ability to communicate. Incorporating signs into songs and rhymes can help the adult, along with their child, learn this language.

Music

Rhythm and melody can soothe a fussy infant and help him regulate movements and find joy in creating sound. Music is inclusive: the caregiver holds a baby and rocks it; a young Down's syndrome toddler creates his own rhythm with a shaker; a child with limited movement delights in the sight and feel of scarves being stroked down her body; a deaf child can feel the vibrations of a drum.

Touch

The importance of touch for a child's early development cannot be emphasized enough. Touch can be soothing, stimulating, and reassuring to a child. Choosing appropriate rhymes and songs will help an adult provide the kind of touch that benefits the child most. A rhyme that encourages tickles gently stimulates the infant and brings an awareness of the environment. A steady rocking rhyme helps a child focus and develop a method for self-soothing when over stimulated.

Teen Parents

Teen parents need all the support they can get. If they do not feel welcome in the library themselves, they may not think of the library as a place to bring their infant or young child. If teen parents cannot come to your location, go to where they are or investigate the possibility getting them transportation to visit your location. Due to life's pressure, they may need an added incentive or assistance in making the additional effort needed to attend a program or accept help. Showing them how to incorporate literacy activities in their daily life helps reassure them they are on the right track. What better place for them to grow in parenting skills and help their child than where they are accepted and supported?

Approach teen parents through alternative high schools, youth centers, local health departments, Head Start and Early Head Start sites, and community centers. Teen parents may have had no role model for parenting skills, let alone for early literacy. The importance of reading aloud to children and how to do it, or the use of nursery rhymes with infants may not occur to teen parents. Their own literacy skills may be lacking or they may be too tired from trying to survive day to day to make an effort to talk to an infant who cannot talk back. It may seem more sensible to them to wait until their infant is older and can respond to them.

Observing a good role model on how, what, and why to read to very young children is a primary reason for teen parents to participate in storytimes. Having someone demonstrate how to use songs and rhymes helps teen parents who possibly did not have such experiences growing up. Being expressive and talking about the pictures to their child could be a totally new way of reading aloud. The positive response their child has from participating in the program prompts them to repeat it. Learning to be comfortable when holding their child and singing or reciting rhymes can strengthen the bond between parent and child. The role extends beyond the librarian to the other adults in the group as well. Seeing how other adults interact with their children helps teens gain insight into their own interaction of self and child.

The information provided through programs and services helps the teen develop parenting skills. Knowing why to do something helps every parent grow. Important resources and services that support teen parents should be made available to teen parents in an informal, nonpressured manner. Some health departments offer mentors to help support teen parents. Workshops to educate these mentors or visiting nurses can be another way to get the importance of reading aloud to children out those who need to hear it.

Grandparents

Recent statistics show that there are approximately 2.4 million grandparents in the United States raising their grandchildren (Watkins, 2006: 13). Once again facing the demands of parenthood, grandparents may be confronted with the additional challenges of physical limitations, emotional tension within the family, the impact of new technology, and their own discomfort with contemporary parenting styles. Parenting for the second time around can be exciting yet exhausting for them. It is contrary to the traditional role of grandparent and can force a sharp change in their personal plans for the future.

What kind of programs and services do they need? Grandparents may feel as isolated as any new parent might. Programs such as storytime give them the opportunity to be part of a supportive group. Since many grandparents have limited finances, they may especially appreciate the fact that these programs are usually free. Storytime provides an opportunity for grandparents to observe their grandchild in a social environment. They get to see children at various levels of development within the same age group. They also have an opportunity to network with other adults.

Be conscious that something as simple as having chairs in the program room, even around the edge of the group, may make the difference between a grandparent participating or not. When demonstrating action rhymes, offer alternatives so that senior caregivers feel included. If a grandparent is not strong enough to lift their grandchild up in the air, have him or her raise the child's arms in the air instead.

Help grandparents to catch up on what is currently available. The latest brain research or the idea of communicating with the very young child using sign may be completely new to them, and they may also welcome new thinking on old topics such as potty training. Create pathfinders, booklists, and displays that help grandparents find their way. Make them aware of resources available to them from educational and government agencies. Consider programs featuring expert speakers from community or legal agencies knowledgeable in areas of child custody, child referral services, services such as federal funds for child support, and so on, and invite grandparents. To encourage attendance, try offering free child care during these programs.

Grandparents raising their grandchildren face not only the challenges of daily life, but in many cases the reason they are caring for their grandchildren is traumatic, sad, or painful. The parents may have been neglectful, abusive, or even be incarcerated. Sometimes the parents may simply need help and the situation is temporary. Regardless of the situation, grandparents want their grandchild to have the best possible environment in which to grow up. They are entitled to enjoy the rewards of raising a grandchild, of sharing their love, and creating a good foundation for their grandchild's future.

Child Care Providers and Early Childhood Educators

Sometimes the person bringing a very young child to programs or using services is not a family member. Nannies, babysitters, and childcare workers may welcome services and programs that help them connect with the child and find a network of support. Some may not speak the same language as the child hears at home, may be unfamiliar with the customs of the majority culture, or may not have an early childhood educational background. Providing them access to materials, services, and caring individuals helps them create an environment that enriches not only the young child's life but their own.

Early childhood care providers and educators are often too busy to be aware of resources outside their own buildings. Reach out to them with mailings, training sessions, and free materials; through them your efforts will reach further out into the community. Help them realize how they can incorporate literacy activities in their daily routine and support them in their quest to offer quality childcare and education to even their youngest clients. To find more ways in which to meet the needs of this group, see Chapter 4.

The Librarian/Presenter

In this book, the terms "librarian" and "presenter" will refer to the person who gives the Baby Rhyming Time program. The person may be the children's librarian, a teen librarian, other librarian staff assigned the responsibility, a nonprofessional, an early childhood caregiver/educator or, perhaps, even a volunteer. No matter who they are, they all require the same information and attitude to make the program a success.

Education

The presenter needs to have an understanding of child development and age appropriate materials. Basic facts regarding the field of early childhood can be introduced through workshop training, classes, or self-education. Presenters can also learn through observation of similar programs and practical experience. Adult participants may believe the presenter is the expert in early childhood development, but, in reality, the presenter's expertise lies in connecting the adult with the materials and resources they need to create an environment and foundation their child can build on.

Materials

Knowing what material is age appropriate is very important. It is often tempting to embellish materials and pack multiple activities into one program because they can be so much fun for everyone. It is the presenter's responsibility to select age-appropriate materials in order to help the adult participants become familiar with what is actually appropriate for the age group. For infants and very young toddlers, keeping it simple and using repetition is best. See Chapter 7 for more information on age appropriate books.

Resources

Resources can include books, CDs and other materials, and extend to agencies and various sources for information. Knowing what local referral agencies exist, what they offer, and how to contact them can help a family that might not be aware of what is available to them. Guiding a new parent to medical books so they can understand what the pediatrician says can be vital. Being able to borrow materials can help families that have limited financial resources. Knowing what is age appropriate can help overzealous adults relax and enjoy each stage their child is at now, rather than rushing on to the next one. By having the resources and knowing how to use them, the librarian/presenter can support the family and build community support.

Sensitivity

All participants want to have a positive learning experience for their children, but backgrounds can vary. The presenter should recognize that new parents may be exhausted, overenthusiastic, or trying to be perfect. Some may feel very confident and others not so confident. Some may have had a good night's sleep while others may have only been able to grab a catnap before coming. Some may feel very self-conscious doing some of the activities in front of other adults, so encourage them to focus on their child. To put them at ease, remind them of the fact that their child looks at them as "the best." If possible, set up the room so their line of sight will be directed on you rather than what is happening outside the room. If an adult seems to feel unease or expresses a concern that his or her child is not keeping up with the others, talk to the adult privately. Offer reassurance that every child develops at his or her own pace or, if appropriate, refer the adult to an expert. Be aware of the children as the program progresses and adjust the program to fit the children's stages of alertness. A sleepy group may not appreciate a rousing bouncing rhyme or march but a rocking rhyme might lead them to a gentle tickle as they approach the "quiet alert" state when they are most open to the world around them. The presenter's sensitivity can have a tremendous effect on the success of a service or program. The presenter is not a performer nor entertainer but a guide and support for adults who want to share a fun learning experience with their child. Praising the adults for making it to the program might be all they need to reassure them on what may have been a less than perfect day.

Attitude

It may seem unusual to include attitude as a section but it is worth a thought or two. A genuine desire to do this type of program is necessary since it demands an investment of self. An attitude of give and take is beneficial. By giving the program, the presenter supports and educates the group while infusing enthusiasm for sharing early literacy experiences with very young children. Invite the group to share what they know, and both sides become active participants. Connections between the individuals form and everyone becomes more invested in what is happening in the program. Remember that doing is one way people learn. Presenters with no parenting background will certainly learn with every program. By staying calm and accepting, they can reassure the adults, who are often venturing into this activity for the first time, perhaps with some reservations. A positive attitude is helpful in every situation.

Support Staff

Everyone who works at the library needs to be involved in serving very young children and their caregivers. Pages can point out the board books to adults holding infants. While checking books out, staff can praise an adult for bringing a very young child to the library and make her aware of program offerings for that age group. People responsible for facilities can make sure the areas are child-safe. Administrators can develop partnerships with outside agencies and organizations that support early literacy services and programs. Those responsible for collection development may need advice on what materials are truly age appropriate and worth purchasing for the very young. Staff input may indicate the need for a parenting collection, or other resources that could support caregivers, as well as the library's mission statement.

Help staff understand the vital importance of serving the very young. Staff members who feel reluctant to interact with caregivers can practice by role-playing various situations where they could promote services and programs for the very young. Supply the staff with "information bites" they can use when dealing with the public. For some "persuasive evidence to share with those who serve young children," see Renea Arnold and Nell Colburn's column in *School*

Library Journal, listed below. Staff need to know that this is an important part of the overall service of the library and that they all play a role in promoting it when they interact with the very young at work, at home, or in their neighborhoods. Keeping staff informed will help engage their support; post information on the staff bulletin board or even by the coffee pot. King County Library System sends out a monthly "Early Literacy Energizer" through e-mail to the entire staff in order to keep the momentum of their early literacy initiative.

Serving the very young child involves many individuals. All participants need to be understanding, willing to communicate, and involved. Helping create a strong foundation for a child's future success is worth the time and energy. It is a rewarding and exciting endeavor for all involved.

Print Resources for Further Information

Arnold, Renea and Nell Colburn. 2006. "Really Good Research: Some Persuasive Evidence to Share with Those Who Serve Young Children." *School Library Journal* 52, no. 11 (November): 31. http://www.schoollibraryjournal.com/article/CA6386670.html.

DeJong, Lorraine. 2003. "Using Erikson to Work More Effectively with Teenage Parents." *Young Children* 58, no. 2 (March): 87–95.

Golinkoff, Roberta and Kathy Hirsh-Pasek. 1999. *How Babies Talk: The Magic and Mystery of Language in the First Three Years of Life*. NY: Dutton.

Madden, Lee. 2006. "Taking It All In." *Children and Libraries* 4, no. 3 (Spring): 15–16.

Katz, Laurie and Teris K. Schery. 2006. "Including Children with Hearing Loss in Early Childhood Programs." *Young Children* 61, no. 1 (January): 86–95.

Watkins, Jan. 2006. "Grandparents Raising Grandchildren: The Growing Task Facing a New Generation." *Children and Libraries* 4, no. 3 (Spring): 13–14.

Waycie, Linda. 2006. "Groups for Grandparents Raising Grandchildren." *Children & Libraries* 4, no. 3 (Spring): 17–18.

Young Children, the Journal of the National Association for the Education of Young Children. 61 (July 2006). Includes a cluster of articles on infants and toddlers, 12–56.

Electronic Resources for Further Information

http://aarp.org
American Association of Retired People
    AARP offers information for seniors in many areas including grandparenting. On their homepage click on "Family, Home and Legal," then "Grandparenting." Topics include raising grandchildren, family relationships, financial health and proving childcare for grandchildren. Links to sites that offer statistics and reports are also available.

http://www.ala.org/ala/pla/plaissues/earlylit/earlyliteracy.htm
American Library Association
    Every Child Ready to Read @ Your Library: This joint project by the Public Library Association and ALSC provides librarians with resources to help teach parents about the importance of early literacy and early brain development in young children.

http://www.ala.org/ala/alsc/alscresources/borntoread/bornread.htm
American Library Association

> *Born to Read: How to Raise a Reader:* Created by ALSC, this site provides tips for reading, book sharing, Web sites, emergent literacy, and booklists that can be shared with parents.

http://www.famlit.org
National Center for Family Literacy

> Created by a grant in 1989, this organization employs an intergenerational approach aimed at low income and at-risk families in order to stop the cycle of poverty and low literacy.

http://www.nectac.org
National Early Childhood Technical Assistance Center

> "The National Early Childhood Technical Assistance Center supports the implementation of the early childhood provisions of the Individuals with Disabilities Education Act (IDEA). Our mission is to strengthen service systems to ensure that children with disabilities (birth through five) and their families receive and benefit from high quality, culturally appropriate, and family-centered supports and services." (description from homepage)

http://library.ppld.org/Kids?ForParentsAndTeachers/LinkPicks.asp
Pikes Peak Library District

> "Grandparents Raising Grandchildren"—can be found from PPLD homepage by going to "Kids Web," click "Parents and Teachers," click "Parents and Teachers Web Picks," which takes you to a list of links for grandparents raising grandchildren.

http://www.readtomeprogram.org/
Read To Me Program, Inc.

> Stresses the importance of reading aloud to babies. Offers many activity ideas to make it fun and interesting for all involved. Uses workshops, DVDs, and videos for training educators and parents about reading to very young children. The DVD/video *Reading with Babies* is great to use with groups to demonstrate exactly how a baby "reads" a book.

http://www.rif.org
Reading Is Fundamental

> The oldest and largest early literacy organization for children birth to eight years of age and families in the United States, the agency provides information for educators and parents. Topics include best books, activities, resources, and partnering.

http://zerotothree.org
Zero to Three

> This site has a great deal of information on all the topics covered in this chapter. There is "Parenting A-Z" and "Professional A-Z" categories/links buttonsthat offer very useful searches. Handouts on some of these topics are available for downloading or purchase.

3
Setting the Stage

Very young children and their caregivers are entitled to the same quality of services that other library users receive. Armed with new knowledge and resources, librarians can evaluate, design, and implement services both within the actual building and outside its walls. Programming will play a major role, but there are other aspects to consider as well: the layout of the facility, décor of the area, materials purchased, type of staffing, outreach services, and partnerships.

Facilities

"The physical and emotional health and safety of young children and their families should be paramount in the design and maintenance of the library's physical environment."—Feinberg, Kuchner, and Feldman (1998: 30)

First, the facility must welcome very young children and their caregivers by creating an environment that feels comfortable and meets these patrons' specific needs. Are there materials, services, and programs that they can use and enjoy? Does the staff treat them with the same regard and understanding as they do other patrons, or do they feel harassed by staff if their child cries? How easy is it to identify and access the children's area? Does this area encourage interaction between books, adult, and child? Does this area invite people to stop and share a book by offering comfortable seating that can be shared by adult and child? Can young children reach the board books or are they on the top shelf? Are changing tables available in both the women's and men's restrooms? The library should be not only a place caregivers *like* to come with their children but a place they *want* to come with their children, a place where they know they matter.

Acoustics should be taken into consideration since very young children are not familiar with "library etiquette" or how to use their inside voices. In a welcoming and friendly space, adults may also forget this. A general statement to the group at the beginning of a program regarding voice level and behavior in a library is often an adequate reminder. Although the silent library has changed over the years, it is still important for everyone in the library to be considerate of each other. Post signs or guidelines for behavior but know in advance they only work if they are read. A crying infant can frustrate the adult trying to quiet him or her and the adult can unknowingly create a louder disturbance. Offering a smile along with the statement, "Some days are like this," can relax the adult and enable him or her to regain control. The adult does not feel scolded, but rather that another adult empathizes. Use a calm, quiet voice and manner to help model the desired behavior. If the situation allows for it, you may find offering a distraction to the child in the form of a book, toy, or puzzle helpful.

Space, Furnishings, and Displays

Consider clean, bright colors, lighting, child-size furniture, and accessibility when evaluating the children's area. A cozy reading nook creates a sense of welcome; use a colorful area rug, a rocking chair, or other comfortable seating for adult and child to indicate the area. If space allows, a couch or window seat is perfect for sharing a book. A low table functions as a standing support for very young children as well as a place to sit and read or do puzzles. Choose seating small children can sit on without tumbling off. Store board books and toys where the littlest ones can safely reach them; brainstorm ways to simplify clean up. On the walls, try posters of children from around the world. Pictures of children's faces have proven to be one of the best ways to direct all ages to the children's area, and infants and young children especially love to look at faces. Early educational curriculum stores and Web sites, such as Lakeshore Learning, offer posters of this kind.

Safety

Monitor your space for uncovered electrical outlets, sharp objects on the floor, rough or sharp edges on furniture or shelving, and small objects that tempt little hands and mouths. Get down on hands and knees to see the room and floor from the very young child's point of view. Consider alarms on doors that exit the area so no child can wander outside alone.

Toys

Keep safety and cleanliness in mind when selecting toys for the children's area. It is not necessary to fill the entire area with toys. Simple puzzles with knobs for little fingers to grasp, puppets, toy vehicles, and stuffed animals can be rotated quarterly or even monthly to keep the collection from becoming stale. Select materials that are washable, easily disinfected, and very sturdy. For safety reasons, check the size of pieces and parts that may detach and become a possible choking hazard. Some children's toys make noise, so be sure to read the full description before purchasing—animal sounds resounding through the library may disturb some patrons. Choose toys that develop the gross motor skills the very young child is learning to master or tie into early literacy. Try a rug printed with a road scene for toy vehicles. Store toys in plastic boxes on the floor or on the lowest shelves for safety. Another storage solution is a hanging shoe bag securely attached to a wall or sturdy surface. For infants and very young children, consider wall toys such as mirrors, touch screens, and basic manipulative toys. Suppliers include Community Playthings, Childcraft, and Lakeshore Learning (see end of this chapter for contact information).

Periodically check toys for wear and cleanliness and replace as needed. Is the intended age group using the toys? Are display materials being noticed and circulated or is it time to introduce a new topic? Are materials accessible to both adults and children? The objective is not to become a daycare or playschool but a place that introduces the world of books and language to the very young and their caregivers in a fun and interactive way.

Collections

Books

A book collection for the very young will consist largely of board books. Whether cataloged or not, they pose a storage challenge. Shelves can be used, but do not expect the very young child (or in many cases the adult caregiver!) to put board books back on the shelf. A better solution may be colorful plastic storage boxes and crates in various sizes. Community Playthings offers a baby toy box that can also hold books. Please refer to Chapter 6 for detailed information about selection and resources for books.

Parenting Collection

If space is at a premium, use booklists and identifying stickers within the general nonfiction collection to help identify this material. If space allows for a parenting collection near the children's area, make sure it is clearly marked. Include materials on parenting, breastfeeding, toilet training, sleep issues, discipline, brain development, child development, children's literature, and nutrition. Having parenting magazines and books, brochures and booklists, videos, DVDs, and audio materials all in one location makes it easier for parents to browse. Try to offer information in all languages spoken in your community.

Nonprint

Offer a selection of recordings that includes lullabies, classical music, children's popular songs, traditional songs, nursery rhymes, and so on. Having such a collection located in the children's area, or as nearby as possible, will encourage browsing by the adult. CDs, tapes, and other media offer the stimulation that infants need for development and support for adults who prefer not to sing on their own. For additional information on the importance of these materials and resources see Chapters 7 and 8 on rhymes and music.

Staffing

Having someone on the staff who is a children's specialist is always advantageous and in many places a requirement. However, this person is only one member of the team that supports and encourages adults and very young children to use the library and venture into the world of language. The specialist can help staff understand their role through training sessions, handouts, and informal conversation. It takes the whole staff to promote programs for the very young, point out and encourage use of age-appropriate materials, and spread the word about the importance of reading aloud to the littlest patrons.

If non-children's staff are resistant to this role, remind them that though they may feel they are not directly serving this age group, they no doubt have contact with adults who care for or educate very young children. They may also interact with very young children outside their work environment. Take time at staff meetings to update everyone on what is happening in the children's department, especially for the very young. Keep them informed through posters or emails of early literacy tips and facts. Go over the materials promoting early literacy and make copies available for staff to hand out at the checkout and information desks. A supply of booklists or bookmarks with tips on how to read to babies can be stored conveniently in an envelope and easily slipped into a book or handed to the adult. Suggest ways staff can support this area of service. For example, they might

- pass along a storytime schedule to an adult with a baby or young toddler,
- point out the collection of board books and remind caregivers that children love repetition and a favorite book is always worth hearing again, or
- reassure an adult with a wiggly baby that, "Yes, the little one is getting something out of the experience."

Staff can be supported by being supplied with tips or "info bites" (see Chapter 12) to share through postings or e-mail.

Programming

Programming for the very young should be integrated into the overall mission statement for the organization. Offer programs for a variety of audiences, such as workshops for adults only as well as programs for child and adult together.

An example of this would be to include the youngest member of the family in the summer reading program, which has traditionally been aimed at school-age children only. Very young children, with the assistance of their caregivers, can participate by completing various activities throughout the time period. A booklet or game board can keep track of these activities. Use a bingo template or a pathway with steps to mark off for each activity. Even a simple handout with age-appropriate early literacy activities and books for the adult and child to enjoy together and then check off would be sufficient.

Activities may include but are not limited to the following: visit the library, sing child a song, do an action rhyme with the child, look at a book together, meet the librarian today, read a story about going to the zoo/farm/store and go there, etc. Incentives could be a board book, bib, baby "sippy" cup, or growth chart. "Leave No Pre-schooler or Toddler Behind: Summer Reading Programs and Our Youngest Patrons," presented by Pamela Marin-Diaz, Sharon Deeds and Debbie Noggle at the Public Library Association's 2006 conference, focused on summer programming for the very young. Handouts from this presentation can be found on the 2006 PLA National Conference site.

Please refer to Section II for additional information regarding all aspects of storytime programming for the very young.

Outreach

The word "outreach" means leaving one's comfort zone, extending beyond the normal boundaries, and finding someone or some group to work with. This can be done in a variety of ways, such as material exchange, information communication, programs, and joint activities. Before reaching out in search of partnerships and off-site opportunities, be prepared with facts and statistics that support the need for new or expanded services. Ask the difficult questions and gather your information first. Consider the following:

- What are you currently offering to families with young children?
- Are there waiting lists for existing programs and services?
- What statistics would support the need for the programs, services, or training you want to offer? What do local demographics tell you about the community?
- What agencies are already serving this population? What services do they offer and what do they need? What percentages of families are using them?
- Would you be duplicating existing services?
- Could a lack of transportation be a major factor preventing families from taking advantage of your in-house programs and services?
- How can you get the most from your investment of time, resources, and budget?
- What can you contribute to a partnership?

Partnerships

Although many of us believe we can "do it all ourselves," the reality of life is that we cannot. Partnerships take time to develop and communication is vital to their existence. For many agencies, working with the public library may be a new concept and you may have to take the initiative. Get to know and understand all involved and do not assume everyone understands things as you do. Just as in any relationship, partnering works when everyone knows the goal, what is expected of them, and their value to the group. Some partnerships are small groups collaborating and sharing information. This can be as simple as displaying each other's flyers, booklists, and informational booklets or as complex as creating a parenting information fair with educational seminars and exhibits. For examples of large partnerships, look online at the "Brooklyn Reads to Babies" and "Read to Me, Charlotte!" projects (URLs below).

Offering training classes to early childhood teachers, visiting nurses, or volunteer mentors who support new mothers is a wonderful way to spread the word about early literacy. It also can create a ripple effect that spreads the message to those who would benefit the most. The *Every Child Ready to Read @ Your Library* Web site has a checklist that will help with finding, creating, and developing partnerships in the area of early literacy.

In addition to sharing the work, these are a few benefits of creating a partnership:

- Adding new points of view about literacy from other agencies and organizations that serve the very young
- Reaching an audience that might never think of the library as a place that would not only offer them services, but welcome very young children
- Broadening the knowledge base for understanding how to prepare children for success in school
- Accomplishing more because of combined resources

You may consider collaborating with one or more of the following agencies and individuals that serve families with very young children:

- State, county, or local departments of health: Collaborating with departments of health at the state, county and local levels provides an opportunity to promote the importance of reading aloud to very young children to those with limited resources and who, perhaps, may be unaware of its importance. Many health departments send mailings at specific intervals for children born in their communities. The library might be able to have their program offerings and an invitation to visit (often with an incentive of some kind) included in these mailings. Also, investigate the possibility of partnering with Women, Infants and Children (WIC) sites in your area. These are set up through the US Department of Agriculture.
- Head Start and Early Head Start
- School districts: These are good sources for demographic statistics.
- Daycares: Those that offer infant care may welcome training in how to incorporate language activities into the daily routine.
- Community colleges: Many community colleges have daycares for their students' children in addition to early childhood development and education classes. Some also offer programs for very young children and their families. For example, Bellevue Community College in Washington State offers parent education courses called "Parent Education Child Study

Laboratories," where parent and child can learn together through experience, observation, and instruction. Labs are divided by age groupings of infant, pre-toddler, toddler, and child.

- Pediatricians and visiting nurses: May be happy to put informational materials in their waiting rooms and pass brochures out to clients. Other possible joint projects might include getting books to children at each checkup. (See "Reach Out and Read" on pages 37–38.)
- Service organizations, such as Rotary, Lions, etc., have a history of contributing time and money to the community.
- High schools and alternative high schools: Many offer workshops for students in early childhood development classes, psychology classes, and education classes. Some alternative high schools have childcare centers where a librarian might conduct a storytime modeling how to read aloud to a child.
- Hospitals: Good places to make contact with new parents; give them information about library cards and services, perhaps include a new board book to welcome the baby to reading, or a coupon for a free book when they bring it to the library.
- Businesses: Some businesses encourage their employees to volunteer in the community, or offer educational programs for their employees during lunch hour.

Use your local phonebook and newspaper to identify community and government agencies, daycares, and early childcare centers that may be possible partners.

Once partnerships are in place, outreach offerings can include these elements:

- Story times
- Workshops: Topics could include reading aloud to very young children and its impact on brain development. Offer training in how to use books and language with very young children or model story programs for parents, early childhood educators, and caregivers. Find out what you need to do so that these workshops can count towards the continuing education credits that licensed care providers and educators need every year in order to maintain their licenses. The Washington Association for the Education of Young Children (WAEYC) oversees, administers, and offers training for STARS (State Training and Registry System) under the State Department of Early Learning. King County Library System libraries serve as locations for these STAR classes and have received approval for the librarians' early literacy workshops to count for STARS credit as well. These workshops can reach a completely new population when offered at an early childhood conference, a new parents' group meeting, or a childcare facility.
- Materials: Consider exchanging materials and creating booklists with partner organizations; producing a joint calendar of events; or perhaps

providing small collections for waiting areas where children can be found, such as in a pediatrician's office, food banks or shelters. Some service organizations not only contribute funds to support the library's early literacy activities but also help organize these materials for distribution and hand them out.

- Fairs and conferences: Information can be distributed, such as children's fairs, back-to-school events, and education fairs.
- Promotions of the library can be held in conjunction with local media such as community newspapers and television stations.
- Book bags containing early literacy and local library information in addition to welcoming the new arrival. These packages might contain developmental information, recommended booklists, local library information, a gift tied to early literacy, and an incentive for the new parents to visit the library. The gift might include a reminder about reading to the infant. In libraries that have undertaken such projects, popular gifts have been bibs, growth charts, sippy cups, placemats, shirts, board books, or CDs that contains songs and rhymes. *The Baby Record* by Bob McGrath and Katharine Smithrim, *Baby Rattle and Roll* by Nancy Stewart, *More Tickles & Tunes* by Kathy Reid-Naiman and *Baby-O!* by MaryLee Sunseri, along with other titles listed in Chapter 8, are highly recommended.

  Bags may be distributed to families as they leave the hospital/birthing center, on designated well-baby check-ups, or on a home visit. An incentive to visit their local public library may be included in the form of a coupon for which the parent will receive an additional gift or token when they bring it to the library.
- Programs with new parents' groups: Presenters can role model how to tell stories to the very young, explain what services the public library offers, and introduce them to a collection which can support both them and their child(ren). Groups of this kind can be located in hospitals, clinics, religious facilities, alternative high schools, community colleges, or by looking through parenting newspapers for play or parenting support groups that meet in the area. An example of this would be a group called "PEPS," which stands for "Program for Early Parent Support." Groups can also be found through the Internet.

Funding

Know what you want to do before asking for funds. Be prepared with documentation and research from federal, state, or local governments or private research groups that supports the importance of your request. The *Every Child Ready to Read @ Your Library* Web site has a resource component that can serve as a good foundation for a funding request. Since sources and requirements for funding are continually changing and developing, review Web sites for most current information.

Resources for Toys, Furniture, and Other Supplies

(Check Web sites for international contact information.)

Childcraft—early childhood supplies and materials.
PO Box 3239
Lancaster, PA 17604
1-888-532-4453
www.childcrafteducation.com

Community Playthings—early childhood furniture, storage, toys, etc.
359 Gibson Hill Rd.
Chester, NY 10918-2321
1-800-777-4244
www.communityplaythings.com

DEMCO—library furniture, learning materials, library supplies, etc.
PO Box 7488
Madison, WI 53707-7488
800-962-4463 (Customer Service)
608-241-1201 (International number)

Environments, Inc.—early childhood classroom equipment, furniture, educational toys and curriculum materials
PO Box 1348
Beaufort, SC 29901-1348
800-342-4453
www.eichild.com

Gaylord—library furniture, learning materials, library supplies, etc.
PO Box 4901
Syracuse, NY 13221-4901
800-448-6160
001-315-457-5070 ext. 8221 (International Division)

International Playthings, Inc.—puzzles, games, educational toys from around the globe
75D Lackawanna Ave.
Parsippany, NJ 07054
800-445-8347
www.intplay.com

Lakeshore Learning—educational products such as puzzles, toys, musical instruments, etc. that support early childhood and elementary curriculum including the areas of language and literacy
2695 E. Dominguez St.
Carson, CA 90895
800-778-4456
www.lakeshorelearning.com

Learning Resources—educational products in language arts, reading, ESL, early childhood, etc.

> 380 N. Fairway Dr.
> Vernon Hills, IL 60061
> 800-333-8281
> www.learningresources.com

Resources for Planning In-House Services

Arnold, Renea and Nell Colburn. 2007. "Read to Me! Summer Reading for Preschoolers." *School Library Journal* 53:7 (July): 25.

http://www.mcpl.lib.ny.us/familyplace
Family Place @ Middle Country Public Library
> "The Family Place project consists of a network of children's librarians nationwide who believe that literacy begins at birth, and that libraries can help build healthy communities by nourishing healthy families. As coordinators of Family Place, Libraries for the Future and the Middle Country Public Library conduct trainings on how to create spaces where young children and their caregivers can play and learn together." (from Web site)

Feinberg, Sandra, Joan F. Kuchner and Sari Feldman. 1998. *Learning Environments for Young Children: Rethinking Library Spaces and Services*. Chicago: American Library Association.

Isbell, Rebecca and Betty Exelby. 2001. *Early Learning Environments That Work*. Beltsville, MD: Gryphon House.

Martin-Diaz, Pamela, Sharon Deeds, and Deb Nobble. 2006. "Leave No Pre-Schooler or Toddler Behind: Summer Reading Programs and Our Youngest Patrons." Public Library Association Conference. http://www.placonference.org/2006/handouts_audiotapes.cfm.

Schickendanz, Judith A. 1999. *Much More Than the ABC's: The Early Stages of Reading and Writing*. Washington, DC: National Association for the Education of Young Children.

Walter, Virginia A. 2001. *Children & Libraries: Getting It Right*. Chicago: American Library Association.

Resources for Funding and Partnerships

Arnold, Renea and Nell Colburn. 2006. "Howdy, Partner: Community Alliances can Help You Reach the Next Generation of Readers." *School Library Journal* 52 (May): 35.

Arnold, Renea and Nell Colburn. 2006. "The Perfect Partner: Head Start is an Ideal Ally for Promoting Early Literacy." *School Library Journal* 52 (March): 37.

Feinberg, Sandra and Sari Feldman. 1996. *Serving Families and Children Through Partnerships*. New York: Neal-Schuman.

Hall, Mary and Susan Howlett. 2003. *Getting Funded: The Complete Guide to Writing Grant Proposals*. 4th ed. Portland, OR: Portland State University, Continuing Education Press.

Electronic Resources for Funding and Partnerships

www.brooklynpubliclibrary.org/first5years/pdf/BRTBALA2007.pdf
Brooklyn Public Library

Brooklyn Reads to Babies: This intensive early literacy campaign was designed to reach Brooklyn's 2.5 million residents (including caregivers of 50, 000 children under the age of five living primarily low-income, immigrant, and underserved neighborhoods), to help themcreate an exciting campaign using visually appealing and ethnically diverse artwork, and to make "Brooklyn Reads to Babies" synonymous with "Brooklyn Public Library." Partners included Target, Astoria Federal Savings, Harcourt Trade Publishers, Snapple & NYC Marketing, the "Read To Me" program created by Susan Straub, and others.

www.loc.gov/loc/cfbook
Center for the Book/Library of Congress

The Center is a partnership between government and the private sector to promote books and literacy. Current projects include those for very young children.

www.firstbook.org
First Book

Giving children from low-income families the opportunity to read and own their first new books.

www.ala.org/ala/pla/plaissues/earlylit/earlyliteracy.htm
American Library Association

Every Child Ready to Read @ Your Library: Web site supplies basic information and resources for developing partnerships in the community. There is a powerpoint presentation online by Garrison Kurts, of the Foundation for Early Learning, entitled "Building, Growing and Sustaining Partnerships" that will be useful to those new to this endeavor. The Web site also provides resources for finding and applying for funding. It is especially useful for identifying reliable research reports to investigate.

www.acf.hhs.gov/programs/hsb
Head Start

"Head Start is a national program that promotes school readiness by enhancing the social and cognitive development of children through the provision of educational, health, nutritional, social, and other services to enrolled children and families" (Head Start mission statement). Offers grant information and opportunities to those who meet its criteria.

http://www.reachoutandread.org
Reach Out and Read

This national, non-profit organization promotes early literacy by making books a routine part of pediatric care. It trains doctors and nurses to advise parents about the importance of reading aloud and to give books to children at pediatric check-ups from six months to five years of age. Children growing up in poverty are its primary focus. It also places books in the pediatric waiting room.

http://plcmc.org/readtomecharlotte/default.asp
Public Library of Charlotte and Mecklenburg County, North Carolina
  Read to Me, Charlotte!: A community-wide initiative coordinated by the Public Library of Charlotte and Mecklenburg County.

4

Finding Answers: Baby Rhyming Time FAQs

You can create programs for your youngest community members and their caregivers. It may be as simple as looking at your current story times from a new perspective. By adding new components and enhancements, you can elevate your program to a completely new level. Remember, story time is not just entertainment. It is a fun, interactive, educational early literacy experience for adults and children. The first part of this book examined how children learn and how involvement, play, and emotional connections affect their development. The following part will provide materials and resources for creating literacy programs for the very young. The program presenter has the opportunity to be a role model for the adults attending the program, presenting not only wonderful materials but the "how to" that empowers participants to continue their own exploration of the world of language and literacy with their children.

For the sake of consistency, the term "baby" or "infant" will refer to the youngest portion of this age group or those not yet moving or walking under their own power. The term "child" or "young toddler" will refer to the older portion of the age group or those able to move about, crawling or walking, on their own.

You may have many concerns and questions regarding programming for the very young. What books do I use? What ages should the program include? How do I get the parents to participate? Why should parents listen to me? Whoa! Each library and each program has its own unique situations and possible solutions. The rest of this chapter is presented in a question and answer format to provide possible solutions to some common "bumps in the road."

Organization

What Ages Should Be Included in the Group?

Ideally, the group would be limited in age range so that the program can focus on that specific age.

- Option 1: Strict age grouping by chronological age: Newborn to 12 months, 12 to 24 months, two to three years of age and three to five years of age. I use these groupings for my programming during the school year. These change in the summer, however, when our library system focuses more on school-age children and families. I am still able to provide younger children with some literary offerings during the summer by scheduling one or two programs for 24 months and younger.
- Option 2: Developmental age grouping. This can be as simple as offering programs for "babes in arms," children just starting to crawl about ("wigglers"), and children who are on the move ("walkers"). Such divisions can also prove helpful when selecting materials. However, this method can cause some confusion as it leaves open to individual (usually parental) interpretation the group to which the child belongs.

I have found that starting with chronological ages enables me to become familiar with the families and the children's development. If necessary, I can then recommend the program that would best suit the child and adult.

In many libraries, staffing, schedule conflicts, and so on can prevent ideal age groupings. Programs with a wide age range are a normal way of life for many librarians. See the section below on a wide range of ages and abilities for more suggestions on programs with wider age ranges.

What about Siblings?

For infant (12 months and younger) story time, I stress the importance of one-on-one time for adult and child, tending to keep strictly to the ages listed. Siblings can be a distraction, especially if they are close in age. An older sibling who can understand that the program is really for the younger sibling can take the part of the "adult" by bringing a doll or stuffed toy to use as the "baby." I have seen three- and four-year-olds showing their "babies" how to do "Head and Shoulders, Knees and Toes" as well as any adult. Many of these older ones have been through the baby and young toddler programs already and know the rhymes as well as I do! It is not necessarily easy to set and keep to age limits since most of us want everyone who shows up to enjoy the experience. If you have set age requirements and need to keep to them no matter what because of room restrictions or program design, do so with a smile and firmly explain why it is necessary. Try offering early registration for the next series to those you had to turn away.

What Happens If There Is a Wide Range of Ages and Abilities?

Each child develops at her own pace, so there will always be a variety of developmental stages present. The presenter can simply suggest and demonstrate various ways of participating as she leads the activity. For example, for "Eensy-Weensy Spider" ⓒⓓ, the presenter may offer the following directions:

Babes *(Held in arms):*

"The eensy, weensy spider went up the waterspout"	*(Adult tickles fingers up child's body)*
"Down came the rain and washed the spider out!"	*(Adult tickles fingers down the child's body from head to toes and ends by tickling or massaging child's feet— use thumb to make circle pattern on sole of child's foot)*
"Out came the sun and dried up all the rain"	*(Adult places both thumbs on baby's forehead, stroking each one downward in opposite directions around the outside of face to chin; the adult gently rubs the baby's tummy in a circular motion)*
"And the eensy, weensy spider went up the spout again!"	*(Adult tickles fingers up the baby's body again)*

Wigglers *(Child may be sitting up, standing, or held by adult):*

"The eensy, weensy spider went up the waterspout"	*([As above or] Raise child above head if holding in arms)*
"Down came the rain and washed the spider out!"	*([As above or] Lower child to floor)*
"Out came the sun and dried up all the rain"	*([As above or] Hold child under arms, swing gently back and forth, or use finger to outline child's mouth, or wiggle with child, smiling of course)*
"Out came the sun and dried up all the rain"	*([As above or] Raise child again)*

Walkers:

At this age, the child has greater control of her large muscles, such as those in her arms and legs, than she has of those needed for fine motor skills, such as her fingers. Add a verse or adapt the rhyme to allow for more physical involvement. Change the spider from an "Eensy" to a "Great Big" spider. Encourage her to use her whole body as the spider (arms up in air and moving legs as if climbing), bending down to the floor when the rain falls, stretching up for the sun, and then doing the spider movements, thereby using her whole body to become the spider, the rain, and the sun.

These types of directions enable and encourage everyone to participate throughout the program. Keeping directions/suggestions brief also allows the program to flow smoothly.

Should There Be Registration?

The size of your program area is not the only reason to require registration. It also depends on what size group you feel comfortable working with and the ages you intend to include. I highly recommend registration for the youngest ages (newborn to 12 months) because too many participants can disturb or overstimulate this age group. The size of your room may also indicate the need to register and is often determined by someone of authority such as the fire marshal. With babies younger than 12 months, I have found that registering 12 to 15 families usually means 10 families attend the program. I am able to focus on each family grouping and our meeting area is not crowded. The 12- to 24-month-old story time does not have registration and the attendance often runs high. This makes this program by necessity a more active program filled with bounces and other action songs. These programs are not better or worse than each other, simply different.

Registration depends on your community. If there is a large population of very young children in the area, registration is one way to manage the size of your group. People who register also tend to be more regular in attending. In addition, registration lists will supply a way to contact and stay connected with the participants outside of class.

Online registration is now becoming more available although paper registration is still often used. The use of tickets to control attendance has also been used by giving them out at a specific time prior to the program.

How Long Should the Program Last?

The actual program for very young children lasts 15 to 30 minutes on average. A typical script might look like this:

Welcome and opening	Rhymes—a bounce, a tickle, a cuddle
Rhymes—a cuddle, a stretch, a tickle	Circle time using a story, music, free dance
Song	Rhymes—a bounce, a stretch, a cuddle
Read a book	Closing routine

It can be tempting to have a program last too long, especially if everyone is enjoying it. Very young children can easily become overstimulated and that can ruin the experience. A short program also encourages the participants to repeat things on their own and to look forward to the next program rather than be exhausted from the present one.

Time may be added prior to or right after the program for interaction between participants and to give them a chance to practice what was demonstrated.

How Often Should I Offer This Kind of Program?

Keep in mind the goals and objectives of your library or school. Is this area of service valued? Can you make a case for serving this age group if it is undervalued? Examine your schedule and make a list of things for which you are responsible.

What are your required activities and programs? What is realistic for you at this time? The answers to all these questions can determine how often you offer programs for the very young. Is it possible to offer a series of four-week programs a few times during the year? Perhaps once a month is all you can currently schedule, so is it possible to maintain this throughout the whole year or at least for a season? If this is a new service for you and your institution, try not to overwhelm yourself. Give yourself time to become accustomed to working with this age group and to become familiar with the materials. Remember the tortoise and the hare—go slow and steady! This program is an introduction to literacy and is meant to encourage participants to explore the world of literacy further on their own. Do not beat yourself up for not offering it every week, year round!

What Is the Best Time for Programs for the Very Young to Be Offered?

If your target audience is working families, an evening or weekend time might be best. A weekday morning program will attract more at-home moms/dads, nannies, or other caregivers. No matter what time you select, it will be someone's naptime. If that comment comes up, simply remind the family that you are available during the library's open hours and encourage them to visit the library so you can assist them in creating their own literacy program.

Should Programs for the Very Young Be Offered Singly or as a Series?

Once again, look realistically at what you can do. When I first began programming for the very young, a four-week series in the spring and another in the fall was all I could offer. Series offer a chance for participants to build relationships and develop early literacy skills in a way that a single program would not. They also enable you to build upon the previous class. However, over the period of a year, once-a-month programs can accumulate to a respectable number of offerings and perhaps reach even more people than one or two four-week series can. Baby Rhyming Time was first offered once a month. Since this was a new program, we were unsure as to what kind of demand there might be. It has since developed into part of the regular story time offerings, with a four- to eight-week series offered throughout the year. It might be best to start slow and simple, especially if this is not only a first-time program offering, but also a stretch of your own professional experience.

How Do You Publicize Program Offerings?

Beyond advertising in the library, newsletters, and the local papers, where else can you publicize programs for the very young? Try hospitals that have new parent classes, childcare fairs, and local meeting places such as shopping malls. (With activity centers in many malls, young families find them convenient meeting places.) Post information in health clinics, alternative high schools, community colleges, and daycare centers. Check with your state department that handles childcare resources. A list of all registered daycare facilities in your area may be available. (See the appendix and accompanying CD-ROM for flyer and handout ideas.)

How Expensive Is This Type of Program?

It depends on you. Simple items made from inexpensive materials such as shakers (see page 120 for more information), cardstock fingerpuppets made by using Ellison dies, or juice lid manipulatives with stickers have proven to be big hits with families. Keeping an eye open for sales on items such as small bottles of bubbles (often found in craft stores in the party section) and sheer scarves (for peek-a-boo) can be another way of limiting the expense. At the other end of the spectrum, you can create a separate collection of board books just for your program or collect multiple copies of the same board book for everyone in your group to use. This may require you to apply for a grant to cover costs.

This Kind of Program Needs a Name, but What?

Trying to think up the right title for a program can be challenging. Luckily, children's librarians tend to believe in sharing ideas and many of the following suggested titles stem from them and have been shared verbally or electronically. A big thank you to all of them!

Babes in Bookland	Infant Time
Babies and Books	Just for Babies!
Babies with Books	Lapsit
Baby and Me	Little Sprouts
Baby Bookworms	Mother Goose Story Time
Baby Bounce	P.I.N.T. (Parents Infants and Toddlers)
The Baby Club	Rattle & Rhyme
Baby Explorers	Rhyming Time
Baby Laptime	Rhymes and Rhythms
Baby Rhyming Time	Rhymes and Songs and Books,
Baby Steps	Oh My!
Baby Story Time	Rock-a-bye Baby *(for evening program)*
Babytime	Rocking & Rhymes
Bibs 'n' Books	Shake, Rattle and Read
Book Babies	Small Wonders
Book Nibblers *(the books*	Snuggle: Story Time for Babies
are short, only a "nibble")	Teddy Time
Books & Babies	Terrific Twos
Books for Babies	Tiny Tales
Born to Read	Tiny Tots
Bouncing Babies	Wee Ones
Bright Beginnings	Wee Read
Bright Start	Wigglers and Jigglers
Bye Baby Bunting	Wonderful Ones

What If No One Comes to the Program?
What If Too Many Come?

This is the double-edged sword! If no one comes to the program, look at adjusting the time your program is offered. Sometimes half an hour earlier or later can make a difference. Consider moving the program to where this age group and their caregivers are. A local hospital's new parent meeting or an alternative high school parenting class creates a ready-made audience. Posting publicity over a larger area or targeting a greater range of people could be a solution. Look beyond the local paper to parenting newsletters and Web sites. Perhaps you can put flyers in other places where families with very young children meet. Think of pediatricians' offices and health departments, gyms, and dance studios. Do not forget to check into local community colleges, especially in the field of early education, to promote your services and programs. Exploring this route often creates the possibility of partnerships!

If your program is wonderfully successful, it may be necessary to create some boundaries. Registration is one way to control the size of the group. Once the class is filled, people on the waiting list may be offered the chance to sign up early for the next program. The fire marshal and safety limits restrict the size of groups in public areas. Pointing this out to the overflow crowd politely does not make it easier to turn away those who want to participate but gives a logical explanation. Extend an invitation to those unable to participate to explore the library, explaining that staff can help them locate material that is age-appropriate for their child. Consider the possibility of offering two identical programs, one right after the other. If necessary, you may have to enlist the assistance of another staff member to control the flow into the program room for you. Whichever solution you choose, present it tactfully, politely, and firmly, keeping in mind realistically what you can do.

Format

How Much Repetition Is Okay?

Repetition is an important way people learn no matter what their age. In the very young child whose brain is still developing, repetition helps with the "hard-wiring." (See Chapter 1 for more information on brain development and the importance of repetition.) I usually do rhymes/stories/songs at least two to three times and if the children show signs of really enjoying something, I will do it again. Offering familiar material is another way of keeping control during the program. Fussy or crying children are sometimes distracted into attentiveness when "The Wheels on the Bus" is sung and you can "Row, Row, Row Your Boat" as often as you like.

What If I Forget Something or Confuse the Rhymes?

Nobody is perfect. Keep an index card in your pocket with some of the rhymes, songs, and activities you want to include written on it. Do not be too shy to refer to it! A handout with all the rhymes used for the program kept by your side can be a great reassurance. The use of an outline for the program or each of the rhymes posted in the room will keep you on track but do not let it be a distraction. Many adults who attend these programs are impressed by what you seem to do so easily. They may also voice dismay at what they believe is their inability to duplicate what you present. If you accidentally "goof," acknowledge it. Doing this indicates to the participants that it is okay to make a mistake and try again. Having fun is a great way to learn for everyone involved, even the presenter!

How Should I Set up My Room/Area?

Whatever space you use, make it as child safe as possible. Check the floor for any objects that little ones might pick up and put in their mouths. Cover electrical outlets with childproof covers. Make sure that there is nothing hanging that might be a danger such as drapery cords, computer cables, or tablecloths. Look around the room from the child's point of view to see what may present a hazard, even getting down on your hands and knees.

Displays and handouts work best when kept to the back of the room to limit distractions. Preferably, center the presenter at the front of the room so no action will be taking place behind the presenter. At my location, I put a plain solid wall behind me so the participants are looking in my direction, not through the glass door where people are passing or at the fountain out in the courtyard. Make sure the presenter is visible and easy to hear so the participants can follow actions and directions.

Arrange chairs in a semi-circle facing the presenter. If attendance is large to overwhelming, remove all the chairs except one for the presenter. Those who absolutely need chairs or those unable to sit on the floor may sit in chairs kept to the side or back of the room. You may need signage to indicate this, especially if the entire group has been using chairs in past programs. (See Chapter 12 for signage ideas.) Another arrangement is to have everyone sit in a complete circle. This works fine with a limited group, as long as everyone can see the presenter. With a large group in a circle, the presenter should stand in the middle and rotate throughout the program to exclude no one. Personally, this is my least favorite setup since my back would always be towards someone.

Should the Program Have a Theme?

To theme or not to theme? Themes can work as long as the materials selected are chosen for their overall appropriateness, not *just* because they fit a theme. Having a theme helps the presenter gather materials, select rhymes, songs, create handouts, and so on. The adult participants enjoy themes because they make the material easier to remember throughout the week. The children just want to enjoy the literary experience. If it is easier for you to use themes, do so. If you need to "grab and go" using an assortment of material, simply present it as "Story Stew." A theme can be represented in the choice of book or rhymes selected, be it one or two. For example: *Brown Bear, Brown Bear* by Bill Martin plus *The Big Hungry Bear* by Don and Audrey Wood plus the rhyme "Teddy Bear, Teddy Bear" constitutes a bear theme no matter what other rhymes/songs are included. For more ideas, consult the subject/theme index.

Materials

Should I Use a Doll or Stuffed Animal to Demonstrate?

If you prefer to use a doll or stuffed animal as your "baby demonstration model" feel free to do so. There are life-size baby dolls and puppets available that are very realistic and may suit your needs. A stuffed animal with flexible joints may also work. Just make sure the children are not overwhelmed or frightened by it. Practice with your "baby" prior to the program so you are comfortable using it. The demonstration doll/stuffed animal may distract children. They may become so attracted to it that they grab for it. Whatever feels the most comfortable is the way to go. If it embarrasses you to use a doll or stuffed animal, do not feel compelled to do so. I will often use an imaginary "baby" to demonstrate, and this does not seem to bother the participants. Quite often by the end of the series, one or more of the very young children in the group will venture forward to become my partner.

I Am Not a Singer—Can I Use a Boom Box, and How?

Very young children are nonjudgmental and are mesmerized by the voices they hear, especially familiar ones. Use a boom box to help you with the tunes if needed, but make sure you have them cued up or have the track numbers marked down so they can easily be located. Remember, safety is very important. Use batteries or keep the power cord out of the children's reach. Try to keep equipment to a minimum and away from the children, especially if they are moving about under their own power. Chanting instead of singing, or making up your own tunes and simply reciting the verses are both acceptable. If the presence of adults in the audience embarrasses you while you sing, remember that they are focused on their babies. As you focus on the youngest of the participants, this may help you be less conscious of the adults. However, one of the best ways to help your singing is to ask the big people to sing, too. With group singing, everyone's voices blend and are enjoyed by all. Maintaining eye contact with the child helps the adult to be less conscious of the adults around them.

I Like to Use Props—How Can I Incorporate Them into the Program?

If you like to use props, keep in mind their size, where they will be located, and how many you will use. Props can help tell a story or rhyme, for instance, holding toy birds in your hands for "Two little birdies (or blackbirds) sitting on a hill." An extremely large prop, such as a four-foot-tall teddy bear, may frighten some of the children as it "turns around."

Props can be distracting, so it helps to have a place to put them out of sight. I simply put mine on top of the covered piano that is about four steps from my chair. A small open box by the presenter's side or behind the chair is useful for stashing items. A basket is good if it is large enough to put your materials in but small enough to move out of sight, or you might use a bag made out of a colorful child's pillowcase.

Leaving props in sight creates a distraction, especially for children who can crawl. With this in mind, I recommend props be kept to a minimum. Fun though they are, they can overcomplicate the straightforward mission of this program—to introduce the words of stories, rhymes and songs. So keep it simple. Use a bag with stuffed animals in it, pulling one out at a time as everyone joins in on "Old MacDonald Had a Farm." Have a ball available when "Roll That Red Ball Down to Town" is part of the program. With each repetition, the presenter can roll the ball to another adult/child couple. The use of a prop can help add variety to a rhyme used more than once during a program. It can encourage repetition and lessen the chance for boredom. See the section on "Enhancements" for additional ideas for using props.

What Do I Do If the Books I Want to Use Are Too Small to Share with a Large Group?

An infant has a limited range of vision. Move around the group to show the illustrations while telling the story. Use a flannel board, enlarge the actual illustrations on a copy machine, create individual pages on card stock that can be passed around the group, tell the story with puppets, or obtain enough copies of the desired book for each adult/child couple to have one to follow along in. This last suggestion might require finding grant funding to purchase enough books.

Should I Include Toys or Other Realia?

Including toys or other realia in your program is helpful if you want to talk to the adults. Occupy the children with the toys, allowing the adults to listen to announcements, parenting education, or literacy education—anything you need to tell them—or to relax together and network. The adult and child can also use the toys/books to practice what you may have demonstrated or suggested during the program. If this is the case, try to observe, give positive feedback, and help adults who are still unsure of how to do this on their own.

- "[Child's name] is watching you so intently when you shake the shaker and move it!"
- "That's a good idea to talk to your baby while the scarf is on your head. That way he knows you are still around."

- "Using lots of descriptive words about the bubbles you are blowing is giving your child a great start on vocabulary."
- "Talking to [child's name] encourages her to try and hit the drum herself."

Should I Use Nametags?

Nametags are helpful if you want the group to get to know each other and you want to get to know them. It is not necessary to use nametags, but they can increase the positive atmosphere of the program and help build relationships. People appreciate it when addressed by name. If the adult wears a nametag, it may not be necessary for the child to wear one. When putting a nametag on a very young child or infant, it is best to put it on the child's back, especially if the child is at the stage of pulling things off or chewing on things.

Nametags are also nice souvenirs for the participants to take home. When deciding on what type of nametag to use, remember to take into consideration how much time you have. Do you make new nametags every week or only once for the series? For safety reasons the use of string, yarn, or ribbon to hang the nametag around the very young child's neck is not recommended. Cut nametags out of construction paper or cardstock using scissors or a die-cut machine. Die-cut supply companies such as Ellison and AccuCut offer shapes usable as nametags. Teddy bears, apples, circles, and books are just a few of the shapes available. Use regular cellophane tape, double-sided tape, or a piece of tape rolled with the sticky side out to attach nametags.

If need be, nametags can be as simple as general white office labels (such as Avery mailing label no. 5163). Be aware that some labels may remove nap from corduroy or damage fabric. Write the adult's name on it with the child's name below. Self-stick labels written on with a marker or pen are stress-free nametags. If time allows or you have volunteers, use stickers or stamps to brighten up the label. Another way to decorate is to use clip art. Purchase reusable plastic badge holders with pins or clips at office supply stores. Companies, such as SmileMakers, specialize in labels and have a selection of nametag stickers. (Search at www.smilemakers.com under "name.") Personalizing these with the name of your program or library is also a great way to get the word out about your program!

Other methods for making nametags are more time-consuming, but they do result in nice keepsakes for the participants at the end of the program. Cut out a shape or simple figure from cardstock or upholstery vinyl. If using cardstock, write the name on with marker and then laminate. Punch one hole or two holes close together at the top and use a large safety pin to attach to back of child's clothing where it cannot be pulled off. The adult wears the nametag attached in the front. If using vinyl material there is no need to laminate, just punch holes and pin on. If you have a button maker, investing the time to make nametags for everyone is a special way to help them remember the experience. Demco, Badge-A-Minit, and Highsmith offer button makers.

Other Concerns

How Can I Get the Adults to Join In?

Be up front with what the story time is about—sharing between adult and child for a fun-filled literacy experience. Let them know that the child may prefer to observe and that this is fine since he is learning the stories, songs, and rhymes. It is a new and unknown activity for the child and he needs the adult to guide him into it. By actively participating, the adults are not only learning the materials presented, thus enabling them to use them on their own, but also showing the children what fun they can be. It may be helpful if you mention the following:

- Children are nonjudgmental and love how the adult presents the story time material.
- Everyone in the room is there for the same reason, to give her child a good start on the road to literacy success.
- Focus on the child and do not worry about the rest of the group.
- It is okay to make "mistakes," sing a different tune, or use different words because that makes the story/song/rhyme unique to the family.
- The child takes cues from the adult he is with and looks to that adult for reassurance and direction.

Encourage eye contact between adult and child when doing the rhymes to help create a bonding experience. Keep in mind how you speak—use a calm and sincere voice and do not forget to wear a pleasant expression.

The Adults Are Always Having Conversations in the Background—How Can I Stop It?

Once again, be right up front with the expectation that the adults take part. Perhaps the room can be reserved half an hour longer than the program to allow for conversation time at the conclusion. This problem tends to arise more with programs for older children such as toddlers or preschoolers. Depending on how big and how long the disruption is, you can simply stop and wait or lower your voice (theirs will seem louder) until they do stop and you can continue, with a smile of course. Mention to the group at the start of each program the importance of active adult participation in the program.

If the situation continues, you may have to talk to the "offenders" privately and explain this to them again. With the 12- to 24-month-old group, I will recruit the children to get the adults back on track. "Oh, boys and girls! The big people don't seem to know this song so let's teach it to them" or "Okay everyone, get into your boats [adults' laps] so we can go on a boat ride with 'Row, Row, Row Your Boat'!" Using a song/rhyme/story that demands interaction between adult and child gets that important sharing back into place.

Keep in mind that some of the adults in your group may not participate because they are unfamiliar with the rhymes/songs/stories. Sometimes there may be a language barrier. By talking to these adults afterwards, you can offer to help them find resources that will help them learn the program material. Speak to the group as a whole; try not to embarrass anyone by singling them out. Remind the adults that they act as role models for their children. Make positive comments to them throughout the program to reinforce that fact. Again, remember to comment gently and firmly with a smile on your face.

How Can I Integrate Early Literacy Information into My Program without Sounding as If I Am Lecturing?

Share early literacy information in small, simple statements throughout the program. They do not have to be elaborate references, just as simple as "Your child loves the sound of your voice, so singing, talking, and reading aloud to them is great. Especially since they believe you are the greatest singer, talker, and reader in the world!"

If you have space, use posters or a whiteboard to promote the message or the objective you plan to demonstrate that day. For example, post one of the early literacy skills from the Public Library Association/Association for Library Service to Children's *Every Child Ready to Read @ Your Library* Web site so you can point to it during the program with a "what we just did relates to this skill." Keep it simple and incorporate one skill into your script rather than trying to fit them all into one program.

Angela Reynolds of Annapolis Valley Regional Library, Bridgetown, Nova Scotia created a "speech balloon" for each of the six early literacy skills listed by the "Every Child Ready to Read @ Your Library" program. When attached to a stick in the manner of a stick puppet, the balloon could then be held up momentarily during a rhyme, song, or story. It could also be pointed to on a wall. (See "Text Balloon Template" ⓒ)

How Do I Get My Staff to Support and Promote Early Literacy?

Individuals can promote early literacy, but when everyone on the staff gets "on board," the train really gets moving! One of the most important things is to keep staff informed about what you are doing and why. Perhaps at a staff meeting you can present some basic information, such as the Public Library Association/Association for Library Service to Children's "Six Steps to Early Literacy." Let staff know how important they are in getting the word out to the community about early literacy. Many of the staff may be parents or grandparents or know children in the neighborhood. In any case, they are individuals who can help children themselves or their caregivers start on the road to school success by promoting the importance of reading aloud to children. To keep the momentum going, share tips and interesting facts on a bulletin board or through e-mail so staff can pass them on to the community through their daily interchanges. (See, e.g., "Early Literacy Ideas" ⓒ on pages 196–197.)

How Do You Keep "Control" of the Program with Such Little Children (Fussing, Crying, Wandering, etc.)?

Suppose an out-of-control child is behaving in such a way that makes it impossible to continue with story time. The disruption is preventing the other participants from hearing and seeing and, perhaps, you are about to lose your train of thought! Be proactive by reminding the participants at the beginning of each program that it is okay to step outside the room if their child has a "meltdown." They are welcome to come back in later or try again next week. This happens at times in the 12- to 24-month-old group. In the infant classes, a baby will cry because of hunger, the need for a diaper change, or over-stimulation. Let the participants know before starting the program if it is all right to meet their child's need there or if there is a special spot for them nearby which might be more comfortable. I have discovered that most participants in the infant story time prefer to move out of the group for a time and rejoin us when they finish.

By remaining calm, the presenter can help relieve a tense parent's embarrassment with the situation. Do not be afraid to enlist the help of the adult in controlling a child and keeping her safe. One of the guidelines you state before starting the program is that each adult should keep an eye on her child! In some cases, you may want to stop what you are presenting, be it a rhyme or story, and start one that is familiar or a favorite of the group. "The Wheels on the Bus" and "Tick-Tock" come to mind, or sometimes a simple, soft clapping pattern will help refocus everyone. Just because you start a story, rhyme, or song does not mean you cannot stop and change direction when the situation calls for it. You may have to stop completely but through it all remain calm and remember some days are like that!

Why Should Parents/Adults Listen to Me?

Let me ask you a question: Why shouldn't they? You, as the presenter, have invested time and energy to develop a program intended to introduce the participants to a world of stories, rhymes, and songs that are age appropriate and fun. The adults appreciate this and come to the program, perhaps, a little unsure of what to expect. They look to the presenter for direction.

If you are a children's librarian, you may feel that adults with children expect you to be the expert in everything parenting- and child-oriented. It is true you are an expert—an expert in helping them find the resources and materials they need. You are an expert in demonstrating good ways to introduce early literacy skill building. You have their interests at heart and can direct them to the real parenting experts who can answer their concerns and questions. That means you are someone worth listening to.

You care about children and their families enough to help them get a good start exploring the world of literacy. Why should they listen to you? Because you have something amazingly important to teach them—"The single most important activity for building the knowledge required for eventual success in reading is reading aloud to children" (Anderson, *Becoming a Nation of Readers*, 1985: 23).

Resources

AccuCut	Customer Service Center 1035 E. Dodge St. Fremont, NE 68025 Toll-Free Telephone: 800-288-1670 Telephone: 402-721-4134 www.accucut.com
Badge-A-Minit	345 North Lewis Ave. Oglesby, IL 61348 Telephone: 800-223-4103 Fax: 815-883-9696 badgeaminit.com
DEMCO, Inc.	PO Box 7488 Madison, WI 53707-7488 USA 800-962-4463 (Customer service) 608-241-1201 (International order line) demco.com
Ellison	Ellison Educational Equipment, Inc. 25862 Commercentre Dr. Lake Forest, CA 92630-8804 800-253-2238 (Toll Free in the USA) 949-598-8822 (Outside of the USA) www.ellison.com
Highsmith	Highsmith, Inc. W5527 State Rd. 106 PO Box 800 Fort Atkinson, WI 53538-0800 Attn: Customer Relations Telephone: 800-558-2110 Fax: 800-835-2329 highsmith.com

SmileMakers

USA	CANADA
PO Box 2543	91 Station St. Unit 4
Spartanburg, SC 29304	Ajax, Ontario L1S 3H2
Telephone: 800-825-8085	Telephone: 800-667-5000
Fax: 800-825-6358	Fax: 800-223-2058
smilemakers.com	

5

Creating Successful Story Times

Library story time has changed considerably over the years. "The preschool story hour was designed to provide an early peer experience; to expose children to books and literary language; and to give them skills in listening, sitting still, and concentrating that would help prepare them for school. Parents were usually excluded, and if their child wasn't ready for the separation, they were told to try again when the child was a little older" (Walter, 2001: 86).

Today, story times for infants and toddlers, and by necessity and intention their parents, are part of the weekly offerings of public libraries and community centers. The concept of emergent or early literacy has come to the forefront in not only the education field but the political field as well, becoming a topic even in recent presidential elections. The importance of teaching children what they need to *know* about reading and writing before they can learn *how* to read and write is being recognized. New research in brain development and how learning takes place has not only caused a change in programming emphasis but has also fostered partnerships among such disciplines as education, librarianship and medicine.

The traditional rules of story time need to be relaxed to be more age appropriate for those who do not yet understand "proper" story time behavior such as sitting still. Materials should reflect the shorter attention spans of the participants, leaning towards rhymes, brief stories, and songs that allow for repetition. Having the adult present and actively engaged with the child throughout the program completely changes the tone of story time and offers a wonderful opportunity to demonstrate the use of age-appropriate materials.

Jane Cobb, children's librarian and coordinator of Parent-Child Mother Goose Programs for Vancouver Public Library, and author or two books on creating story times for young children, says this about programming for the very young child: "Baby Programs required a paradigm shift for me. I was so used to addressing the children in my preschool and toddler programs. I had to learn how to relax and address the parents, to include them, communicate with them, and show them how to play in a way that would foster their children's early language and literacy development" (Cobb, 2007: 12).

Room Arrangement

If a meeting room is available, it is probably the most likely place to have the program. In some cases, however, you may find yourself in the middle of a shopping mall or out in an area that is usually used for something else, such as the picture book section of a library. Whatever the case, try to make an arrangement that you feel comfortable in and works with your style of presentation.

When arranging your participants keep in mind simple shapes, such as a circle or semicircle, whenever possible. A small group of 10 or 12 pairs creates a circle while larger groups seem to call for a semicircle.

Baby story time tends to work best when participants are in a circle. They can be sitting on the floor, perhaps, around a large blanket or bedspread (a child's twin size works well), or in chairs. Use a colorful area rug as a centering location. Encourage adults to bring their own blankets or have extra receiving blankets on hand. (Watch for sales!) Using a blanket or bedspread means washing it on occasion, but it can also help center and focus the group. If using mats or carpet squares for sitting on, remind people to be careful when doing a standing and/or moving activity such as "Ring Around the Rosie." Depending on the size of the circle, the presenter may choose to sit among the participants.

For large groups, arrange the participants in a semicircle shape with the presenter as the focal point. When using a circle arrangement, the presenter can join the circle or stand in the middle. Being in the center of a circle means that you will need to walk around, constantly turning to demonstrate, making sure everyone can hear you and see whatever it is you are reading or showing. Whatever arrangement you choose, try to place yourself slightly above the group, using a stool or chair. Make sure there is space for movement and that everyone can easily see the presenter.

Materials used during the program, such as a CD player or rhythm instruments, will need to be within your reach. Placing materials on a slightly elevated plane such as a table or in a crate, basket, or bag behind you will keep them from becoming a distraction. "Out of sight, out of mind" helps if the babies are crawling or grabbing at things. Sometimes my demonstration doll finds its way out of sight if it proves to be a bit too fascinating for the youngest participants. If you plan to use an easel, make sure it is safe and will not tip over easily. Posting the guidelines/expectations for the class will help remind adults what is expected.

If the program needs to be out in a public area, try to keep distractions to a minimum. Can the computers nearby be turned off during the program? Face the group away from the windows; watching people playing outside may seem more interesting than the story you are sharing. Keep the program focused and moving so that the colorful books on the shelves go unnoticed. As the presenter, you must focus on what is going on in your program; by staying calm and on track, you can have a successful program just about anywhere.

A table for displays and handouts is always important. Placed by the door or away from the activity, this table keeps things out of the reach of little fingers and lets you highlight items or materials you want to bring to the participants' attention. Place paper handouts, nonprint materials, magazines, and adult books furthest away from the edge of the table but feel free to put board books along the edge just in case little fingers can reach that high. Display materials can include the following:

- Sheets with rhymes used during the program (e.g., "Today's Books and Rhymes" ᴄᴰ on pages 205–210)
- An outline of that day's program, including books and rhymes
- Resources and booklists on parenting topics, early literacy, and so on (e.g., "Babies and Language" ᴄᴰ on page 190)
- Flyers/booklets from community agencies
- Guidelines or "rules" for the class (e.g., "Story Time Guidelines" ᴄᴰ on page 204)
- Applications for library cards; brochures listing open hours, locations and services, and so on
- Activity sheets detailing finger plays, music books, crafts, and activities that the adult can use at home to create a language experience with the child
- Presenter's business card and contact information
- Free parenting newspapers or magazines (check in your area for such publications)
- Age-appropriate books and media for this age along with bibliographies

Check with national and local agencies that may sell or distribute booklets on topics of interest: for example, "Every Child Ready to Read @ Your Library" from the Public Library Association and Association of Library Services to Children (PLA/ALSC), "Zero To Three," and "Parent Action" (formerly "I Am Your Child").

In addition to these types of display materials, I also set out a box of tissues and a package of baby wipes . . . just in case!

Format

The program length for infants and very young children is usually about twenty to thirty minutes. Use the time before or after the class to allow participants the opportunity to interact, or to present an educational segment or directed activity time. It is often tempting to extend the time frame of the program, especially if the group is active and enthusiastic. Remember that infants and very young children need time to take in and process what is happening around them. You do not want the experience to become a crying, chaotic mess due to over stimulation! If your group consists of infants that are still "babes in arms," you may at times want to consider a quiet or more introspective cuddle time rather than a bouncy exuberant one. Be aware of the levels of alertness within the group of children. Ideally, an infant is in what some call the "quiet alert" stage, well rested, tummy full, diaper dry, and actively engaged with someone with whom she has a positive relationship. In reality, rarely will *all* the participants in your group be at the same stage of alertness, but being aware can help you adjust the flow of the program. In addition, acknowledging the different levels can help reassure the adult who may tend to compare her baby to the others. A mom humming a song with the group while she holds her sleeping infant is giving that child an important literacy learning experience. A dad walking in the back of the room to quiet a cranky baby may learn that literacy experiences can help calm things down as "The Grand Old Duke of York" goes marching.

Here are a few possible formats from which to select:

Format 1: Activity at the end of program:

- Arrival and Settling In: Music playing in background and informal conversation
- Welcome, Explanation of Guidelines, and Introductions: Introduce self first, and then ask each adult to introduce herself and her child and give the child's age. If time allows or you feel it would help the group get to know each other better, use an ice-breaker. An example would be "What is your child's favorite book or rhyme?"
- Story Time: Program consisting of rhymes, songs, and stories
- Closing
- Activity/Education: For example, Blowing bubbles while music is playing or putting board books on the floor for children to handle while you explain early literacy concepts to the adults

Format 2: Activity at the beginning of program:

- Arrival and Settling In (Activity): Board books, plastic letters, or other early childhood educational toys set out for children to examine
- Welcome/Guidelines: Allow time to put away the toys or books
- Story Time: Rhymes, stories, and songs
- Closing Routine: Song or activity
- Announcements and Explanation of What Is on Display

Format 3: Activity during the program:

- Arrival and Settling In
- Welcome/Guidelines
- First Half of Story Time Materials: Rhymes, songs, stories
- Activity: Demonstrate how to read to a baby and then give participants board books to practice. During this time, you can verbally encourage, reinforce participants' actions, and give directions/advice to those who need it.
- Second Half of Story Time Materials: Rhymes, songs, stories

- Closing Routine: Song or activity
- Hand out souvenir or item that encourages an early literacy experience at home

These formats are suggestions to get you started. You may find that you use one of them consistently or you may prefer to vary them. Routine is important, especially to 12-to-24-month-olds, and adults with infants will appreciate knowing the general flow of the program. Each format has common elements that help the participants become comfortable and familiar with it.

Outlines

The outline of a program provides the frame into which you can set your choice of stories, rhymes, and songs. (For sample program outlines and ready-to-go programs, see Chapter 10.) Flexibility is a key component since the children can have such a big impact on what you are doing. Sometimes you may have to close a book due to an excessively restless group, or the chosen story just may not work that day with that group. Better to stop and move to a favorite song or activity. "The Wheels on the Bus" can literally call back distracted children and making the adult the boat for "Row, Row, Row Your Boat" helps everyone regroup physically and focus on the program.

Guidelines for Participants

Use a handout or sign titled, for instance, "Tips to Make This a Good Time for All," to share the ground rules for the program. (See, for example, "Story Time Guidelines" ⓒ on page 204.) It should include rules or suggestions the presenter feels important to bring to the participants' attention. For example:

- Please turn cell phones off or switch to vibrate mode.
- It is fine to let the child observe; do not force the child, but the adult should participate.
- If child becomes overstimulated or just needs a break from the group, please feel free to step out for a moment and then return.
- It is okay to make a mistake or use the words that are more familiar; rhymes can change!
- The adult knows the child best and can judge how much participation the child can handle.
- Relax and remember the more fun the adult has, the more the child will have.

Resources

Cobb, Jane. 2007. *What'll I Do with the Baby-O? Nursery Rhymes, Songs, and Stories for Babies*. Vancouver, BC: Black Sheep Press.

Ernst, Linda L. 2001. *Lapsit Services for the Very Young II*. New York: Neal-Schuman.

Ghoting, Safoj Nadkarni and Pamela Martin-Diaz. 2006. *Early Literacy Storytimes @ Your Library*. Chicago, IL: American Library Association.

Marino, Jane. 2003. *Babies in the Library*. Lanham, MD: Scarecrow Press.

PART II
BABY RHYMING TIME PROGRAMS

6
Books That Work

When selecting books, keep in mind the developmental level of your group, the size of your group and what you feel comfortable using. Size of the book and illustrations are important since an infant's range of vision is not fully developed. Taking a book to each adult/child couple to view is time-consuming and best used with small groups; limit to once during the program.

Publishers are coming out with larger size board books and "Big Books" that are good for sharing with large groups. Practice beforehand to make sure you can comfortably hold an oversize book, turn the pages and still keep the flow of the program going. Repetition is important when programming for the very young, so have a core book or books you use at every program. Through experience, selecting age-appropriate materials will become easier. The following bibliography of books used successfully in storytimes for the very young contains a summary and subject headings for each book as well as program tips where applicable.

Acredolo, Linda and Susan Goodwyn. 2003. *Baby Signs for Animals*. New York: HarperFestival.
> Intended to help infants/babies communicate what they need, see and feel. Full color photographs on heavy board book pages. Small size limits its use to small groups or couples. Signs are from *Baby Signs* by Acredolo and Goodwyn. (Animals/Sign Language)

_____. 2003. *Baby Signs for Bedtime*. New York: HarperFestival.
> A board book which gives the most popular signs for bedtime experiences. Intended to help infants/babies communicate what they need, see and feel. Full color photographs. Small size limits its use to small groups or couples.

> **Tip**
> With the two books above, demonstrate baby signs while reading the book. Have the adult repeat the sign two or three times. Read the book at least twice; encourage the adults to do the sign with you each time.

Signs are from *Baby Signs* by Acredolo and Goodwyn. (Bedtime/Daily Life/Sign Language)

Alborough, Jez. 2000. *Duck in the Truck.* New York: HarperCollins.
Large illustrations and rhyming text make this story fun to share. Duck and the other animals try to get the truck out of the muck. (Animals/Ducks/Things That Go/Trucks)

Aliki. 2001. *One Little Spoonful.* New York: HarperCollins.
A fun and rhyming story about feeding a baby. Short text, lots of sound effect possibilities and bright illustrations. (Babies/Daily Life/Food)

Appelt, Kathi. 2001. *Bubbles, Bubbles.* New York: HarperFestival.
A little girl takes a bath. Rhyming text; illustrations are made to look muddy but are still bright enough for sharing with a group. Part of the Harper Growing Tree series. (Baths/Daily Life)

TIP

Try blowing bubbles to music before or after reading *Bubbles, Bubbles.* A bubble machine is particularly effective.

_____. 2000. *Toddler Two-Step.* New York: HarperFestival.
Wonderful rhyming couplets that can be acted out by child and adult. Counting one, two to nine, ten and back again, the action moves in fun ways. Part of the Harper *Growing Tree Series.* (Movement)

TIP

Toddler Two-Step is great action rhyme—have the adults simply clap to the beat using their own hands or those of the child.

Baicker, Karen. 2005. *You Can Do It Too!* New York: Handprint Books.
Big sister teaches her toddler brother all kinds of things, encouraging him by saying "You can do it too!" Illustrations are in bold colors outlined in black. Text is somewhat long and detailed but may be shortened. (Families/Daily Life/Family)

Barry, Frances. 2004. *Duckie's Rainbow.* Cambridge, MA: Candlewick Press.
Trying to get home before it rains, Duckie passes through areas that match each color of the rainbow. Curved edges of the pages form a rainbow on the last page. Bold and bright primary colors on sturdy pages. (Animals/Colors/Ducks/Rain/Weather)

Barton, Byron. 1986. *Boats.* New York: HarperCollins.
Very simple sentences describe boats in the harbor and what they do. Bright and simple illustrations. (Boats/Things That Go)

Beaumont, Karen. 2004. *Baby Danced the Polka*. New York: Dial.
Instead of napping, the baby wants to dance. Rhyming text with foldout pages add to the fun. Small size may limit usage. (Babies/Dance/Movement/Music/Sleep)

Bell, Babs. 2004. *The Bridge Is Up!* New York: HarperCollins.
The bridge is up; a long line of vehicles waits for it to come down so they can go. A cumulative story with fun repetition of line. You can really be expressive on the line "So everyone has to wait!" (Animals/Flannel Board/Things That Go)

> **TIP**
>
> *The Bridge Is Up!* works as flannel-board story and can vary in length.

Bloom, Suzanne. 2001. *The Bus for Us*. Honesdale, PA: Caroline Press.
A little girl asks, "Is this the bus for us?" as different vehicles drive up and let off riders. Finally the school bus arrives and everyone gets on. Pages are large enough for sharing with groups and story has possibilities as a flannel-board story. (Bus/Flannel Board/Things That Go)

> **TIP**
>
> In *The Bus for Us*, you can add "Nooooo" to answer the little girl's question. Encourage adults to ask child, "What is that? [pause] It's a _____!" Do this even if the child is too young to reply by asking the adult to say the answer.

Bowie, C. W. 1998. *Busy Toes*. Dallas: Whispering Coyote Press.
Toes can do so many things like wave, tickle, dance, and taste good! Rhyming text. (Body/Stories in Rhyme)

Boynton, Sandra. 2004. *Moo, Baa, La, La, La!* New York: Simon & Schuster.
This extra large board book makes it easy for a group to share in the barnyard musical chorus. (Animals/Farms/Music/Sounds/Stories in Rhyme)

> **TIP**
>
> Encourage participants to make the animal sounds during *Moo, Baa, La, La, La!*

_____. 2003. *Fuzzy Fuzzy Fuzzy! A Touch, Scratch, & Tickle Book*. New York: Little Simon.
Large board pages illustrated with Boynton's fun-loving animals have something to touch on every page. Boynton's answer to *Pat the Bunny* is great for reading to a group and passing around. Good for building vocabulary. (Animals/Touch/Vocabulary)

Brown, Anthony. 1988. *I Like Books*. Cambridge, MA: Candlewick.
This little monkey loves all kinds of books be they funny, fat, song, scary, and so on. (Animals)

Butler, John. 2003. *Who Says Woof?* New York: Viking. "Who says _____?"
Turn the page to find the answer and an illustration of the animal that makes that sound. (Animals/Sounds/Question and Answer Story)

TIP

For *Who Says Woof?*, add the different animal sounds while reading aloud. Encourage the adult to make eye contact with the child while making the sound.

_____. 2004. *Whose Nose and Toes?* New York: Viking.
Each question page shows a different baby animal's nose and toes; turn the page for the answers. Illustrations of jungle animals and farm animals alternate. Similar to *Who Says Woof?* but more of a challenge. (Animals/Question and Answer Story)

Carle, Eric. 1990. *The Very Quiet Cricket*. New York: Philomel Books.
Little Cricket tries to talk to other animals but is unable to make a sound till the very end. (Animals/Sounds)

TIP

The Very Quiet Cricket can be shortened to fit the attention span of the group. Have participants rub their hands or wrists together every time the little cricket rubs his wings. Pause before turning to the last page to draw everyone's attention, creating a quiet moment. The electronic cricket sound at the end of the book can then be heard.

Carr, Jan. 1999. *Frozen Noses*. New York: Holiday House.
Lively poem about winter; bright, bold, colorful illustrations with a 3D look of layers. (Seasons/Stories in Rhyme/Winter)

Carroll, Kathleen Sullivan. 1992. *One Red Rooster*. Boston: Houghton Mifflin.
Counting book about very noisy farm animals. (Animals/Colors/Farms/Sounds/Stories in Rhyme)

Cartwright, Reg. 2004. *What We Do*. New York: Henry Holt & Co.
All kinds of creatures tell who they are and what they do. Shorten as needed. (Animals/Movement)

Charlip, Remy. 2002. *Baby Hearts and Baby Flowers*. New York: Greenwillow Books.
Rhyming story about all kinds of babies and their things ending with a quiet lullaby line. (Babies/Bedtime/Stories in Rhyme)

Church, Caroline Jayne. 2002. *Do Your Ears Hang Low?* New York: Scholastic.
Bold colors illustrate the silly camp song. (Body/Song/Interactive)

> **TIP**
> Of course, using the actions during *Do Your Ears Hang Low?* is a great way to get adults and children to participate.

Cimarusti, Marie Torres. 1998. *Peek-A-Moo!* New York: Dutton's Children's Books.
An oversize lift-the-flap book with a different farm animal on each page. Wonderful for encouraging interaction between reader and participants. (Animals/Board Book/Farms/Interactive/Lift-the-Flap/Sounds)

> **TIP**
> *During Peek-A-Moo!,* making the animal sounds is a must.

_____. 2004. *Peek-A-Pet!* New York: Dutton's Children's Books.
A different pet on each page plays peek-a-boo with the reader. (Animals/Pets/Interactive/Lift-the-Flap/Pets)

_____. 2003. *Peek-A-Zoo!* New York: Dutton's Children's Books.
An oversized lift-the-flap board book with a different zoo animal playing peek-a-boo on each page. Animal sounds help listeners guess the animal. (Animals/Board Book/Interactive/Lift-the-Flap/Sounds/Zoo)

Cousins, Lucy. 1999. *Maisy Dresses Up.* Cambridge, MA: Candlewick Press.
Maisy the mouse needs to find a special costume for a dress-up party. Simple illustrations are in bright primary colors. (Animals/Clothing/Mice/Parties/Seasons/Fall)

_____. 2000. *Maisy Drives the Bus.* Cambridge, MA: Candlewick Press.
Maisy is the bus driver and picks up riders at each stop. Bright, simple pictures. (Animals/Bus/Things That Go)

_____. 2000. *Maisy's Morning on the Farm.* Cambridge, MA: Candlewick Press.
Maisy the mouse takes care of the animals on the farm one morning. Bright, clear illustrations. (Animals/Farms/Mice)

Cravath, Lynne. 2000. *My First Action Rhymes.* New York: HarperFestival.
Heavy pages with bold illustrations. Ten finger and action rhymes with words and directions for each. (Stories in Rhyme)

Deegan, Kim. 2001. *My First Book of Opposites.* New York: Bloomsbury.
Board book with one concept per page or per double-page spread. (Concepts)

Demarest, Chris. 1995. *Ship*. New York: Harcourt Brace & Co.
Very simple rhyming couplets about boats. Illustrations are bold colors or black, purple, yellow, red, white and a slash of green. (Boats/Things That Go)

Ehlert, Lois. 1995. *Snowballs*. San Diego: Harcourt Brace.
Snowballs become a snow family when clothes and props are added. Since each snow person is a full vertical double-spread illustration, this works well with groups. Fun to use with 12- to 24-month-olds. (Families/Snow/Stories in Rhyme/Winter)

Emberley, Ed. 1992. *Go Away, Big Green Monster!* Boston: Little, Brown & Co.
Clever cutouts help a colorful monster "go away" piece by piece as the pages are turned. (Colors/Interactive)

TIP

During *Go Away, Big Green Monster!*, have the audience wave their hands and say "Shoo, shoo, shoo" each time a part of the monster is told to "go away."

Fitch, Sheree. 2005. *Peek-A-Little Boo*. Custer, WA: Orca Book Publishers.
This text lends itself to numerous ways of telling. The 26 letters of the English alphabet are playfully introduced by use of a rhyming couplet that always ends with the adult and child playing "peek-a-little boo!" Multicultural with big, bright illustrations. (Babies/Games/Multicultural)

TIP

While reading *Peek-A-Little Boo*, select only a few of the letters to introduce. Read the rhyme or point out where the item is on the page that is indicated on the bottom of the page. Objects like the apple or kite can be pointed to or touch the body part mentioned.

Floca, Brian. 1999. *Five Trucks*. New York: DK Publishing.
Five different trucks work at the airport. Each one helps to get the plane and its passengers ready to fly. (Things That Go/Trucks)

Florian, Douglas. 1987. *A Winter Day*. New York: Greenwillow Books.
This rhyming story recounts a family's activities on a winter day. (Seasons/Stories in Rhyme/Winter)

Fox, Mem. 2004. *Where Is the Green Sheep?* New York: Harcourt.
The reader can find all kinds of sheep but the green sheep seems to be missing. Simple, bright illustrations. (Animals/Farms/Question and Answer Story)

Frazee, Maria (illus). 1999. *Hush, Little Baby: A Folk Song with Pictures*. San Diego: Browndeer Press.
A favorite old-fashioned lullaby that encourages cuddling between adult and child. Illustrations will be mostly for the adults' enjoyment. (Bedtime/Songs)

> **TIP**
> Have adult holding baby or child gently rock in rhythm, singing or humming along with *Hush, Little Baby: A Folk Song with Pictures*.

Genechten, Guido Van. 2001. *Ha! Ha!* Singapore: Pleasant Co.
Farm animals laugh as a little boy drapes cherries over his ears. Illustrations are bright colors on heavy board pages. (Animals/Sounds)

> **TIP**
> Encourage giggles from group while reading *Ha! Ha!*

_____. 2001. *Hello!* Singapore: Pleasant Co.
All the animals say hello. (Animals)

> **TIP**
> During *Hello!*, have participants wave hello back to each of the animals.

_____. 2001. *Too Loud!* Singapore: Pleasant Co.
A number of jungle animals groan, moan, grumble, etc. that "it's" too loud. The last page shows a boy playing a trumpet with a TOOT-TOOT! Vibrant colors in board book form. Book is large enough to share with moderate-size groups. (Animals/Sounds)

> **TIP**
> While reading *Too Loud!*, cover ears after each animal says "Too loud!"

Gliori, Debi. 2002. *Can I Have a Hug?* New York: Scholastic.
The bear family explains why a hug is wonderful to share. Full color only four pages long. Nice size book for lap reading or sharing. This one will be read multiple times. (Families/Feelings/Love/Stories in Rhyme)

Greenspun, Adele Aron and Joanie Schwarz. 2000. *Bunny and Me.* New York: Scholastic.
Photos tinted yellow and purple give this rhyming story a quiet charm. For small group sharing due to lack of contrast in the illustrations. (Animals/Friends/Photographs)

Halpern, Shari (illus). 1994. *Little Robin Redbreast: A Mother Goose Rhyme.* New York: North-South Books.
This traditional rhyme is wonderfully illustrated using bold colors, white space and paper. (Birds/Cats/Mother Goose/Spring/Stories in Rhyme)

> **TIP**
>
> Gently lift or rock child up and down to appropriate passages of *Little Robin Redbreast: A Mother Goose Rhyme.*

Henderson, Kathy. 2001. *Baby Knows Best*. New York: Little, Brown.
Rhyming verse of what baby has alternating with a two-page spread of what baby *really* has. Wonderful illustrations and large size makes this book easy to share with groups. (Babies/Daily Life/Toys)

Horacek, Petr. 2004. *A New House for Mouse*. Cambridge, MA: Candlewick Press.
Mouse is looking for a new house large enough to fit the big yummy apple she has found. Die-cut holes throughout allow readers to join Mouse in her search. (Animals/Apples/Mice)

> **TIP**
>
> Insert questions such as, "Do you think this will fit?" while reading *A New House for Mouse*, and wait for replies. These will come mostly from the adult, but usually after the adult and child have talked about it.

Hru, Dakari. 2002. *Tickle, Tickle*. Brookfield, CT: Roaring Brook Press.
Playing with Daddy is lots of fun. Illustrations using bold colors and black outlines help make this book easier to share. (Families/Daddy/Family/Play)

Hurt-Newton, Tania. 2001. *Let's Go!* New York: Scholastic.
Elephant takes Giraffe for a ride in his car to a surprise destination. A simple story in dialogue form. Board book large enough to share with small groups. (Animals/Cars)

Isadora, Rachel. 2002. *Peekaboo Morning*. New York: G.P. Putnam's Sons.
Toddler plays peek-a-boo from the moment he wakes up. Last illustration is "I see you!" (Babies/Daily Life/Games/Multicultural)

> **TIP**
>
> With *Peekaboo Morning*, try incorporating a mirror as a prop. Play peek-a-boo with the child when indicated by the text.

Johnson, Kelly. 2002. *Look at the Baby*. New York: Henry Holt.
Photos and simple rhyming text about different parts of the body. Photographs are very clear, color shots that are large enough to share with groups. (Babies/Body/Photographs/Stories in Rhyme)

> **TIP**
>
> Encourage adult to touch/tickle child's body part as it is referred to in the text of *Look at the Baby*.

Katz, Karen. 2001. *Counting Kisses*. New York: Margaret K. McElderry Books.
How many kisses does it take to quiet a crying baby to sleep? Very simple text on one page with clear, colorful pictures of actions on opposite pages. (Babies/Body/Bedtime/Feelings/Love)

> **TIP**
>
> *Counting Kisses* is another book to encourage adult to interact with child by touching/kissing/ tickling the respective body part.

_____. 2006. *Mommy Hugs*. New York: Margaret K. McElderry Books.
Mommy counts the hugs baby receives throughout the day. (Daily Life/ Feelings/Mothers/Families/Love)

_____. 2000. *Where Is Baby's Bellybutton?* New York: Simon & Schuster Books for Children.
A lift-the-flap book that engages the reader to look for baby's bellybutton everywhere. (Baby/Games/Lift-the-Flap)

> **TIP**
>
> Tickle child's bellybutton during *Where Is Baby's Bellybutton?*

Krauss, Ruth. 1949. *The Happy Day*. New York: Harper & Row.
All the animals are sleeping (hibernating) when a new smell, the first spring flower fills the air. (Seasons/Winter)

Kubler, Annie. 2004. *Baa, Baa, Black Sheep*. Sydney, Australia: Child's Play (International).
Kubler introduces basic sign vocabulary with illustrations of babies from around the world singing a familiar children's song. Illustrations of babies from around the world show the sign with the actual word printed next to the child using it. This board book is large enough to share with a group. Part of the *Sign & Singalong* series. (Babies/Multicultural/Music/Sign Language/Song)

> **TIP**
>
> Use *Baa, Baa, Black Sheep* and others in the series to introduce sign language to the group.

Kutner, Merrily. 2004. *Down on the Farm*. New York: Holiday House.
This one is a keeper! Simple rhyming text with clear bright illustrations shows life on a farm. Repeated refrain is "Down on the farm." (Animals/Farms/Stories in Rhyme)

TIP

For *Down on the Farm*, repeat the line "Down on the farm" each time and encourage participants to chime in with you, clapping on "down" and "farm."

Larranago, Ana Martin. 2004. *Pepo and Lolo and the Red Apple*. Cambridge, MA: Candlewick.
Two friends, Pepo (pig) and Lolo (chick), figure out a way to get the apple out of the tree with some help from the ants. Sturdy pages, bright color, and simple text for sharing with groups. (Animals/Fall/Farms/Friends/Seasons)

_____. 2004. *Pepo and Lolo Are Friends*. Cambridge, MA: Candlewick Press.
Pepo and Lolo have many things in common—they both love to sing and play—but they have differences as well. Sometimes they get mad at each other but they learn to make up. Sturdy pages (8" x 8"), bright color, and simple text. (Animals/Farms/Feelings/Friends)

Lawrence, John. 2002. *This Little Chick*. Cambridge, MA: Candlewick Press.
Little Chick looks for playmates around the farm. Bold, black-outlined art, animal sounds, and a repeating phrase make this a fun story to share. (Animals/Farms/Friends/Sounds)

TIP

Encourage making animal sounds while reading *This Little Chick*.

Lawston, Lisa. 1999. *Can You Hop?* New York: Grolier.
Frog looks for someone to hop around with him. (Animals/Movement)

TIP

During the reading of *Can You Hop?*, encourage children 12 months and older to do the action stated independently. Adults can also do the action while holding a very young child.

Lewis, Kevin. 1999. *Chugga-Chugga, Choo-Choo*. New York: Hyperion Books for Children.
A rhyming story about a toy freight train's busy day. Bold artwork. (Stories in Rhyme/Things That Go/Trains)

> **TIP**
> Make *Chugga-Chugga, Choo-Choo* an interactive story by having the audience repeat the refrain "Chugga-Chugga, Choo-Choo" and adding a few "train whistles" for fun.

Lewison, Wendy Cheyette. 2004. *Raindrop, Plop!* New York: Viking.
A young girl and her dog count the things they play with outside and inside on a rainy day. Read the whole story or use as two shorter stories divided into outside time (counting 1–10) and inside time (counting 10–1). (Rain/Stories in Rhyme/Weather)

Linch, Tanya. 2001. *Three Little Kittens*. London: Gullan/Winchester House.
Large size and simple illustrations for this familiar nursery rhyme. (Animals/Cats/Nursery Rhymes/Stories in Rhyme)

Lionni, Leo. 2003. *Let's Play*. New York: Random.
Small size (6½" x 5½") limits sharing with large groups, but it has a nice story line. Lots to do from the start of the day until night falls. (Daily Life/Sign Language)

> **TIP**
> *Let's Play* is a possible flannel-board story; can be used with sign language.

Little White Duck. 2000. Lyrics by Walt Whippo, illustrations by Joan Paley.
New York: Little, Brown.
This popular children's song is illustrated with bright colors and begs to be shared. Book is a good size for sharing with groups. Score included. This is a definite hit with the group. (Animals/Ducks/Music/Children's Song)

> **TIP**
> Encourage those who know this song to sing *Little White Duck* along with you.

London, Jonathan. 2000. *Snuggle Wuggle*. New York: Harcourt.
How do various animal mothers hug their babies? Fun rhyming phrases describe hugs, such as "Swing-a-ling, swing-a-ling" for the monkeys. (Animals/Families/Feelings/Mothers)

> **TIP**
> Throughout *Snuggle Wuggle*, encourage hugs between the adult and child.

MacDonald, Suse. 2004. *Here a Chick, Where a Chick?* New York: Scholastic.
This lift-the-flap book is a good size for sharing. Illustrations are cutouts from handmade paper. Text is repetitive and fun to read aloud. Idea is to

look for chicks, but no chicks are to be found under the flaps until the last page. (Animals/Farms/Lift-the-Flap)

TIP

To add interaction in *Here a Chick, Where a Chick?*, read the line like this: "Here a chick, chick, chick. . . Where a chick, chick, chick? . . . [Pause] . . . Here? . . . [Point to flap] Let's see . . . [lift flap] . . . No!"—return to written text.

Mallat, Kathy. 2002. *Just Ducky*. New York: Walker.
Baby Duck is looking for a playmate till he finally finds one in his own reflection. Simple repetitive story with bold colors and simple illustrations. (Animals/Ducks/Friends/Play)

Manuel, Lynn. 1996. *The Night the Moon Blew Kisses*. Boston: Houghton Mifflin.
Quiet story of a grandmother and granddaughter taking a walk one snowy winter night. Child blows a kiss goodnight to the moon, and the moon sends down frozen kisses in the form of snow. (Bedtime/Families/Feelings/Family/Seasons/Winter)

TIP

Adult can kiss the child's body parts to add interaction to *The Night the Moon Blew Kisses*.

Martin, Bill. 1967. *Brown Bear, Brown Bear, What Do You See?* New York: Henry Holt.
A popular title for this age group, a question/answer rhyming story uses bold artwork and encourages the listeners to join in the storytelling. (Animals/Bears/Colors/Flannel Board/Sign Language/Stories in Rhyme)

TIP

Sign language is easy to incorporate while telling *Brown Bear, Brown Bear, What Do You See?*; it also can be made into a simple flannel-board story.

McDonnell, Flora. 1994. *I Love Animals*. Cambridge, MA: Candlewick Press.
A little girl who lives on a farm names each of the animals she loves—all of them! Realistic, large illustrations for sharing with groups. (Animals/Farms/Sounds)

TIP

In *I Love Animals*, use animals sounds after naming the animal; use when singing "Old McDonald Had a Farm" or "When Cows Get Up in the Morning."

McGee, Marni. 2001. *Sleepy Me*. New York: Simon & Schuster.
Calm, cool colors illustrate two-page spreads that are accompanied by a simple two-word text in rhyme: "Sleepy cat, sleepy mouse, sleepy sounds inside the house." (Animals/Bedtime/Stories in Rhyme)

_____. 2002. *Wake Up, Me!* New York: Simon & Schuster.
Great book to use with the very young. Big illustrations fill the pages. A rhyming story of a young child greeting the world at the start of the day. (Daily Life/Games)

> **TIP**
> Fun to have the adult and child point and tickle parts of the body as mentioned in *Wake Up, Me!*

Miller, Margaret. 1998. *Baby Faces*. New York: Little Simon.
Color photographs of different baby faces expressing various feelings. Board book that is a good size (7" x 7.5") for group sharing. (Babies/Body/Feelings/Multicultural/Photographs)

> **TIP**
> While reading *Baby Faces,* allow time for the adult to duplicate each facial expression while looking at his or her own child and to name the feeling aloud.

_____. 1998. *What's On My Head?* New York: Little Simon.
Color photographs of babies wearing different objects on their heads. A board book that is a good size for mid-size groups. (Babies/Clothing/Multicultural/Photographs)

> **TIP**
> Act out *What's On My Head?* by putting objects on your head or on your demonstration doll's head.

Miller, Virginia. 2002. *Ten Red Apples: A Bartholomew Bear Counting Book*. Cambridge, MA: Candlewick Press.
A simple story about collecting apples that can also be used as a counting book. Book large enough to share with groups. (Animals/Apples/Bears/Counting/Fall/Flannel Board/Numbers/Seasons)

> **TIP**
> *Ten Red Apples: A Bartholomew Bear Counting Book* works well as a flannel board.

Mockford, Caroline. 2001. *Come Here, Cleo!* New York: Barefoot Books.
A simple story about Cleo the cat told in rhyming couplets. (Animals/Cats/Stories in Rhyme)

Murphy, Mary. 1999. *Caterpillar's Wish*. New York: DK Publishing.
Caterpillar wishes to fly as her friends do, but she cannot until she turns into a butterfly. Bold, clear, colorful illustrations with a very simple text. (Friends/Seasons/Spring)

_____. 2004. *How Kind!* Cambridge, MA: Candlewick Press.
A circle of kindness touches all the animals on the farm when Hen gives Pig an egg. (Animals/Farms)

TIP

Adult gives child a hug whenever the word "kind" is said in *How Kind!*

O'Connell, Rebecca. 2003. *The Baby Goes Beep*. Brookfield, CT: Roaring Brook Press.
Baby makes sounds throughout the day children can imitate. Large size aids in sharing, with sharp contrast in illustrations using bold primary colors with black outlines. Repetitive text encourages audience participation. (Babies/Daily Life/Sounds)

O'Hair, Margaret. 2005. *Star Baby*. New York: Clarion Books.
This story in rhyme describes the many things that babies do throughout the day. (Babies/Daily Life/Stories in Rhyme)

TIP

While reading *Star Baby,* have the adult tickle or touch each part of the baby's body as indicated by the text.

One Little Duck. 2003. New York: DK Publishing.
Based on the children's song "Six Little Ducks That I Once Knew" and large enough to share with a group (7" x 9"). (Animals/Ducks/Songs)

TIP

Since some of your group will know *One Little Duck,* encourage the adults to sing with you.

Oxenbury, Helen. 1993. *It's My Birthday*. Cambridge, MA: Candlewick Press.
A little boy asks his animal friends to help him gather the ingredients for his birthday cake. (Animals/Daily Life/Flannel Board/Food/Friends)

> **TIP**
>
> *It's My Birthday* is a possible flannel-board story, or use props pulled from bag or box. Storyteller mimes mixing the cake.

_____. 1993. *Tom and Pippo and the Bicycle*. Cambridge, MA: Candlewick Press.
  Tom has trouble keeping his toy monkey Pippo on his bicycle until he gets help from a big friend. (Daily Life/Friends/Things That Go/Toys)

Prater, John. 1999. *Number One, Tickle Your Tum*. New York: Random House.
  Two bears count to ten using rhyming words. Heavy pages and big enough for sharing. (Animals/Bears/Counting/Stories in Rhyme)

Raschka, Chris. 1992. *Charlie Parker Played Be-Bop*. New York: Scholastic.
  This story of the famous saxophone player has a wonderful rhythm to read aloud. Introduces be-bop rhythm to children. (Music/Stories in Rhyme)

> **TIP**
>
> *Charlie Parker Played Be-Bop* is a board book version of the picture book by the same title. It's fun to read aloud and bounce, clap, or move to. Play jazz music as background while reading aloud or during activity part of program.

Rosen, Michael. 1989. *We're Going On a Bear Hunt*. London: Mantra.
  This follow-the-leader story may be used with children 12–24 months as a participation story. Oxenbury's illustrations enhance the story, but with large groups they may be difficult to see. (Animals/Bears/Participation)

> **TIP**
>
> Before starting *We're Going on a Bear Hunt,* ask everyone to clap their hands to its rhythm and do actions to get past each obstacle. Length of story can be varied if necessary.

Schertle, Alice. 2002. *All You Need for a Snowman*. San Diego: Harcourt.
  This story lists everything needed to build a snowman. (Snow/Winter)

> **TIP**
>
> During *All You Need for a Snowman,* have listeners roll their hands around each other to make "snowballs." Tie story to activity, such as dancing to "The Waltz of the Snowflakes" from the Nutcracker ballet or play with tulle circles as snowflakes (see page 118).

Scott, Ann Herbert. 1972. *On Mother's Lap*. New York: Clarion Books.
  Simple story of a little boy bringing his treasures one by one to join him

rocking on his mother's lap. When the baby wants to join, he learns that his mother's lap has room for them all. (Baby/Daily Life/Families)

> **TIP**
>
> While reading *I Love Trains*, have adults rock the children to the refrain "back and forth, back and forth."

Siddals, Mary McKenna. 1998. *Millions of Snowflakes*. New York: Clarion Books.
 A child counts snowflakes as they fall. Small book that has a playful and rhyming text. Best for small groups. (Counting/Flannel Board/Numbers/Seasons/Winter)

> **TIP**
>
> Turn *Millions of Snowflakes* into a flannel-board story. Using a die-cut machine or your own pattern, you can make paper snowflakes to toss in the air after the story or to give as a take home souvenir.

_____. 2001. *Morning Star*. New York: Henry Holt & Co.
 A little boy wakes up and happily greets the day. (Daily Life/Stories in Rhyme)

Simmons, Jane. 2000. *Daisy's Day Out*. New York: Little, Brown.
 Little Daisy Duck and her mother take a trip to Granny's part of the pond. (Animals/Ducks/Family/Sounds)

> **TIP**
>
> Make animal sounds when reading *Daisy's Day Out* aloud.

Stoeke, Janet Morgan. 1994. *A Hat for Minerva Louise*. New York: Dutton.
 A charming story about everyone's favorite hen. To stay out longer in the snow, Minerva Louise looks for something to keep her warm. (Animals/Chickens/Clothing/Farms/Seasons/Winter)

> **TIP**
>
> When reading *A Hat for Minerva Louise*, use scarves to put on infant's head as hat. Have different kinds of hats for the children to try on (these will need to be disinfected after using).

Sturges, Philemon. 2001. *I Love Trains*. New York: HarperCollins.
 Reminiscent of Byron Barton's books, this title features bold colors and simple rhyming text to tell of a little boy's love of trains. (Things That Go/Trains)

_____. *Rainsong/Snowsong*. 1995. New York: North-South Books.
    Two simple poems, one about rain, the other about snow, with clear illustrations made of cut paper. (Rain/Seasons/Snow/Spring/Stories in Rhyme/Winter)

Suen, Anastasia. *Red Light, Green Light*. 2005. Orlando: Harcourt.
    Playing with his toy cars and town, a little boy uses his imagination to create a world full of action. (Cars/Stories in Rhyme/Things That Go)

Tafuri, Nancy. 2006. *Five Little Chicks*. New York: Simon & Schuster Books for Young Readers.
    Mother hen teaches her chicks where to find breakfast. (Animals/Chickens/Farms)

_____. 2002. *Mama's Little Bears*. New York: Scholastic Press.
    Simple story of three little bears exploring the woods "on their own"—with Mama always in the background adding a sense of security. The cubs find the answers to their questions of what is over, under, in, etc? The large size of this book makes it easy to share with groups. (Animals/Bears/Families/Mothers/Question and Answer Story)

> **TIP**
> While reading *Mama's Little Bears*, pause to give the children time to locate objects in the pictures and perhaps answer the questions that the little bears ask. You can also ask them if they see Mama and point her out in each of the pictures.

Thompson, Lauren. 2006. *Mouse's First Fall*. New York: Simon & Schuster Books for Young Readers.
    Bright fall colors illustrate this simple story of Mouse and Minka sharing a windy autumn day. (Animals/Fall/Friends/Mice/Play/Seasons)

Tracy, Tom. 1999. *Show Me!* New York: HarperCollins.
    A rhyming story about body parts that is a good size for sharing with a group. (Body/Stories in Rhyme)

Turner, Ann. 1998. *Let's be Animals*. New York: HarperFestival.
    Children visiting a farm copy the animals' movements. (Animals/Farms/Movement)

> **TIP**
> Fun to have group move as the animals do while reading *Let's Be Animals*.

Van Laan, Nancy. 2001. *Tickle Tum!* New York: Atheneum Books for Young Readers.
    Mother Rabbit and her child have fun at suppertime. (Animals/Rabbits/Stories in Rhyme)

> **TIP**
>
> Tickles are a great follow-up to *Tickle Tum!*

Walsh, Melanie. 2002. *My Nose, Your Nose.* Boston: Houghton Mifflin Press.
Children show their differences but also their similarities. For example, one child has curly hair, another has straight hair, but both of them do not like shampoo. (Body/Individuality/Multiculutural)

> **TIP**
>
> While reading *My Nose, Your Nose,* touch child's body parts as they are mentioned and add phrase "That's (child's name) _____!"

Weeks, Sarah. 2006. *Overboard!* New York: Harcourt.
A little bunny loves to toss everything he gets his paws on "overboard!" The gravity game at its best. (Animals/Daily Life/Games/Play/Rabbits)

Wellington, Monica. 2000. *Bunny's First Snowflake.* New York: Penguin Putnam Books.
Everyone but playful Bunny is ready to sleep through the winter. Best used with small groups. (Animals/Rabbits/Seasons/Winter)

Wild, Margaret and Bridget Strevens-Marzo. 2004. *Kiss Kiss!* New York: Simon & Schuster Books for Young Readers.
Rushing out to play, Baby Hippo forgets to kiss his mama, but all the noises he hears around him finally jog his memory. Very sweet and good size for sharing. (Animals/Families/Feelings/Jungle/Love/Mothers)

> **TIP**
>
> Encourage the adult to "kiss" the child when line is said during *Kiss, Kiss!*

Wood, Jakki. 1992. *Dads Are Such Fun.* New York: Simon & Schuster Books for Young Readers.
The dads in the zoo are as much fun as any human dad. Double-page spread illustrations, simple and understandable text. (Animals/Dads/Families/Jungle/Zoo)

Yolen, Jane. 2002. *Time for Naps.* New York: Simon & Schuster.
Getting all one's stuffed animals ready for a nap takes time. Rhyming text with soft illustrations. A quiet story best used with small groups. (Bedtime/Toys)

Zuravicky, Orli. 2005. *Baby Faces.* New York: Rosen.
Each double-page spread of this board book offers something for child and adult. One side is a clear photograph of an infant's face showing emotion

while on the other side are words that clue the adult to which emotion it is. Next to the words there is a stylized dot similar to a "smilie" face that depicts the emotion as well. This format will enable this book to be shared with a group. (Babies/Feelings/Multicultural/Photographs)

TIP

During *Baby Faces,* allow time for the adult to duplicate each facial expression while looking at his or her own child and to name the feeling aloud.

Print Resources for Further Information

Butler, Dorothy. 1998. *Babies Need Books.* Rev. ed. Portsmouth, NH: Heinemann.

Ernst, Linda L. 1995. *Lapsit Services for the Very Young.* New York: Neal-Schuman.

_____. 2005. *Lapsit Services for the Very Young II.* New York: Neal-Schuman.

Ghoting, Saroj Nadkarni, and Pamela Martin-Diaz. 2006. *Early Literacy Storytimes @ Your Library.* Chicago: American Library Association.

Marino, Jane, and Dorothy F. Houlihan. 1992. *Mother Goose Time: Library Programs for Babies and Their Caregivers.* New York: H.W. Wilson.

_____. 2003. *Babies in the Library!* Lanham, MD: Scarecrow Press.

Odean, Kathleen. 2003. *Great Books for Babies and Toddlers: More Than 500 Recommended Books For Your Child's First Three Years.* New York: Ballantine Books.

Raines, Shirley, Karen Miller, and Leah Curry-Rood. 2002. *Story S-t-r-e-t-c-h-e-r-s for Infants, Toddlers, and Twos: Experiences, Activities and Games for Popular Children's Books.* Beltsville, MD: Gryphon House.

Electronic Resources for Further Information

www.prge.lib.md.us/Bks-Info/ParentsBIB.html
Babies Into Books Handbook.
   Kathy Kirchoefer (Prince Georges County Memorial Library System) created a handbook based on her program Babies Into Books. Look under "Appendices" for booklist.

http://www.itg.uiuc.edu/people/mcdowell/laptime/index.html
Babies' Lap Time: by Kate McDowell, Children's Librarian at The Urbana Free Library

www.unc.edu/~sllamber/pathfinder/mothergooseindex.html
Mother Goose Time Pathfinder: Library Programs with Books and Babies by Sylvia Leigh Lambert.
   King County Library System, Washington
   kcls.org
   Montgomery County Public Libraries, Maryland montgomerycountymdgov/content/libraries
   Multnomah County Library, Oregon
   multcolib.org

Sources for "Big Books"

Amazon: http://www.amazon.com
Bound-to-Stay-Bound: http://www.btsb.com
Childcraft: http://www.childcraft.com
Scholastic (in the Teachers Store): http://shop.scholastic.com

7
Rhymes and More Rhymes

Even before birth, rhythm surrounds a baby through the mother's beating heart. An adult holding a baby will often unconsciously begin to rock back and forth. To calm a fussy infant an adult may croon in a sing-song manner. Some nursery rhymes may have originated as political satire, but rhymes work with young children because they are essentially rhythmic play with sounds. Rhymes are often children's first language-building experience; they are short "conversations" between adult and baby in which both can actively participate, verbally and nonverbally. No matter what their culture or language, adults around the world use rhymes with their infants and young children.

Action rhymes and finger plays are learning experiences that involve the senses. They help build language skills by presenting the sounds that make up the language. Active one-on-one play between a child and a caring adult promotes relationship building. The child is stimulated when an adult uses rhymes to play with him. The sounds of the rhyme, the touch of the adult acting out the rhyme using the child, eye-to-eye contact, and following the adult's lead and movements are all ways of stimulating brain development. Sharing an experience like this helps excite emotions that, as we have seen though research, also help development and learning take place. "Sensory stimulation is very important for babies. These rhymes, which focus on touching the baby, also make a wonderful bonding experience between baby and caregiver" (Maddigan, 2003: 18). For more information on brain development and how learning takes place see Chapter 1.

Rhymes are a major component of any story time for very young children. They are short and lend themselves to repetition. Some adults may need encouragement to overcome their self-consciousness about using rhymes, especially in a group setting. While adults tend to be more at ease around babies, they may need your reassurance that slightly older young children are not going to critique them. They need to realize that babies and young toddlers love to share the rhyming experience with adults and, after all, infants cannot initiate the experience on their own. There are various ways of teaching rhymes, so experiment with the following methods to see which fits your style.

Teaching Rhymes Orally

Teach a rhyme by saying its title and reciting it completely. Then break it down line by line, explaining the motions for each line. Using a doll or stuffed toy to demonstrate can be helpful for this, but an "imaginary baby" works just as well. Simply perform the actions as if you were interacting with a baby on your lap, in your arms, or lying in front of you. Repeat rhymes two or three times (or more) before moving to the next component of the program. This will help everyone remember them. Keep in mind that not everyone will have grown up with the same rhymes, let alone with the same versions or melodies. There may be multiple cultures present at the program with each one having its own traditional rhymes. This presents an opportunity to encourage participants to be involved and enrich the experience. It also allows the children to hear the sounds of other languages.

Teaching Rhymes Visually

Handouts with the printed text of rhymes (see "Rhymes Only" ⓒⒹ) can be incorporated into a program in various ways. Distribute a handout with the rhymes you intend to use before each story time begins, at the start of a series, or at the conclusion. It would be preferable for the adults not to hang onto it for security. You may need to distribute the handouts at the end of the storytime to prevent this. If you distribute them before or during the story time, ask them to put the handout to the side and glance at it only as needed. They will learn the rhymes as they participate in the program. Either way, taking the handouts home enables the adults to practice the rhymes on their own. Another way to assist in visually learning rhymes is to make a poster with the rhyme written large enough to see from a distance and post it where participants can see it—on a wall behind the leader, taped to the table, box, or other piece of furniture the presenter uses, or on a sturdy easel slightly to the side. This method is useful when introducing new or unfamiliar rhymes to the group. Remember to keep these posters out of reach and secure for safety reasons.

The following section offers rhymes and actions to use during baby and young toddler story time. (See "Rhymes and Directions" ⓒⒹ.) The first column supplies the text for each rhyme in alphabetical order. The middle and right-hand columns offer directions for infant and young toddler respectively. Some are action rhymes requiring the participants to stand and move around. Others are tickles, bounces or rhymes that encourage physical contact between adult and baby. Some are perfect for cuddles. Increase your repertoire by asking colleagues, friends, and family members for rhymes they remember, encourage participants to share a favorite, or explore the resources listed at the end of this chapter, which includes non-English resources. Remember also that rhymes and music go hand in hand. (The ⓒⒹ icon shows which rhymes have audio versions on the accompanying CD-ROM.) See Chapter 8 for additional music and resources.

Rhymes and Directions

Rhyme	Directions for Babies	Directions for Young Toddlers

Acka Backa ⓒᴰ

Rhyme	Directions for Babies	Directions for Young Toddlers
Acka backa soda cracker, acka backa boo!	*(Rock baby back and forth)*	*(Bounce child on knee)*
Acka backa soda cracker, I love you!	*(Give baby a hug)*	*(Give child a big hug)*
Acka backa soda cracker, acka backa boo!	*(Rock baby back and forth)*	*(Bounce child on knee)*
Acka backa soda cracker, up goes you!	*(Lift baby over your head)*	*(Lift child into air)*
Acka backa soda cracker, acka backa boo!	*(Rock baby back and forth)*	*(Bounce child on knee)*
Acka backa soda cracker, I love you!	*(Give baby a hug)*	*(Give child a big hug)*

All Around the Mulberry Bush—*see* POP—Goes the Weasel

Apple Tree ⓒᴰ

Rhyme	Directions for Babies	Directions for Young Toddlers
Way up high in the apple tree	*(Raise baby above head)*	*(Raise arms above head)*
Two little apples did I see.		*(Make two fists)*
So I shook that tree as hard as I could,	*(Jiggle baby)*	*(Shake whole body)*
And d-o-w-n came the apples,	*(Lower baby)*	*(Bend down to floor)*
Umm! They were good!	*(Rub tummy)*	*(Rub tummy)*

(With baby lying on back—raise arms above head; massage circles around eyes; jiggle tummy; rub tummy; kisses OR adult lying on back—bring knees to chest with baby on shins; straighten legs to slide baby down and give kisses)

Baa, Baa, Black Sheep ⓒᴰ

Rhyme	Directions for Babies	Directions for Young Toddlers
Baa, baa, black sheep, have you any wool?	*(Clap baby's hands together)*	*(Clap hands)*
Yes sir, yes sir, three bags full.		
One for my master,		
And one for my dame,		
And one for the little boy who lives down the lane.		

Rhyme	Directions for Babies	Directions for Young Toddlers

Beehive ⊕

Here is the beehive,	*(Adult makes fist with one hand)*	*(Make fist with one hand)*
Where are the bees?	*(Point to fist)*	*(Point to fist)*
Hidden inside where nobody sees.	*(Wave finger "no")*	*(Wave finger "no")*
Soon they'll come out, out of the hive,		
One, two, three, four, five!	*(Open fist and tickle)*	*(Open fist and tickle)*

Cheek, Chin (Reprinted with permission from *Hippety-Hop Hippety-Hay* by Opal Dunn and Sally Anne Lambert, published by Frances Lincoln Limited, copyright © 1999)

Cheek, chin, cheek, chin, cheek, chin,	*(Touch baby's body parts)*	*(Touch body parts)*
NOSE.	*(Tap nose)*	*(Tap nose)*
Cheek, chin, cheek, chin, cheek, chin,	*(Touch baby's body parts)*	*(Touch body parts)*
TOES.	*(Tickle toes)*	*(touch toes)*
Cheek, chin, cheek, chin, cheek, chin,	*(Touch baby's body parts)*	*(touch body parts)*
Up baby goes!	*(Lift baby up)*	*(swing up into air)*

Choo-Choo Train ⊕ (Reprinted with permission from *Little Songs for Little Me*, written by Nancy Stewart, copyright 2007)

This is a choo-choo train	*(Standing, gently bounce baby)*	*(Bend arms at elbows)*
Puffing down the track.		*(Rotate arms in rhythm)*
Now it's going forward,	*(Move forward)*	*(Walk forward)*
Now it's going back.	*(Move backward)*	*(Walk backward)*
Now the bell is ringing,	*(Tap baby's nose gently)*	*(Pull cord with closed fist)*
Now the whistle blows.	*(Blow on baby's head)*	*(Hold fist near mouth)*
What a lot of noise it makes	*(Cover ears)*	*(Cover ears)*
Everywhere it goes.	*(Turn around in a circle)*	*(Stretch arms out)*

Clap Your Hands

Clap your hands—one, two, three!	*(Clap baby's hands together)*	*(Do as directed)*
Clap your hands, just like me!		

(Add verses by including: Roll your hands, Nod your head, Wave bye-bye, or use other body motions)

Rhyme	Directions for Babies	Directions for Young Toddlers
Cobbler, Cobbler (CD)		
Cobbler, cobbler, mend my shoe.	*(Pat baby's foot)*	*(Pat child's or adult's foot)*
Give it one stitch, give it two.		
Give it three, give it four,		
And if it needs it give it more!		
Criss, Cross, Applesauce (CD)	*(Baby on tummy)*	*(Child faces away from adult)*
Criss, cross, applesauce,	*(Draw X on back)*	*(Draw X on back)*
Spiders climbing up your back!	*(Walk fingers up baby's back)*	*(Walk fingers up back)*
Cool breeze, tight squeeze,	*(Blow hair, give hug)*	*(Blow hair, give hug)*
And now you've got the shivers!	*(Tickle)*	*(Tickle)*
Diddle Diddle Dumpling (CD)		
Diddle diddle dumpling, my son John,	*(Rock baby)*	*(Bounce)*
Went to sleep with his stockings on!		
One shoe off	*(Pat one foot)*	*(Pat one foot)*
And one shoe on.	*(Pat other foot)*	*(Pat other foot)*
Diddle diddle dumpling, my son John!	*(Rock)*	*(Bounce)*
Eensy, Weensy Spider (CD)		
The eensy, weensy spider went up the water spout.	*(Walk fingers up body)*	*(Walk fingers up back or arm)*
Down came the rain and washed the spider out!	*(Tickle fingers down head to toe)*	*(Tickle fingers downward)*
Out came the sun and dried up all the rain,	*(Massage baby's back)*	*(Arms above head)*
And the eensy, weensy spider went up the spout again.	*(Walk fingers up body)*	*(Walk fingers up back or arm)*
The Engine (CD)		
Here is the engine that runs on the track.	*(Bounce baby)*	*(Rotate arms like engine)*
It whistles—"toot toot!"	*(Tap baby's nose)*	*(Pat belly)*
And then it runs back.	*(Tickle down from nose)*	*(Wiggle backwards)*

Rhyme	Directions for Babies	Directions for Young Toddlers

From Wibbleton to Wobbleton ⓒⒹ

From Wibbleton to Wobbleton is 15 miles,	*(Bounce baby)*	*(Clap hands or bounce)*
From Wobbleton to Wibbleton is 15 miles,		
From Wibbleton to Wobbleton, from Wobbleton to Wibbleton,		
From Wibbleton to Wobbleton is 15 miles.		

The Grand Old Duke of York ⓒⒹ

Oh, the grand old Duke of York, He had 10,000 men.	*(March holding baby)*	*(March in place)*
He marched them up to the top of the hill	*(Lift baby up into air)*	*(Lift up/hold arms over head)*
And he marched them down again.	*(Lower baby)*	*(Lower or touch floor)*
And when they were up, they were up.	*(Baby up)*	*(Lift up/arms up)*
And when they were down, they were down.	*(Lower)*	*(Lower or touch floor)*
But when they were only halfway up,	*(Stand)*	*(Stand)*
They were neither up nor down!	*(Hop)*	*(Hop)*
They marched them to the left,	*(Turn to left)*	*(Turn to left)*
They marched them to the right,	*(Turn to right)*	*(Turn to right)*
They even marched them upside-down,	*(Tip upside-down)*	*(Turn upside-down)*
Now isn't that a sight!	*(Bounce)*	*(Clap)*

Grandma's Glasses ⓒⒹ

These are Grandma's glasses,	*(Massage circles around eyes)*	*(Fingers circle eyes)*
This is Grandma's hat.	*(Pat baby's head)*	*(Hands on head)*
This is the way she folds her hands	*(Hold baby's hands together)*	*(Put hands together)*
And lays them in her lap.	*(Hands together in lap)*	*(Put hands in lap)*

Rhyme	Directions for Babies	Directions for Young Toddlers
Gray Squirrel ⓒⓓ		
Gray squirrel, gray squirrel, swish your bushy tail.	*(Rock baby back and forth)*	*(Child on knees/swing side to side)*
Gray Squirrel, gray squirrel, swish your bushy tail.		
Wrinkle up your little nose,	*(Tickle baby's nose)*	*(Wiggle nose)*
Hold a nut between your toes.	*(Tickle toes)*	*(Pat hands together)*
Gray Squirrel, gray squirrel, swish your bushy tail.	*(Rock baby back and forth)*	*(Child on lap/swing knees)*
Great Big Spider ⓒⓓ	*(Baby on tummy)*	*(Standing)*
The great big spider went up the water spout.	*(Massage up baby's back)*	*(Climbing/arms above head)*
Down came the rain and washed the spider out!	*(Tickle fingers down back and rub feet)*	*(Bend over/touch ground)*
Out came the sun and dried up all the rain,	*(Rub in circle on baby's back)*	*(Arms over head in circle)*
And the great big spider went up the spout again.	*(Massage up baby's back)*	*(Climbing/arms above head)*
Head and Shoulders, Knees and Toes ⓒⓓ		
Head and shoulders, knees and toes, knees and toes.	*(Touch baby's body parts)*	*(Touch own or child's body)*
Head and shoulders, knees and toes, knees and toes.		
Eyes and ears and mouth and nose.	*(Use thumbs to circle these)*	
Head and shoulders, knees and toes, knees and toes.		
Here Comes a Mouse ⓒⓓ		
Here comes a mouse— mousie, mousie, mouse.	*(Walk finger up baby's body)*	*(Wiggle finger towards child)*
On tiny light feet, and a soft pink nose,	*(Tap nose)*	*(Tap nose)*
Tickle, tickle, wherever he goes.	*(Tickle)*	*(Tickle)*
He'll run up your arm and under your chin!	*(Do as directed)*	*(Do as directed)*

Rhyme	Directions for Babies	Directions for Young Toddlers
Here Comes a Mouse *(Continued)*		
Don't open your mouth or the mouse will run in!	*(Tap lips)*	*(Circle around mouth)*
Mousie, mousie, mouse.	*(Tap nose or chin)*	*(Tap nose)*
Here Is Baby (CD)		
Here is baby ready for a nap.	*(Rock baby in arms)*	*(Hold up hand)*
Lay her down in her mother's lap.		*(Cross arms together)*
Cover her up so she won't peep.	*(Cuddle)*	
And rock her till she's fast asleep.	*(Rock baby)*	*(Rock arms back and forth)*
Here's a Ball (CD)		
Here's a ball and here's a ball,	*(Bounce baby)*	*(Form circles with hands . . .*
And a great big ball I see.		*each increasing in size)*
Shall we count them? Are you ready?		
One, two, three!	*(Swing baby)*	*(Repeat above)*
Here's a Ball for Baby (CD)	*(Adult does actions)*	
Here's a ball for baby,	*(Hands make circle shape)*	*(Hands make circle shape)*
Big and soft and round.		
Here is baby's hammer,	*(Make fist)*	*(Make fist)*
Oh, how he can pound.	*(Pound hands together)*	*(Pound hands together)*
Here is baby's music, clapping clapping so.	*(Clap hands)*	*(Clap hands)*
Here are baby's soldiers,	*(Hold fingers upright)*	*(Hold fingers upright)*
Standing in a row.		
Here is baby's trumpet,	*(Bring fist to mouth)*	*(Bring fist to mouth)*
Toot toot-toot, toot-toot, toot.		
Here's the way that baby		
Plays at peek-a-boo.	*(Peek-a-boo)*	*(Peek-a-boo)*
Here's a big umbrella	*(Hands together over head)*	*(Hands together over head)*
To keep a baby dry.		
Here is baby's cradle,	*(Arms folded)*	*(Arms folded)*
Rock-a-baby bye.	*(Rock arms back and forth)*	*(Rock arms back and forth)*

Rhyme	Directions for Babies	Directions for Young Toddlers

Here We Go 'Round the Mulberry Bush/Cobbler's Bench (CD)

Here we go 'round the mulberry bush,	*(Baby in arms, rock or walk around)*	*(Walk in circle)*
The mulberry bush, the mulberry bush.		
Here we go 'round the mulberry bush		
Early in the morning.		

Here We Go Up–Up–Up (CD)

Here we go up–up–up,	*(Lift baby up)*	*(Jump up three times)*
And here we go down–down–down.	*(Lower baby)*	*(Bend to floor)*
And here we go back-and-forth and back-and-forth.	*(Rock gently)*	*(Rock from side to side)*
And here we go around and around and around.	*(Turn in circle)*	*(Spin around)*

Hey Diddle, Diddle (CD)

Hey diddle, diddle, the cat and the fiddle,	*(Clap)*	*(Bounce child on knee)*
The cow jumped over the moon.	*(Hop)*	*(Lift child to other knee)*
The little dog laughed to see such fun,	*(Tickle)*	*(Tickle)*
And the dish ran away with the spoon.	*(Clap)*	*(Bounce)*

Hickory, Dickory Dock (CD)

	(Holding baby)	*(Holding child)*
Hickory, dickory dock, the mouse ran up the clock.	*(Rock and tickle up body)*	*(Rock then lift child up)*
The clock struck one, the mouse ran down!	*(Tap baby's nose and lower)*	*(Lower child)*
Hickory, dickory dock.	*(Rock)*	*(Rock)***

***(For child standing alone: hands held together in front of body; swing gently back and forth; lift hands above head; clap; lower hands and swing)*

Rhyme	Directions for Babies	Directions for Young Toddlers
Humpty Dumpty 💿	*(Hold baby in arms)*	*(Hold child on knees)*
Humpty Dumpty sat on a wall.	*(Rock)*	*(Bounce)*
Humpty Dumpty had a great fall!	*(Lower baby)*	*(Drop child between knees)*
All the king's horses and all the king's men,	*(Rock)*	*(Bounce)*
Couldn't put Humpty together again.	*(Rock)*	*(Bounce)*
Jack Be Nimble 💿 *(You can also demonstrate "over" by jumping a stuffed animal over something)*		
Jack be nimble,		
Jack be quick.		
Jack jump over the candlestick!	*(Jump)*	*(Jump on "over")*
Jeremiah, Blow the Fire 💿 *(Baby on back in front of adult)*		
Jeremiah, blow the fire,		*(Bounce)*
Puff, puff, puff.	*(Blow on tummy three times)*	*(Blow child's hair three times)*
First you blow it gently…	*(Blow soft and long on tummy gently)*	*(Blow soft and long on hair gently)*
Then you blow it rough.	*(Big blow and tickle on tummy)*	*(Big blow and tickle)*
Leg Over Leg 💿		
Leg over leg, the dog went to Dover.	*(Hold baby and rock)*	*(Bounce child on knee)*
He came to a stile—Jump!	*(Dramatic pause, then slight jump)*	*(Dramatic pause, then lift up)*
He went over!		*(Move to other knee)*
Mother and Father and Uncle John 💿		
Mother and Father and Uncle John	*(Bounce baby)*	*(Bounce child on lap)*
Went to town, one by one.		
Mother fell off,	*(Tip to one side)*	*(Tip to one side)*
And Father fell off,	*(Tip to other side)*	*(Tip to other side)*
But Uncle John went on and on and on and on and on!	*(Bounce)*	*(Bounce)*

Rhyme	Directions for Babies	Directions for Young Toddlers

My Pony Macaroni (cd)

I have a little pony,	*(Bounce)*	*(Bounce)*
His name is Macaroni.		
He trots and trots and then he STOPS!	*(On "STOPS"—long pause)*	*(On "STOPS"—long pause)*
My funny little pony, Mac-a-<u>RO</u>-ni!	*(Bounce and jiggle on "RO")*	*(Bounce and jiggle on "RO")*

One, Two (cd) (Reprinted with permission from *Baby Rattle and Roll*, written by Nancy Stewart, copyright 2007) *(Use pointer fingers on both hands to count "one" and "two")*

One, two, one, two	*(Hold up your fingers to count)*	*(Follow actions for baby but
I have two eyes, so do you.	*(Point to your eyes, then baby's)*	encourage child to point to
One, two, one, two	*(Hold up your fingers to count)*	his or her own body parts)*
I have two ears, so do you.	*(Point to your ears, then baby's)*	
One two, one, two	*(Hold up your fingers to count)*	
I have two lips, so do you.	*(Point to your lips, then baby's)*	
One, two, one, two	*(Hold up your fingers to count)*	
I have two hands, so do you.	*(Point to your hands, then baby's)*	
So do you!	*(Tap nose of baby or give a hug)*	

One, Two, Buckle My Shoe (cd)
(Do as a clapping rhyme or part of a simple exercise/stretch routine)

One, two, buckle my shoe

Three, four, shut the door

Five, six, pick up sticks

Seven, eight, lay them straight

Nine, ten, a big fat hen.

Open, Shut Them (cd)

Open, shut them, open, shut them,	*(Spread baby's arms wide)*	*(Spread arms wide)*
Give a little clap, clap, clap.	*(Clap hands together)*	*(Clap hands together)*
Open, shut them, open, shut them,	*(Spread baby's arms wide)*	*(Spread arms wide)*
Put them in your lap, lap, lap.	*(Put hands in lap)*	*(Put hands in lap)*
Creep them, crawl them, creep them, crawl them,	*(Walk fingers up chest)*	*(Walk fingers up chest)*

Rhyme	Directions for Babies	Directions for Young Toddlers

Open, Shut Them (Continued)

Right up to your chin, chin, chin.	(Tap chin three times)	(Tap chin three times)
Open up your little mouth,	(Massage circle around mouth)	(Draw circle around mouth)
But do not let them in!	(Tickle fingers down chest)	(Tickle fingers down chest)

Patty-Cake, Patty-Cake ⊙ (Insert child's name and initial—start of letter recognition!)

Patty-cake, patty-cake, baker's man,	(Clap hands)	(Clap hands)
Bake me a cake as fast as you can!		
Roll it and pat it	(Roll hands around together)	(Roll hands around toegether)
And mark it with a "B"	(Draw letter on tummy)	(Draw letter on tummy)
And put it in the oven for baby and me!	(Clap)	(Clap)

Pease Porridge Hot ⊙ (Clap hands together for all ages)

Pease porridge hot, pease porridge cold, pease porridge in the pot nine days old.

Some like it hot, some like it cold, some like it in the pot nine days old.

POP—Goes the Weasel ⊙ (Use "mulberry bush" or "cobbler's bench" melody)

All around the mulberry bush,	(Bounce baby on your hip)	(March in a circle)
The monkey chased the weasel		
The monkey thought 'twas all in fun—		
POP—Goes the weasel!	(Give a slight jump)	(Jump on "POP")

Pussycat, Pussycat ⊙
(Do as clapping rhyme, feltboard story, or part of simple exercise/stretch routine)

Pussycat, pussycat, where have you been?	(Rock baby)	
I've been to London to visit the queen.		
Pussycat, pussycat, what did you there?		
I frightened a little mouse under her chair.	(Tickle tummy)	

Rhyme	Directions for Babies	Directions for Young Toddlers

Rain Is Falling Down (CD) *(Remember to "splash" by patting hands in lap—great in the tub!)*

Rain is falling down, splash!	*(Tickle fingers down body)*	*(Wiggle fingers above head)*
Rain is falling down, splash!		
Pitter-patter, pitter-patter, rain is falling down,		
SPLASH!	*(Big splashing movement)*	*(Big splashing movement)*

Ride a Cock Horse *(Bouncing rhyme)*

Ride a cock horse to Banbury Cross, to see a fine lady upon a white horse.

With rings on her fingers, and bells on her toes, she shall have music wherever she goes.

Ride Baby Ride (CD) *(For even more action—gallop around the room)*

Ride baby ride—Ch, ch, ch, ch, ch, ch.	*(Rock baby in arms)*	*(Bounce child on knee)*
Ride that horsey ride—Ch, ch, ch, ch, ch, ch.		
Ride baby ride—Ch, ch, ch, ch, ch, ch.		
Ride that horsey ride—Ch, ch, ch, ch, ch, ch.		
Whoa . . . !	*(Hug to chest)*	*(Give big hug)*

Riding on My Pony (CD)

Riding on my pony, my pony, my pony	*(Rock baby)*	*(Bounce child on knee)*
Riding on my pony, trot, trot, trot	*(Tap nose three times)*	*(Big bounces on "trot")*

Roly-Poly (CD) *(Rhyme also can be done standing in a circle and following these directions: Hands up, hands down, walk towards center, back out)*

Roly-poly, roly-poly, up–up–up.	*(Raise baby up)*	*(Roll hands upwards)*
Roly-poly, roly-poly, down–down–down.	*(Lower baby)*	*(Continue roll and lower hands)*
Roly-poly, roly-poly, out–out–out.	*(Swing baby outwards)*	*(Spread arms wide)*
Roly-poly, roly-poly, in–in–in.	*(Hug baby to self)*	*(Move hands back together)*

Rhyme	Directions for Babies	Directions for Young Toddlers
Rooster Crows 🆑		
One, two, three,	*(Bounce baby on knee)*	*(Bounce child on knee)*
Baby's on my knee.		
Rooster crows and away (child's name) goes!	*(Lift up)*	*(Lift up and twirl)*
'Round and 'Round the Garden 🆑		
'Round and 'round the garden goes the teddy bear,	*(Draw circle on tummy)*	*(Draw circle on hand)*
One step, two step,	*(Walk fingers up chest)*	*(Walk fingers up arm)*
Tickle (child's name) under there!	*(Tickle)*	*(Tickle)*
'Round the World 🆑		
'Round the world, 'round the world	*(Draw circle on tummy)*	*(Turn in circle)*
Catch a big bear.	*(Clap hands)*	*(Clap hands)*
Where you gonna find him?	*(Shrug shoulders)*	*(Shrug shoulders)*
Right in there!	*(Tickle–poke)*	*(Tickle–poke)*
Shoe a Little Horse 🆑		
Shoe a little horse.	*(Pat one foot)*	*(Pat one foot)*
Shoe a little mare.	*(Pat other foot)*	*(Pat other foot)*
But let the little pony run bare, bare, bare.	*(Lift legs and pat baby's bottom)*	*(Tap feet together)*

Snow Is Falling Down 🆑

(Use actions similar to "Rain Is Falling Down" but slower with no splashing movement)

Snow is falling down,	*(Tickle down baby's body)*	*(Wiggle fingers)*
Shhhhh!	*(Put finger to mouth—"shhhh"*	*(Put finger to mouth—"shhh")*
Snow is falling down,	*(Tickle down baby's body)*	*(Wiggle fingers)*
Shhhhh!	*(Put finger to mouth—"shhhh")*	*(Put finger to mouth—"shhh")*
Slowly, slowly, very slowly,	*(Tickle down baby's body)*	*(Wiggle fingers)*
Snow is falling down,		
Shhhhh!	*(Put finger to mouth—"shhhh")*	*(Put finger to mouth—"shhh")*

Rhyme	Directions for Babies	Directions for Young Toddlers
Teddy Bear, Teddy Bear ⓒ�	*(Adult holding baby does actions)*	

Teddy Bear, Teddy Bear ⓒᴰ *(Adult holding baby does actions)*

Teddy Bear, Teddy Bear turn around.		*(Turn in circle)*
Teddy Bear, Teddy Bear touch the ground.		*(Bend and touch ground)*
Teddy Bear, Teddy Bear show your shoe.		*(Tap shoe)*
Teddy Bear, Teddy Bear that will do.		*(Clap)*
Teddy Bear, Teddy Bear go to bed.		*(Stretch)*
Teddy Bear, Teddy Bear rest your head.		*(Rest head on hands)*
Teddy Bear, Teddy Bear turn out the light.		*(Cover eyes)*
Teddy Bear, Teddy Bear say good night.		*(Blow kiss and wave)*

Ten Little Firefighters ⓒᴰ

Ten little firefighters sleeping in a row.	*(Tickle fingers)*	*(Child on adult's lap)*
Ding-dong goes the bell	*(Tap baby's nose)*	*(Give child jiggle)*
and d-o-w-n the pole they go.	*(Drag fingers down body)*	*(Slide down adult's legs)*

There Was a Little Man ⓒᴰ

There was a little man,		*(Point to child)*
He had a little crumb,	*(Tickle cheek)*	*(Tickle cheek)*
And over the mountain he did run.	*(Run fingers over baby's head)*	*(Run fingers over head)*
With a belly full of fat and a big, tall hat,	*(Jiggle belly and tap head)*	*(Jiggle belly and tap head)*
And a pancake stuck to his bum, bum, bum.	*(Pat baby's bottom)*	*(Lift child up and pat bottom)*

This Is the Way the Ladies Ride ⓒᴰ

This is the way the ladies ride— Prim, prim, prim.	*(Give soft gentle bounce)*	*(Bounce child on knee)*
This is the way the gentlemen ride— Trim, trim, trim.	*(Give firm bounce)*	*(Give stronger bounce)*
This is the way the farmer rides— Trot, trot, trot.	*(Give uneven bounce)*	*(Bounce one knee then other)*
This is the way the hunter rides— A-gallop, a-gallop, a-gallop.	*(Give fast bounce)*	*(Give fast bounce)*

Rhyme	Directions for Babies	Directions for Young Toddlers
This Little Piggy 🆒		
This little piggy went to market.	*(Wiggle one finger or toe at a time)*	*(Shake one arm)*
This little piggy stayed home.		*(Shake other arm)*
This little piggy had roast beef		*(Shake one leg)*
And this little piggy had none.		*(Shake other leg)*
And this little piggy ran wee, wee, wee,	*(Tickle all over)*	*(Tickle all over)*
All the way home.		
Tick-Tock 🆒		
Tick-tock, tick-tock,	*(Rock back and forth)*	*(Stand up to rock or hold child on lap)*
I'm a little cuckoo clock.		
Tick-tock, tick-tock,		
Now it's almost one o'clock.		
Cuckoo!	*(Peek-a-boo one time)*	*(Lift child up one time)**
Tick-tock, tick-tock,	*(Rock back and forth)*	*(Rock)*
I'm a little cuckoo clock.		
Tick-tock, tick-tock,		
Now it's almost two o'clock.		
Cuckoo! Cuckoo!	*(Peek-a-boo two times)*	*(Lift child up two times)**
Tick-tock, tick-tock,	*(Rock back and forth)*	*(Rock)*
I'm a little cuckoo clock.		
Tick-tock, tick-tock,		
Now it's almost three o'clock.		
Cuckoo! Cuckoo! Cuckoo!	*(Peek-a-boo three times)*	*(Lift child up three times)**

(With child on lap, adult may hold one arm around child's waist and the other under child's knees to lift child securely)

Rhyme	Directions for Babies	Directions for Young Toddlers
To Market, to Market ⓒⓓ *(Bouncing rhyme with child on lap)*		
To market, to market to buy a fat pig,	*(Hold baby and walk around while reciting)*	*(Bounce or march)*
Home again, home again, jiggity jig.	*(Bounce baby on "jiggity jig")*	
To market, to market to buy a fat hog,	*(Walk around while reciting)*	
Home again, home again, jiggity jog.	*(Bounce baby on "jiggity jig")*	
Tommy Thumbs ⓒⓓ		
Tommy Thumbs up,	*(Lift baby up)*	*(Thumbs up in air)*
And Tommy Thumbs down.	*(Lower baby)*	*(Point thumbs down)*
Tommy Thumbs dancing all around the town.	*(Dance in circle)*	*(Move thumbs)*
Dance them on your shoulders,	*(Tap shoulders)*	*(Touch shoulders)*
Dance them on your head,	*(Tap head)*	*(Touch head)*
Dance them on your knees	*(Tickle knees)*	*(Touch knees)*
And tuck them into bed.	*(Rock baby)*	*(Cross arms in front)*
Trot, Trot to Boston ⓒⓓ		
Trot, trot to Boston,	*(Bounce baby)*	*(Bounce child)*
Trot, trot to Lynn.		
Look out little *(child's name)*		
You might fall in!	*(Lower baby between knees)*	*(Slide down legs)*
Trot, trot to Denver,	*(Bounce)*	*(Bounce)*
Trot, trot to Dover.		
Look out little *(child's name)*		
You might fall over!	*(Tip baby to one side)*	*(Tip child to one side)*
Trot, trot to Boston,	*(Bounce)*	*(Bounce)*
Trot, trot to town.		
Look out little *(child's name)*		
You might fall down!	*(Lower baby between knees)*	*(Slide down knees)*

Rhyme	Directions for Babies	Directions for Young Toddlers
Wash the Dishes 💿	*(Baby lying on tummy)*	
Wash the dishes, wipe the dishes,	*(Draw "X" pattern on back)*	*(Draw "X" pattern on back)*
Ring the bell for tea. DING!	*(Tap baby's nose)*	*(Tap nose)*
Three good wishes, three good kisses,	*(Draw "X" pattern on back)*	*(Draw "X" pattern on back)*
I will give to thee.		
One, two, three!	*(Kisses)*	*(Kisses)*

Way Up High in the Apple Tree—see Apple Tree

Wiggle Wiggle

Wiggle, wiggle little finger	*(Wiggle and move pointer finger above child)*	*(Do the same)*
Wiggle, wiggle in the air.		
Wiggle, wiggle little finger		
And come down . . . THERE!	*(Tickle child)*	*(Do the same)*

Wiggle Your Fingers 💿 *(Touch and wiggle body parts as indicated)*

Wiggle your fingers,

Wiggle your toes,

Wiggle your shoulders,

Now wiggle your nose.

Programming Resources
Books

Ada, Alma Flor, and F. Isabel Campoy. 2003. *Pio Peep! Traditional Spanish Nursery Rhymes*. New York: HarperCollins.

Cobb, Jane. 2007. *What'll I Do With the Baby-O? Nursery Rhymes, Songs, and Stories for Babies*. Book with CD. Vancouver, BC: Black Sheep Press.

Cole, Joanna. 1991. *The Eentsy, Weentsy Spider: Fingerplays and Action Rhymes*. New York: Mulberry Books.

Dunn, Opal. 1999. *Hippety-Hop Hippety-Hay: Growing with Rhymes from Birth to Age Three*. New York: Henry Holt.

Ernst, Linda. 2001. *Lapsit Services for the Very Young II*. New York: Neal-Schuman.

Feierabend, John, comp. 2000. *The Book of Bounces: Wonderful Songs and Rhymes Passed Down from Generation to Generation for Infants & Toddlers*. Chicago: GIA First Steps.

_____. 2000. *The Book of Tapping & Clapping: Wonderful Songs and Rhymes Passed Down from Generation to Generation for Infants & Toddlers*. Chicago: GIA First Steps.

_____. 2000. *The Book of Wiggles & Tickles: Wonderful Songs and Rhymes Passed Down from Generation to Generation for Infants & Toddlers*. Chicago: GIA First Steps.

Flint Public Library. 2000. *Ring a Ring o'Roses: Stories, Games and Fingerplays for Pre-School Children*. 11th ed. Flint, MI.: Flint Public Library.

Herr, Judy, and Terri Swim. 2003. *Rattle Time, Face to Face, and Many Other Activities for Infants: Birth to 6 months*. Clifton Park, NY: Delmar Learning.

Maddigan, Beth. 2003. *The Big Book of Stories, Songs and Sing Alongs: Programs for Babies, Toddlers and Families*. Westport, CT: Libraries Unlimited.

Marino, Jane. 2003. *Babies in the Library!* Lanham, MD: Scarecrow Press.

_____. 1992. *Mother Goose Time: Library Programs for Babies and Their Care-givers*. New York: H.W. Wilson.

Orozco, Jose-Luis. 1997. Diez Deditos: *Ten Little Fingers & Other Play Rhymes and Action Songs from Latin America*. New York: Puffin Books.

Schiller, Pam, Rafael Lara-Alecio, and Beverly J. Irby. 2004. *The Bilingual Book of Rhymes, Songs, Stories, and Fingerplays*/El Libro Bilingue de Rimas, Canciones, Cuentos y Juegos. Beltsville, MD: Gryphon House.

Schiller, Pam. 2005. *The Complete Resource Book for Infants: Over 700 Experiences for Children from Birth to 18 Months*. Beltsville, MD: Gryphon House.

Silberg, Jackie, and Pam Schiller. 2003. *The Complete Book of Rhymes, Songs, Poems, Fingerplays, and Chants*. Beltsville, MD: Gryphon House.

Stetson, Emily, and Vicky Stetson. 2001. *Little Hands Fingerplays & Action Songs*. Charlotte, VT: Williamson Publishing.

Willner, Isabel, comp. 2000. *The Baby's Game Book*. New York: Greenwillow.

Yolen, Jane. 2006. *This Little Piggy: Lap Songs, Finger Plays, Clapping Games, and Pantomime Rhymes*. Cambridge, MA: Candlewick.

Videos

Jaeger, Sally. *From Wibbleton to Wobbleton*. Toronto: 49 North Productions, 1998. Videocassette (40 minutes), also available in DVD format.

Kleiner, Lynn, and Dennis Devine. *Babies Make Music*. Music Rhapsody, 1996. Videocassette (52 minutes), also available in DVD format.

Audio (Cassette & CD)

Cobb, Jane. *What'll I Do With the Baby-O? Nursery Rhymes, Songs, and Stories for Babies*. Vancouver, BC: Black Sheep Press, 2007. Compact disc with book.

Feierabend, John, and Luann Saunders. *'Round and 'Round the Garden: Music in My First Year!* Chicago: GIA Publications, 2000. Compact Disc.

McGrath, Bob, and Katharine Smithrim. *The Baby Record*. Racine WI: Golden, 1990. Audio Cassette. 41007. Also available in compact disc.

Monet, Lisa. *Circle Time: Songs and Rhymes for the Very Young*. Redway, CA: Music for Little People, 1994. Audio Cassette.

Reid-Naiman, Kathy. *More Tickles & Tunes*. Aurora, ON, Canada: Merryweather Records, 1997. Compact Disc. M9702cd.

_____. *Tickles and Tunes: Tickles, Songs and Bounces for Children 6 Months to 6 Years Old*. Aurora, ON, Canada: Merryweather Records, 1997. Compact Disc. M9701.

Stewart, Nancy. *Baby Rattle and Roll*. Mercer Island, WA: Friends Street Music, 2006. Compact Disc. FS114.

_____. *Little Songs for Little Me*. Mercer Island, WA: Friends Street Music, 1992. Compact Disc.

Sunseri, MaryLee. *Baby-O!* Pacific Grove, CA: Piper Grove Music, 2003. Compact Disc. PGM222.

_____. *Mother Goose Melodies: Four & Twenty Olde Songs for Young Children*. Pacific Grove, CA: Piper Grove Music, 2003. Compact Disc. PGM220.

Web Sites

http://gardenofsong.com
KidzSing Garden of Song
> This site plays the melodies to Mother Goose rhymes and popular children's songs.

http://www-personal.umich.edu/%7Epfa/dreamhouse/nursery/rhymes.html
Mother Goose Pages
> This site shows the words to popular Mother Goose rhymes, recommends books and resources, and artwork.

www.preschoolrainbow.org/preschool-rhymes.htm
Gayle's Preschool Rainbow
> This site groups fingerplays, action poems, nursery rhymes and songs for circle times according to early childhood education themes.

8
Music That Works

"Hearing is the first sense to develop. Sometime between 20 and 30 weeks of gestation, the human fetus can hear" (Shore and Strasser, 2006: 62). "Thump, thump, thump" . . . the steady rhythm of the mother's heartbeat is a child's first music. Sound stimulates the brain, activating neurons, causing them to grow, connect, and create pathways. The growing neural networks eventually become the foundation upon which all other learning is based" (Shore and Strasser, 2006). In fact, "listening to it [music] actually causes that electrical activity to occur, resonating within the brain to enhance learning, and probably laying the neural pathways that create a better foundation for learning" (Shore, 2003: 57). Music stimulates movement; even very young children will bounce to a tune. The movement and sound helps build and reinforce pathways in an infant's brain.

Music has the power to affect moods and helps create emotional bonds between listeners. In a program setting, you might use lullabies to encourage relaxation, ethnic music to explore different heritages, and action songs to make exercise fun. Music for very young children tends to be repetitive, creating patterns for brain and body to respond to together. A musical experience for young children can reinforce language awareness through clapping in rhythm and singing in rhyme. It can introduce social skills such as creating a circle with others, from the safety of the caregiver's arms, and following a leader (Zero to Three, 2002). In her book *Baby Teacher*, Rebecca Shore presents documented scientific research on music and its influence on the very young child in a manner that is accessible and practical. The final chapter offers age-appropriate tips on how to stimulate development in young children and recommended materials to use.

"Music enhances an inclusive classroom [or storytime] by leveling the playing field so everyone can be a participant. Whether a child is a listener or a player, music is accessible and partial participation does not detract from its positive effects" (Humpal and Wolf, 2003: 104). An infant cannot respond to a marching tune in the same manner as a child who can walk, but both benefit from the experience. With a mixed age group, the presenter can suggest ways for everyone to participate; for instance, an older child can rotate his or her own hands while the adult "bicycles" an infant's legs to "The Wheels on the Bus." Music allows the child to participate at his/her own level, be it by singing along, rocking to the beat, squealing with delight, or simply observing.

As with other storytime activities, adults may need more encouragement than children to participate in music portions of the program. Some adults believe they are incapable of any musical expression. Relieve this anxiety by repeating the truth: Children are nonjudgmental; they see their caregivers as the best at everything!

Music has many uses in programs for the very young. Music played as people enter helps everyone feel more comfortable than they would if the room was silent. Used at the program's conclusion, music can encourage conversation and interaction. I prefer to play music that is quiet and soothing while people arrive for the infant program; Pachelbel's "Canon in D" or something similar to help keep the atmosphere non-threatening and calm. This gives the infants a chance to observe and settle in. Young toddlers of 12 to 24 months may respond to well-known songs and rhymes that create a sense of familiarity and help them anticipate the program. The key is to use the music to invite the participants in without exciting them to the point of being overwhelmed. Try opening and concluding the program with the same song or songs each week; adults and children will learn to recognize when the program begins and ends by the sounds they hear. During the reading of a story, carefully chosen background music can add atmosphere. And, of course, everyone enjoys a free dance or movement time, whether the music is recorded or live. There are many creative movement recordings that can be used to introduce concepts of rhythm and timing; many incorporate directions into the lyrics, making it easy to follow along.

The following are tried-and-true recordings and performers, recommended foundation works used successfully in programs with the very young. Information includes the performer, recording title, a summary, and recommended songs with which to start. Many of them contain material that works as fingerplays, as well. There is a wealth of suitable music to explore, with new material constantly being introduced, often first appearing in the early childhood field. Since fingerplays and rhymes are so closely connected with music, see the previous chapter for more information and resources.

Recordings and Videos

Chappell, Eric. *Music for Creative Dance, Vol. III*. Seattle, WA: Ravenna Ventures, 1998. Compact Disc. RVCD9801.

> Part of the *Music for Creative Dance* series, this offers 20 different contrast and continuum musical pieces for movement and instrument play. The styles range from Native American to Celtic, fiesta to fiddles. Creative dance ideas by Anne Green Gilbert are included.

Cobb, Jane. 2007. *What'll I Do With the Baby-O? Nursery Rhymes, Songs and Stories for Babies.* Vancouver, British Columbia: Black Sheep Press. Book and Compact Disc.

> An excellent resource for rhymes and songs that work with infant and young toddler programs. The CD that comes with the text is perfect to help learn tunes and rhythms. Rhymes/Songs are divided by type including welcome and goodbye songs, lullabies, rhymes in other languages, (Japanese, Cantonese, Dutch, Norwegian, Mandarin, and German), tickles, bounces, and more.
> - Canadian Lullaby works wonderfully to sooth a restless crowd.
> - Very good for learning multicultural material.

Feierabend, John M. and Luann Saunders. *'Round and 'Round the Garden: Music in My First Year.* Chicago: GIA Publications, 2000. Compact Disc. CD-437.

> More than 60 songs performed by one voice, guitar, and string bass.
> - Offers a variety of bounces, wiggles, circle games, clapping rhymes, and lullabies that emphasize adult-child interaction.

Hegner, Priscilla and Rose Grasselli. *Diaper Gym: Fun Activities for Babies on the Move.* Long Branch, NJ: Kimbo Educational, 1985. Compact Disc. KIM 9096C.

> Gives directions for two age groups, six weeks to seven months, and eight months to one year old. Includes massage, mirror play, stretches, and other games that match actions to the music.
> - "Butterfly Kisses" and "Blow Me a Kiss" make great good-bye songs.
> - "Peek-A-Boo" is fun to use with scarves.
> - "How Big Is Baby?" is good for stretching.

Jaeger, Sally. *Sally's from Wibbleton to Wobbleton.* 40 minutes. Toronto: 49 North Productions. Videocassette, 1998.

> This video is a live recoding of an actual Music with Young Children program and is a good way to learn new ways of using traditional material.

Jenkins, Ella. *Early, Early Childhood Songs.* Washington, DC: Smithsonian Folkways, 1990. Compact Disc. SF 45015.

> Ella Jenkins, with a group of three-and four-year-olds, sings some of the most familiar English-language children's songs with simple accompaniment.

Kleiner, Lynn and Dennis Devine. *Babies Need Music.* 52 minutes. Redondo Beach, CA: Music Rhapsody, 1996. Videocassette.

> Music Rhapsody combines live action to demonstrate songs and rhymes, followed by puppets, toys, etc., to demonstrate a varied presentation. Recommended for infants to age two, this video introduces a sense of timing, pitch, aural, and language skills for babies in an exciting interactive manner. Also available are the books *Toddlers Make Music!* and *Babies Make Music!* which offer lyrics, directions, activities, photographs, and a CD of musical games for each age group.

Lawrence-Kuehn, David. *Baby Dance: A Toddler's Jump on the Classics.* New York: Erato, 1994. Compact Disc. 4509-96887-2.
> An introduction to classical music that encourages the adult to interact with the child verbally, physically, and emotionally.

McGrath, Bob and Katharine Smithrim. *The Baby Record.* Racine, WI: Golden. Cassette: Golden Music, 1990. Compact Disc. Bob's Kids Music 41007-03.
> Classic nursery rhymes and activity songs with directions are arranged by type: bouncing, action, using instruments, finger and toe plays, songs, and lullabies. This is a first choice for learning traditional English-language rhymes and songs.

Monet, Lisa. *Circle Time: Songs & Rhymes for the Very Young.* Redway, CA: Music for Little People, 1994; distributed by Kid Rhino. Compact Disc. R2 75594.
> Thirty favorite songs are sung with a folk guitar to supply backup for presenter if needed.

Raffi. *Singable Songs for the Very Young.* Universal City, CA: Shoreline; MCA, 1976. Compact Disc. 8051.
> Presents popular, traditional English and French children's songs; helpful for those who are unfamiliar with the tunes.

Reid-Naiman, Kathy with Ken Whiteley. *More Tickles & Tunes.* Aurora, ON, Canada: Merriweather Records, 1997. Compact Disc. M9702cd.
> Primarily traditional songs, this recording also includes additional lyrics for some familiar songs and several original pieces. Lyric sheet with directions makes it easy to follow along.
> - "A Smooth Road" is a wonderful bouncing rhyme.
> - "Nelly Go 'Cross the Ocean"—Everyone will get moving, and the children will enjoy being swung around.

Roberts, Sheena, compiler. *Playsongs: Action Songs and Rhymes for Babies and Toddlers.* London: Playsongs Publications, 2001. Book and Compact Disc. 0-9517112-1-0.
> New and traditional English-language songs, rhymes, and games for adult and child to enjoy.
> - "Spots, Spots, Spots." An original tickle song by Cynthia Raza that, once learned, the participants will never want to stop.

Sharon, Lois and Bram. *Mainly Mother Goose.* Toronto: Casablanca Kids, 2002.
> Popular children's musicians bring life to Mother Goose nursery rhymes.

Stewart, Georgiana. *Baby Face.* Long Branch, NJ: Kimbo Education, 1983.
> Vintage songs that add fun to exercise and games for adult and child to play together.

- "Baby's Hokey Pokey," an arm and leg exercise, is so much fun everyone will want to do it over and over again.
- "Baby Face" helps add music to the game of peek-a-boo.

Stewart, Nancy. *Baby Rattle and Roll: Songs for Babies and Toddlers*. Mercer Island, WA: Friends Street Music, 2006. Compact Disc. FS114.

Original songs presented with guitar and solo voice. Perfect to use to create programs for the very young and materials are easy to learn. Songs are arranged by type such as touch, massage, etc. Companion activities and felt patterns available at www.nancymusic.com. Some original music also available online at her Web site.

- "All Gone!"—This song teaches signs for familiar words such as "more, milk, banana, cracker, please" and "all gone" with easy to follow tune. ASL directions available online.
- "Baby, Who Do You See?—Sing while showing pictures of people (animals) or while adult and child view family pictures. Recorded with pauses that allow for time to turn the page.
- "Hello My Friend"—Great welcome song to start a program incorporating sign language.

_____. *Little Songs for Little Me: Activity Songs for Ones and Twos*. Mercer Island, WA: Friends Street Music, 1995. Compact Disc.

More than just an easy-to-follow music CD, this kit includes lyric sheets, directions and suggestions on how to use the songs, flannel figures and a flannel board all contained in one binder!

- "Mr. Turkey and Mr. Duck" has a surprise ending that always elicits giggles.
- "One Little Baby" has a simple tune and fun actions that climax with a peek-a-boo everyone enjoys.

Sunseri, MaryLee. *Baby-O! Activity Songs for Babies*. Pacific Grove, CA: Piper Grove Music, 2005. Compact Disc. PGM222.

Offers three individual sets of songs and rhymes perfect for lap-sit programs and playtime.

_____. *Wee Chant: Chants, Songs and Lullabies from Around the World*. Pacific Grove, CA: Piper Grove Music, 2001. Compact Disc. PGM218.

A collection of songs with repeating words and simple melodies that even those who "can't sing" will be able to manage successfully.

Tickle Tune Typhoon. *Patty-Cakes and Peek-a-Boos: Activity Songs, Dances and Lullabies for Infants and Toddlers*. Seattle: Tickle Tune Typhoon, 1994. Compact Disc. TTTCD008.

Classic children's music with vocals and full instrumentation, lyrics included.

- "Cuddle Up and Sing" is perfect for reinforcing that intimate bond between adult and child as the two cuddle and rock together.

- "Clap Your Hands Melody" combines a fun activity song with the classic "Open, Shut Them."

Print Resources

Cass-Beggs, Barbara. 1978. *Your Baby Needs Music.* New York: St. Martin's Press.

Feierabend, John M. 2000. *The Book of Simple Songs & Circles.* Chicago: GIA First Steps.

Humpal, Marcia Earl and Jan Wolf. 2003. "Music in the Inclusive Environment." *Young Children* 58, no. 2 (March): 103–107.

Levine-Gelb Comunications, Claire Lerner, and Lynette A. Ciervo. 2002. *Getting in Tune: The Powerful Influence of Music on Young Children's Development.* Washington, DC: Zero to Three.

Miller, Anne Meeker. 2007. *Baby Sing & Sign. Communicate Early with Your Baby: Learning Signs the Fun Way Through Music & Play.* New York: Marlowe.

Preschool Services and Parent Education Committee/Association for Library Services to Children. 2000. *How to Learn and Grow with Music: A Selective Audio List for Infants and Toddlers.* Chicago: American Library Association.

Shore, Rebecca. 2002. *Baby Teacher: Nurturing Neural Networks from Birth to Age Five.* Lanham, MD: Scarecrow Education Book.

Shore, Rebecca, and Janis Strasser. 2006. "Music for Their Minds." *Young Children* 61, no. 2 (March): 62–67.

Silberg, Jackie. 1998. *I Can't Sing Book for Grownups Who Can't Carry a Tune in a Paper Bag . . . But Want to Do Music with Young Children.* Beltsville, MD: Gryphon House.

Web Sites

gardenofsong.com
Kidzsing Garden of Song
> Don't know the melody? This site has audio of tunes for English-language nursery rhymes songs and links to other children's music websites.

nancymusic.com
Nancy Stewart
> Web site of award-winning, professional musician and songwriter. Site includes activity pages for making homemade instruments, games to play with music, information about how to share music with babies, and links to sites related to music and children. Downloadable music to original songs for infants to preschoolers.

www.niehs.nih.gov/kids/musicchild.htm
National Institutes of Health
> Web site for lyrics and MIDI tunes for many popular children's songs.

www.playsongs.co.uk
Playsongs Publications Limited

ravennaventures.com
Ravenna Ventures, Inc.

www.tsl.state.tx.us/ld/projects/ninos/index.html
Texas State Library/El Día de Los Niños: El Día de Los Libros
 This site features traditional songs, rhymes, finger plays, and games in Spanish and
 English; includes lyrics and directions, and some audio.

www.zerotothree.org
Zero to Three
 Web site of a national, nonprofit, multidisciplinary organization whose mission is
 to inform, educate, and support adults who influence the lives of infants and toddlers. Offers well-documented and carefully written brochures for handouts to
 hand out; many can be downloaded and others purchased.

Major Distributors

Kimbo Educational: the Children's Music Company
 www.Kimboed.com
 Phone: 800-631-2187
 Mail: PO Box 477M
 Long Branch, NJ 07740-0477

Music for Little People
 www.mflp.com
 Phone: 800-409-2457
 Mail: PO Box 757
 Greenland, NH 03840

9

Great Programming Enhancement Ideas

Once you have created your core program of books, rhymes and music, you can add materials and activities—enhancements—that create another level of learning, participant involvement, and fun. Remember, the primary focus of the program is not the enhancement; be careful to maintain a balance when adding them. It can be very tempting to spend time developing extra material and activities, especially since they can be so much fun. It is also possible to overstimulate the children or lose control of the group if you have too many props of which to keep track.

Incorporate only one or two enhancements into a program. Combining puppets, flannelboards, scarves, a parachute activity, and bubbles all in one program can overwhelm the children. Keep it simple. For instance, read the *Carrot Seed* by Ruth Krauss, retell the story using felt pieces on a flannelboard, and then give each adult/child pair a smaller flannelboard and the pieces to retell the story to each other. By allowing participants time to interact with the enhancement and explore its possibilities, you encourage them to continue these fun literacy activities on their own.

Enhancements may be objects or activities: puppets, balls, and bubbles, or creative movement, reading together, or massage. Early childhood curriculum books are excellent resources for ideas. Authors Pam Schiller, Judy Herr, and Karen Miller are well respected in early childhood education and their works indicate age levels for each activity. Jackie Silberg, another expert in the field, not only has outstanding books but offers a Web site as a resource for ideas (www.jackiesilberg.com). Children's librarians who have written programming books for this age group include Jane Marino, Linda Ernst, Sue McCleaf Nespeca, Saroj Ghoting with Pamela Martin-Diaz, and Betsy Diamant-Cohen. Books by these individuals provide materials, resources, and ideas that have been tried out in library programs for the very young. A list of books by these experts is included at the end of this chapter in the resource section.

An excellent Web site worth investigating is *Every Child Ready to Read @ Your Library*, http://www.ala.org/ala/alsc/ECRR/ECRRHomePage.htm. A joint venture of Association of Library Services for Children (ALSC) and Public Library Association (PLA), it offers links to many early childhood education and library sites with additional resources. The list at the end of this chapter has more recommended sites.

Enhancements can be incorporated wherever they are best situated for the flow of the program. They may have a tendency to cause some disruption, especially if they have to be put away. Incorporate a ritual or routine to help the transition. For example, wave goodbye as the shakers are put back into the storage box/bag. It is even possible to use a song to ease the transition such as singing, "Goodbye shakers, goodbye shakers, goodbye shakers, we'll play another day" to the tune of "Goodnight Ladies."

At times, the enhancement portion may be at the conclusion of the program rather than during it. Some adult participants may see this as a relaxed or "free time" to socialize amongst themselves. For safety reasons, remind the adult to be aware of what his/her child is doing. Bring this to the group's attention prior to handing out the enhancement. Explain this is not "playtime" but actually part of the literacy experience. The child needs the adult's guidance and encouragement to benefit fully from the experience. Little ones have no real idea about or experience with the objects or activities presented. Without a caring adult actively participating with him or her, a book or activity has no meaning or value to the very young child.

To reinforce the desired interactions, the presenter may move around the area offering encouragement, praise, and suggestions:

"I like the way you talk about the pictures and give [child's name] time to look, before letting her turn the page herself."

"[Child's name] really likes to roll the ball back and forth with you. Saying it is a red ball will add another word to her vocabulary!"

"I like the way you copy what [child's name] is doing with the musical instruments—smiles on both your faces!"

"You and [child's name] really enjoyed the free dance today. She was really focused on what you were saying and doing together."

If giving this kind of feedback is not something you usually do, do not force it. Try making one or two comments until it feels more natural. Above all else, be sincere and brief.

Following are some enhancements that have proven popular with very young children and their caregivers. When you have gained confidence in your ability to evaluate activities and props for age appropriateness, explore the resources provided at the end of this chapter and build your own.

Activities (Free Dance, Reading, Art, etc.)

Most of the enhancements are activities, but here are a few more ideas to add variety.

Free Dance

Put on music and encourage the adult to dance around the room with the child. An infant is held in the adult's arms until able to stand on his or her own. For older children, the adult can guide by holding hands with him or her. The music can be any kind the presenter would like to use. Try classical one week and country the next. Vary soft music and jazz to change the intensity of the activity. Stop the music and have the participants "freeze" in place until it starts again. The presenter should move around as well and offer praise and encouragement to the group, lessening the self-consciousness adult participants may feel.

Toys

Have a selection of age appropriate toys that children can play with. Select ones that are simple and easy to sanitize. Brought out after the conclusion of the program, these will allow the children an activity while the adults have a chance to socialize. Remind the adults about safety issues if necessary. Depending on your facility and budget, the collection may include washable baby dolls, blocks (plastic are lighter than wooden ones), activity boxes, sit-on and steer toys, a tunnel that can be crawled through, plastic animals, toy dishes, pots, and so on. Instead of giving one toy per child, it might be best to offer more toys than the children in the group and let each select from a pile for themselves. What happens if more than one child wants a particular toy? Then it is time for the adults to practice their "distraction" tactics or put the toys away.

Reading

Pass out board books to all the adults to allow them practice at reading to their child. The board book distributed can all be the same title, perhaps, one used for the program, or a variety of titles. The books should be in good condition since dirty or well-worn books may create a poor impression. If they are in poor condition, remove them from your collection. Again, the presenter needs to observe and give feedback to the adults during or directly after this activity. (Children are not the only ones who respond to praise!)

- "You are doing a good job building vocabulary by pointing out objects as you name them."
- "I like the way you are letting [child's name] practice turning the pages."
- "Cuddling when you read together makes this a pleasurable experience and learning is impacted by emotions. You are making this a good one!"
- "Allowing [child's name] to set the pace enables you to both share in this activity."

Art

Depending on the age range of the group, this may be a take-home sheet of ideas instead of part of the program time. Art for the very young focuses on the process, the "doing," rather than the final result. For infants, art activities may include finger-painting with baby food on a tray, splashing water and making wet splotches on the ground (or bathroom wall!), poking holes into mashed potatoes, and manipulating the bubbles in the tub into shapes. As the child develops, so can the art projects. Use paintbrushes to swish water onto an outside wall or sidewalk, or cover a low table with butcher paper and let the children draw on it with crayons. Since little ones have more control over their large muscles, make sure that the entire coloring surface is covered. Check early childhood curriculum books for more art ideas. Remember to keep this activity simple with a minimum of materials and, of course, safe.

Games

Circle games such as "Ring Around the Rosie" may be a challenge since little ones do not particularly want to hold a stranger's hand. Begin with just the adult and child as a group, holding hands or walking in a circle. As participants become comfortable and familiar with each other, small groups may form and eventually you can create one big circle. You might also try having the children and adults hold scarves, hula-hoops, or a parachute. The Hokey-Pokey may be used with infants and children under two years old if the adult moves the child's body parts as directed while the infant is lying on his or her back. If standing and holding the child, changing the words to "put the baby in, take the baby out, put the baby in and shake'um all about!" can lead to lots of giggles. *Baby Face* by Georgiana Stewart has a great baby hokey-pokey song on it with lots of tickles, wiggles and giggles. This CD is available from KIMBO Educational. John Feierabend's "First Steps in Music" series also has simple circle games. (See page 191 for titles.)

Massage

Touch is an important component of a child's healthy physical, social and emotional development and massage is one way to encourage it. Action rhymes can be adapted to involve touch, such as the adult running fingers down the body of a child as a mouse runs down a clock in "Hickory Dickory Dock." Massage is a more than just a way to touch; it is another way to connect adult and child. It allows parents to gain confidence in handling their baby, increases their ability to interpret the baby's behavior, and strengthens the bond with their baby (Heath and Bainbridge, 2000). Heath and Bainbridge's *Baby Massage* has simple directions and color photographs that are extremely helpful when learning the "how-to" of baby massage. *Infant Massage: A Handbook for Loving Parents* by Vimala McClure is also helpful. Sign up for a class to learn basic massage or check in the area for a licensed infant massage instructor that might be willing to come to a class. It is best if you have some experience with infant massage before introducing it into the program. Keep in mind issues such as allergies and health of the child. During a program, children will be fully clothed for the most part and a full massage is not possible. Since this is to be an enhancement only, offer books, videos, DVDs, periodicals, and other materials that promote and instruct infant massage for adults who want to learn more.

Balls

Consider adding balls to literacy programs, even with very young children. Inflatable beach balls come in various sizes, and their bright colors always attract children's attention. Their light weight also makes them safer than heavier playground balls. The six-inch size is perfect for a small child to roll back and forth with an adult, while the larger sizes supply a manipulation challenge. Since beach balls deflate, they are easy to store between programs. Look for them seasonally, in novelty store catalogs, and online; the Oriental Trading Company is one good source.

Playing with balls is fun for the adult and child and introduces the round circle shape to the child. As the child gets older, recognizing shapes will be an important skill for letter recognition. Following directions—"roll the ball to me"—is another skill children need to develop as they get older.

Balls also allow the very young child to learn about cause and effect. It can be so much fun to observe their facial expressions! Roll a ping-pong ball or plastic practice golf ball with holes in it through a mailing tube. The child will lose sight of it until it reappears at the bottom. Help the child retrieve the ball, then drop it into the tube. Tip one end of the tube up to let the ball roll down it. This gives the child an opportunity to practice skills like grasping, moving, inserting, etc., and allows the adult to introduce vocabulary. The infant, in the role of little "scientist," will find this activity fascinating, watching what consistently occurs and learning to predict what will happen when the ball is dropped into the tube.

Baby Play, part of the Gymboree Play & Music series, suggests other ways to use balls in your program, i.e., gently rolling the infant on his tummy while balanced on a soft ball. "Nurturing Pathways," a program created by Christine Roberts, emphasizes growing the mind through movement. *Nurturing Pathways: Nursery Rhymes and Chants* includes activities using balls with babies, "waddlers," and toddlers. (See the Web site list at the end of this chapter for contact information.)

Bubbles

Nothing brings out the young child in everyone like blowing bubbles. Music makes a nice background to this activity. Bubbles can be purchased at most toy, drug, and retail stores. You can also make your own by using liquid dish washing soap (about 2–3 tablespoons) with water (1 cup). Other bubble recipes can be found in children's craft magazines and online. You may want to try using tearless baby shampoo to make bubbles for baby story time. To keep things simple, the presenter can blow bubbles into the air while walking around the group. During this time, the adults may interact with their children by talking to them about the bubbles or dancing to music while holding the children. Let the child catch a bubble to discover what bubbles can do—POP! Supplying a bottle of bubbles to every adult in the group fosters more interaction. Craft and party stores often have miniature bubble bottles that make a great program give-away. For more bubble fun, consider purchasing a bubble machine. These are found at craft and party stores and can be relatively inexpensive. One type plugs into the wall, so the length of the cord limits the area it can cover. Others are battery powered and therefore much more portable. If you intend to move around with the bubble machine in your hand, look for a model that is battery powered and check that the bubble solution container does not slide around or spill easily. Keep in mind that bubble machines will produce bubbles quickly and may leave surfaces slippery if left in one place too long.

Flannel/Magnetic Board

Flannel boards and magnetic boards enable the presenter to tell a story to a large group or repeat a story in a different manner. The board can be flannel or felt-covered cardboard, an artist's portfolio, the inside cover of a binder, the outside of a pizza box (clean of course!), a metal cookie sheet, or can be purchased commercially. Size depends on the individual presenter. A small board, about 11" by 15", is easy to hold with one hand or to rest on your lap. Smaller boards are also easy to place out of sight when not in use, but can be challenging if multiple pieces are necessary to tell the story. A larger board requires an easel, table or ledge to prop it against. A large board is easier to see and frees up both hands, but it can be a distraction when not an active part of the program. It also must be secure enough so that children practicing their walking skills will not be able to tip it over.

Judy Sierra's second edition of the *Flannel Board Storytelling Book* (Wilson, 1997) has an excellent section of easy-to-use patterns for nursery rhymes. The focus of *Flannelboard Stories for Infants and Toddlers* by Ann Carlson and Mary Carlson (ALA, 1999) is stories for the very young. *Felt Board Fun* by Liz and Dick Wilmes (Building Blocks, 1994) also provides patterns. For simplicity, enhance felt or paper pieces cut using dies (from companies such as Ellison or Accucut) with fabric paints or securely glued-on sequins. Such decorations

---

Example: You might first tell the story of *Brown Bear, Brown Bear* by Bill Martin using the book. Then hand out small-size flannel boards (8.5" x 11") with felt pieces representing the characters from the book to each adult/child pair. A kit can be created by first mounting flannel or felt material on 10" x 10" cardboard, taping around the edges, and then placing it with the required story pieces in a Ziplock bag. This makes the materials easier to distribute, recover, and store. Have the adult tell their child the story again using the felt pieces. If printed clip art is used, first mount on sturdy material such as heavyweight copy paper, cardstock or cardboard, then laminate. Place small felt pieces, felt tape, or velcro purchased at material and craft stores on the back of each piece to attach it to the flannel board.

should be used only on the presenter's pieces for safety's sake. To enable each participating child/adult pair to retell the story, make multiples of the same pieces but omit glued-on objects.

Magnetic boards obviously need the story/rhyme pieces to have magnets on them. Check these pieces to ensure that the magnets are firmly attached and do not pose a health hazard to the child.

Recommended stories/songs/rhymes that work as flannel board/magnetic board stories are:

Brown Bear, Brown Bear (Bill Martin)
The Carrot Seed (Ruth Krauss)
Freight Train (Donald Crews)
Go Away, Big Green Monster! (Ed Emberley)
"Hickory, Dickory Dock"
"Hush Little Baby"
"Two Little Blackbirds"

Parachute

Parachutes can be purchased at toy stores, early childhood curriculum stores and, of course, online. They range in diameter from 12 feet to as large as 45 feet across. Select the size that will fit your space but not overfill it. If the parachute is too big, it can prove a challenge when there are too few people to hold it safely.

The adults can walk in a circle holding the parachute up while the children are under it. Infants and nonmobile children placed in the center on top of a parachute while it is flat on the floor can enjoy a ride as the adults walk the parachute in a circle. The parachute can also help children play circle games—have the children hold onto its edge. *Parachute Play* by Liz and Dick Wilmes, and various Totline publications, have more parachute ideas. When selecting a parachute activity remember to keep safety in mind and select an age-appropriate activity.

Props

One of the most useful props for early childhood programs is a demonstration "child" to be the presenter's partner. Some may prefer to use an imaginary baby. As time goes on, one of the child participants may become the presenter's partner.

A "demonstration child" should be of a size that is comfortable for the presenter to hold and manipulate; moveable arms and legs are an advantage. A stuffed animal may be used, but if it interests the children more than the intended activity you may have to reconsider. Baby dolls are always a good choice, try using a Cabbage Patch doll in a sleeper, or a rag doll. Folkmanis also makes a character baby puppet that would work.

Some program themes may suggest a prop. During the winter, snow is a very popular theme. To reinforce the theme and tie in music with an activity, put on a classical recording that suggests the sense of snowfall and encourage the adults to free dance using the babies as the snowflakes. Have a supply of paper snowflake cutouts (Ellison dies work great) and toss them in the air to simulate falling snow. Do not expect these snowflakes to survive; make extras that can be take-home souvenirs. Tulle circles also make great snowflakes and can be found at party, craft, or fabric stores. Basic white is the natural choice, but colored ones are easier to see. Hand out one per adult, instruct them to hold them flat above their child and let them float down like snowflakes. Tulle circles can be easily picked up, tossed in the wash, and reused.

Stuffed animals can be used as props in many ways. A brightly colored bag or pillowcase can hold all the animals for "Old MacDonald Had a Farm." Use a dog, a cat, a bird and your finger (the "worm") to help you tell *The Big Fat Worm* by Nancy Van Laan. Action rhymes can incorporate stuffed animals when they are placed on body parts as directed or used with such songs as "Put Your Finger/Stuffed Animal in the Air."

Puppets

Puppets enable the presenter to:

- Capture the group's attention
- Demonstrate how to do something, e.g., read aloud to a baby
- Vary material previously used in the program
- Feel less selfconscious when working with very young children because their focus is on the puppet, not the presenter

It is important to introduce the puppet to the children since it may upset or frighten some of them. To very young children a puppet is "real" and alive, so give them time and space/distance to get used to the puppet. For example, when saying "hello" with a puppet, let the child approach the puppet rather than putting the puppet in the child's personal space. Some children, of course, want to grab and hold the puppet themselves. If that is the case, you may want to have a box or shelf that the puppet can disappear to when its part of the program is over. Use your judgment when trying to separate a puppet from a child and encourage the adult to let the child give it back. Nothing adds tension to a program like forcing a child to do what he or she does not want to do. If gentle persuasion does not work, moving on to the next part of the program can allow the puppet fall by the wayside so it can be retrieved subtly. Finger puppets have the wonderful ability to disappear into pockets, baskets or other hiding places to minimize distractions.

Look for relatively simple puppets that clean easily. The infant's ability to see detail is still developing, so bright colors and basic faces work best. If participants will be using the puppets, check them weekly as a safety precaution. A puppet can be as simple as a tube sock with a face made by firmly gluing on felt pieces, using permanent fabric paint, or embroidering with brightly colored yarn. Simple stick puppets can be made by laminating pictures and taping them to a stick. In place of wooden chopsticks or small dowels, try plastic/paper straws or tubes made from copy paper rolled tightly on the diagonal. These "sticks" can easily bend if a young toddler should fall. Try making a puppet from an odd mitten or oven mitt; add a simple face and shaggy yarn hair to complete the character.

Most puppets represent animals or people, but they can be more abstract. Represent feelings with simple facial expression outlines; concepts such as sleepy and awake can be opposite sides of the same paper plate puppet. Even an inanimate object like a baby brush can become a puppet. Environments, Inc. has a wonderful set of puppets called Winky Mitts for playing "peek-a-boo." Folkmanis offers a large selection of puppets, as do many early childhood curriculum companies. For contact information see the end of this chapter. To make your own puppets, check the early childhood education books, puppetry books and Web sites listed in the resource section.

Rhythm Instruments

Since music is such a central part of a program, rhythm instruments are an easy enhancement to add. Whether purchased or homemade, it is essential that they be safe for little ones to use. Check weekly that all pieces are securely attached and cannot be pulled apart. For safety, select rhythm instruments sized for tiny hands and made from lead-free materials with no sharp edges since most instruments will end up in a child's mouth. Clean with baby wipes or wash in a solution of $1/4$ teaspoon of bleach to 1 quart of cool water. Many early childhood curriculum stores carry rhythm instruments. Shakers, drums, and bells are the most popular items. Castanets, tambourines, and rhythm sticks are often included in rhythm instrument sets. Offer one type of instrument to the entire group or give a variety. If offering different instruments, give each child—even the babies—time to select the one he/she wants to use. Dump the instruments in the middle of the floor and spread them out for easy "inspection." The adult and child can look at all the instruments, talk about them, and the adult can offer the baby the one that seems to interest him or her most. Another possibility is to let the babies crawl into the pile and select for themselves.

Look for rhythm instruments in toy stores, variety stores such as Target, and even children's bookstores. Early childhood education stores such as Lakeshore Learning Materials and Environments, Inc. also have these available for purchase. When funds are limited, simple rhythm instruments can be handmade. Again, it is important to keep in mind safety, durability, and sanitizing guidelines. The following directions will help you create two very simple rhythm instruments. For additional information on making your own rhythm instruments, check the resources list at the end of this chapter.

- Drum: Thumping empty plastic containers, formula cans, or coffee cans make nice drum sounds. Clean and dry the container thoroughly. Use a hot glue gun to seal the lids on by running a line of glue around the inside lip of the cover. (Applying the glue to the inside lip of the cover prevents glue from oozing onto the outside of the container when you put on the lid.) Hands and wooden or large plastic spoons make good thumpers. Children will often create their own thumpers by using what they find around them.
- Shakers: One of the most common ways to make shakers is to use plastic eggs, best purchased during seasonal sales. Prescription bottles with childproof tops also work well. Colorful eggs do not need additional decoration. Prescription bottles can be decorated with stickers or colorful vinyl electric tape, but keep in mind that stickers or tape can come off when sanitizing the instruments. Inside the shaker put one or two tablespoons of dried beans for a louder sound or uncooked rice for a softer sound. If you are using plastic eggs, run a line of hot glue around the inside of the top of the egg. Press the top and bottom together carefully, holding upright until firm to prevent glue from getting on the contents. Eggs are easy to store in clean egg cartons. Shakers can also be stored in boxes or cloth bags such as a colorful pillowcase or laundry bag.

Retrieve the instruments by taking a basket, bag, or box around to each child, encouraging them to drop the shakers in, and offering lots of praise when he/she does so. Other methods to minimize the "trauma" of letting go are to encourage the child to wave bye-bye to the shaker or sing "Goodbye shakers, goodbye shakers, goodbye shakers, we'll play another day." (tune: "Good Night Ladies")

A shaker makes an inexpensive and simple souvenir for participants to take home. Having it at home will encourage repetition of the songs, rhymes, and activities.

Scarves and Streamers

Using scarves and streamers can be great fun and incorporates the sense of touch into the program. Thrift stores and garage sales can be good sources for them. Make sure all are washable, since most will end up in a little one's mouth.

Scarves made of chiffon or other soft, see-through material are recommended for playing peek-a-boo, as some children may become frightened when the adult "disappears." The gauzy material will allow them to see enough that they should not feel afraid. If a child seems to show signs of anxiety (crying or flailing arms), suggest the scarf be held between the adult and child instead of being put over one of their heads. Fabric and craft stores carry chiffon in many different colors. Cut to the desired size (18" x 18" is good) and either hem or serge the edges, or use a product such as FrayCheck® to minimize fraying. Juggling scarves "float" beautifully and they can be found in toy stores, curriculum stores and even magic shops!

For activities that do not call for see-through fabric, bandanas are another choice, but they can be rather stiff until washed repeatedly. Lycra material, though opaque, is bright, shimmery, and stretchy and does not require hemming. Cut the material into one-and-a-half to two-yard squares. Gently pull the material with the child on top of it and slide across the floor. For safety reasons do not let the child stand on the fabric, but sit or lie on it. Infants and non-walkers particularly enjoy this activity. Of course, this works best on uncarpeted floors and needs to be done carefully. Don't jerk the fabric; keep it steady and slow.

Silk or satin scarves have wonderful textures to use with the very young child. The adult may use the fabric to trace slowly down the child from head to toe while singing "Rain Is Falling Down" or "Rain, Rain Go Away." The sensation can be soothing or tickly depending on how the adult manipulates the material.

Tie scarves in with other activities. Fill a box that has a hole in it, like a tissue box, with scarves and encourage the children to pull them out. An oatmeal container with a circle cut out of the lid works fine too. To make the activity a bit more challenging, tie multiple scarves together end to end using loose knots before putting in the container. These knots provide enough resistance that the child will have to vary the pull necessary to remove them.

Play different kinds of music or sing songs while participants wave their scarves all around to the tempo. The presenter may find it helpful to supply some directions (wave high, low, fast, slow, toss it in the air, etc.) during the activity. The CD *Musical Scarves & Activities* by Georgiana Stewart (Kimbo Educational, 2002) has many movement ideas using scarves, some of which can easily be adapted for use with very young children. Check Totline's *Toddler-Theme-A-Saurus* for additional songs to use with scarves.

Cut streamers from colorful fabric or use wide satin ribbon or blanket binding. Make sure any ribbon you choose does not have wired edges or attached sparkles since these pose a health hazard to very young children. Paper streamers have edges that may cut tender skin and colors may bleed when dampened by little mouths, so they are not the best choice to use with children who still put things in their mouths.

One streamer activity is to have the adult hold the streamer slightly out of reach and encourage the child to try to grab for it. Watching bright streamers or scarves moving from side to side will exercise the child's ability to track or follow, an important early literacy skill. Make a wand for each adult by attaching several thin streamers to a straw or a tube of paper made by rolling copy paper on the diagonal. The adults can use these wands to mimic the wind or rain or to help keep the tempo while singing or reciting rhymes.

Sign Language

Over the last few years, teaching sign language to very young children has become more predominant and has created a difference of opinion. There are those who believe teaching hearing children to sign will delay their vocalization. There are those who believe only American Sign Language should be taught, not gestures. Others feel sign language is too difficult and will confuse the child.

Using sign language in a program simply introduces it to adults who, if they so choose, may pursue additional information and instruction on their own. Sign language allows the young child to communicate with the adult before they have the ability to vocalize. It can ease the tension between adult and young child by enabling the child to convey what he or she wants, needs, or feels.

A study by Ohio State University in 1999 investigated using sign language with the children in their infant-toddler laboratory school. "It is so much easier for our teachers to work with 12-month olds who can sign that they want their bottle, rather than just cry and have us try to figure out what they want. This is a great way for infants to express their needs before they can verbalize them," said Dr. Kimberlee Whaley, coordinator of the laboratory school and an associate professor of human development and family science at Ohio State's College of Human Ecology. The signs were not formally taught but were included with daily activities, with words and phrases signed while they were simultaneously spoken. Infants were introduced to signs as early as six weeks and as late as nine months. These children began using sign before verbalizing to communicate with adults. The ability to understand what very young children are trying to convey is very beneficial to the adult working with them. Research does not indicate children who sign have difficulty communicating later in life. In fact, they seem to have a larger vocabulary and are better at expressing themselves. Dr. Linda Acredolo and Susan Goodwyn have presented studies that support this. These studies and additional research information can be found on the BabySigns Web site under "Research."

Two recommended resources for using sign language with very young children are:

- *Baby Signs: How to Talk with Your Baby Before Your Baby Can Talk* by Linda Acredolo and Susan Goodwyn. (Contemporary Books, 1996) Information is available in print, informative video, DVD, and board books for use with little ones. Instructional classes are available in some areas, see Web site for more information (www.babysigns.com).

- *Sign with Your Baby: How to Communicate with Infants Before They Can Speak* by Joseph Garcia (Stratton-Kehl Publications, 2001) Printed text, video, and a music CD with activity guide all using American Sign Language. Classes are also available; information on these can be found on their Web site (www.sign2me.com).

Musicians that specialize in children's music have begun to add signing to songs both traditional and original. Instructions for these signs are included on their CDs and/or Web sites. For instance, Nancy Stewart's (Friends Street Music) Web site includes signing directions on some of her "Song of the Month" activity pages. Links to sites such as the American Sign Language Web and HandSpeak can be found on her resource page. Some books adapt easily to sign language. A couple of titles to start with are *Brown Bear, Brown Bear* by Bill Martin and *I Love Animals* by Flora McDonnell, both of which are easy to sign. For more on using sign with music and rhymes see the music and rhymes chapters earlier in this book.

Incorporating sign language into stories is not intended to be word for word. Focus first on nouns, then verbs. This follows the natural pattern of how language is learned. Before you read a story aloud or recite a rhyme or song, select a key noun or action to sign. For example, sign "apple" when reciting "way up high in the apple tree." Say the word out loud as you sign it. Use signs for things children see or do daily to help reinforce them. Such signs could be water, apple, cat, eat, milk, sing, duck, dance, sleep, and so on. Make this a fun activity. If you would like to learn sign language, check with community colleges, many of which offer classes, or see the resources at the end of this chapter.

Resources

Print

Acredolo, Linda, and Susan Goodwyn. 1996. *Baby Signs: How to Talk With Your Baby Before Your Baby Can Talk*. New York: Contemporary Books.

Albrecht, Kay, and Linda G. Miller. 2000. *The Comprehensive Infant Curriculum: A Complete, Interactive Curriculum for Infants from Birth to 18 Months*. Beltsville, MD: Gryphon House.

Anderson-Wright, Judith, Robert Berg, and Joseph Garcia. 2003. *Pick Me Up! Fun Songs for Learning Signs*. Seattle: Sign2me/Northlight Communications.

Carlson, Ann, and Mary Carlson. 1999. *Flannelboard Stories for Infants and Toddlers*. Chicago: ALA.

Carlson, Ann, and Mary Carlson. 2005. *Flannelboard Stories for Infants and Toddlers, Bilingual Edition*. Chicago: ALA.

Ernst, Linda. *Lapsit Services for the Very Young II*. 2001. New York: Neal-Schuman.

Garcia, Joseph. 2001. *Sign With Your Baby: How to Communicate With Infants Before They Can Speak*. Bellingham, WA: Stratton-Kehl.

Heath, Alan, and Nicki Bainbridge. 2004. *Baby Massage: The Calming Power of Touch*. New York: DK Publishing.

Herr, Judy, and Terri Swim. 2002. *Creative Resources for Infants and Toddlers*, 2nd ed. Clifton Park, New York: Thomson Delmar Learning.

_____. 2003. *Making Sounds, Making Music, and Many Other Activities for Infants: 7 to 12 Months*. Clifton Park, New York: Thomson Delmar Learning.

_____. 2003. *Rattle Time, Face to Face, and Many Other Activities for Infants: Birth to 6 Months*. Clifton Park, New York: Thomson Delmar Learning.

_____. 2002. *Sorting Shapes, Show Me, and Many Other Activities for Toddlers: 13 to 24 Months.* Clifton Park, New York: Thomson Delmar Learning.

Hewitt, Karen. 2001. "Blocks as a Tool for Learning: A Historical and Contemporary Perspective." *Journal of the National Association for the Education of Young Children* 56, no. 1 (January), 6–13.

Koralek, Derry, ed. 2004. *Spotlight on Young Children and Play.* Washington, DC: National Association for the Education of Young Children.

Leiderman, Roni Cohen, and Wendy S. Masi, eds. 2001. *Baby Play: 100 Fun-Filled Activities to Maximize Your Baby's Potential.* San Francisco: Creative Publishing International.

McClure, Vimala. 2000. *Infant Massage: A Handbook for Loving Parents.* New York: Bantam Books.

Miller, Anne Meeker. 2007. *Baby Sing & Sign. Communicate Early with Your Baby: Learning Signs the Fun Way Through Music & Play.* New York: Marlowe.

Miller, Karen. 1999. *Simple Steps: Developmental Activities for Infants, Toddlers, and Two-Year-Olds.* Beltsville, MD: Gryphon House.

Raines, Shirley, Karen Miller, and Leah Curry-Rood. 2002. *Story S-T-R-E-T-C-H-E-R-S for Infants, Toddlers, and Twos: Experiences, Activities, and Games for Popular Children's Books.* Beltsville, MD: Gryphon House.

Schiller, Pam. 2005. *The Complete Resource Book for Infants: Over 700 Experiences for Children from Birth to 18 Months.* Beltsville, MD: Gryphon House.

Sierra, Judy. 1997. *The Flannel Board Storytelling Book.* New York: Wilson.

Silberg, Jackie. 1999. *125 Brain Games for Babies.* Beltsville, MD: Gryphon House.

_____. 2001. *Games to Play with Babies,* 3rd ed. Beltsville, MD: Gryphon House.

_____. 2002. *Games to Play with Toddlers,* rev. ed. Beltsville, MD: Gryphon House.

Wilmes, Liz, and Dick Wilmes. 1994. *Felt Board Fun.* Elgin, IL: Building Blocks.

_____. 1985. *Parachute Play.* Elgin, IL: Building Blocks.

Woodfield, Julia. 2004. *Healing Massage for Babies and Toddlers.* Great Britain: Floris Books.

Web Sites

General

www.beyondplay.com
Beyond Play: Early Intervention Products for Young Children with Special Needs.
Phone: 877-428-1244
Mail: 1442A Walunut St. #52, Berkeley, CA 94709

www.environments@eichild.com
Environments, Inc.
Phone: 1-800-EI-CHILD (1-800-342-4453)
Mail: Environments, Inc., PO Box 1348, Beaufort, SC 29901-1348

www.folkmanis.com
Folkmanis
Phone: 510-658-7677

www.kimboed.com
KIMBO Education
   Phone: 800-631-2187 or 732-229-4949 Fax 732-870-3340
   Mail: PO Box 477, Long Branch, NJ 07740

www.lakeshorelearning.com
Lakeshore Learning
   Phone: 800-421-5354
   Mail: Lakeshore Learning Materials, 2695 E. Dominguez St., Carson, CA 90895

www.nurturingpathways.com
Nurturing Pathways
   Phone: 425-280-3805
   Mail: 18429 12th Ave. W., Lynnwood, WA 98037

www.orientaltrading.com
Oriental Trading Company
   Phone: 800-875-8480

jsilberg@interserv.com
Miss Jackie Music Company
   Mail: 5000 West 112th St., Leawood, Kansas 66211

Flannel Boards

www.accucut.com
AccuCut: die cut machines and dies
   Phone: 1-800-288-1670

www.childwood.com
ChildWood
   Wooden magnetic characters
   Phone: 800-362-9825
   Mail: 8873 Woodbank Dr., Bainbridge Island, WA 98110

www.ellison.com
Ellison
   Phone: 800-253-2238 (Toll Free in the USA)
   Mail: Ellison Educational Equipment, Inc., 25862 Commercentre Dr., Lake
   Forest, CA 92630-8804

Preschoolexpress.com
Preschool Express
   Preschool activities and idea site created by Jean Warren that includes "Pattern
   Station" useful for making flannel pieces.

sisters-in-stitches.com
Sisters-in-Stitches: Hand crafted flannel characters and story sets
   Phone: 425-259-4140, 866-259-4140
   Mail: 2423 Virginia, Everett, WA 98201

Sign Language

http://commtechlab.msu.edu/sites/aslweb/browser.htm
American Sign Language Web

babysigns.com
Baby Signs
    Phone: 800-995-0226
    Mail: 871 Cotting Ct., Ste. I, Vacaville, CA 95688

www.handspeak.com
HandSpeak
    This is a subscription-based Web site.

www.sign2me.com
Sign2me
    Phone: 877-744-6263
    Mail: 12125 Harbour Reach Dr., Ste. D, Mukilteo, WA 98275

10

A Dozen Ready-to-Go Programs

When one is just starting to venture into programming for the very young, it is helpful to have an outline or script to work from. This chapter offers program outlines and scripts that have been created by librarians in the field and presented successfully. Program scripts are in the first part of the chapter and the outlines of these scripts are in the second half. The numbers for scripts and outlines match, so you can select which format feels comfortable.

Programs 1 through 6 are designed primarily for babies, newborns to 12 months, and their caregivers. Programs 7 through 10 are designed for children 12 to 24 months and their caregivers. Programs 11 and 12 are examples of programs with these age groups combined. These outlines and scripts offer a variety of individual programs. It is not necessary to use them as a series: 1, 2, 3, etc. Keep in mind the importance of repetition. A core selection of material for each program can be varied by changing one or two books, rhymes, or songs. Most importantly, keep it simple. Too much variety can be unsettling to many young children. If you create a routine, the group becomes familiar with the material and more willing to participate. For instance, you may want to have the first book in each program remain constant while changing the other books you want to use. Every program I do starts with Bill Martin's *Brown Bear, Brown Bear, What Do You See?* You may choose to sing the same songs at every program. If you want to add bits of information, such as facts on brain development or early literacy, select one that you want to highlight instead of constantly interjecting different ones throughout the program. Pace yourself so there is time for the participants to take in what you are sharing verbally and allow time for them to respond to it.

These programs and outlines are a format to which to add and subtract materials, depending on your own personal favorites and the length of the program. Books and rhymes that have been used successfully in programs for the very young can be found in Chapters 6 and 7 with suggested themes in Chapter 11. (CD icon indicates an audio version is included on the CD-ROM.)

Each script and outline has lines that say "Tips" and "Tips to make this a good time for all," which indicate where guidelines to help the program move smoothly should be inserted. If you need ideas here are a few suggestions:

- Please turn cell phones off or at least to vibrate.
- It is fine to let the child observe. Do not force the child, but the "big people" should participate.
- If child becomes over-stimulated or just needs a break from the group, please feel free to step out for a moment and then return.
- Sharing is something that children this age are still learning about so please keep snacks or security items to the side if possible. If a child needs to be breast-fed, they will often move slightly out of the group and then rejoin it so there is usually minimal interruption.
- It is okay to make a mistake or use the words that are more familiar. Rhymes can change!
- The adult knows the child best and can judge how much participation they can handle.
- Relax and remember the more fun the adult has, the more the child will have.

Programs for Newborn to 12 Months

Program 1—Script

Introduction: "Welcome to story time"—Introduce yourself and then have each participant introduce him or herself and his or her child. Offer tips to make this a good time for all.

Welcome song: "The More We Get Together" from *If You're Happy and You Know It, Sing Along with Bob #1* by Bob McGrath

(Rock baby back and forth on lap or in arms)

Clapping rhyme: "Patty-Cake, Patty-Cake" CD

(Baby is lying on back on floor or sitting on adult's lap. Do actions to the rhyme by manipulating baby's arms. Instead of "B," baby's name and initial may be used.)

Patty-cake, patty-cake, baker's man
Bake me a cake as fast as you can.
Roll it and pat it and mark it with a "B"
And put it in the oven for baby and me!

Cuddle rhyme: "Wash the Dishes" CD

(Make criss-cross pattern across baby's chest and abdomen or back)

Wash the dishes, wipe the dishes,
Ring the bell for tea. DING!
Three good wishes, three good kisses,
I will give to thee.
One, two, three!

(Kiss each cheek and then belly or nose)

Stretch rhyme: "Apple Tree" ⓒ

(Directions are for baby lying on back)

Way up high in the apple tree

(Stretch baby's arms gently over his head)

Two little apples did I see.

(Gently make circles around baby's eyes)

So I shook that tree as hard as I could,

(Jiggle baby's tummy back and forth)

And d-o-w-n came the apples,

(Tickle fingers down baby's body from head to toe)

Umm! They were good!

(Give baby a hug)

Rocking rhyme: "Tick-Tock" ⓒ

(In a sitting position, hold the baby and gently rock back and forth. On the last line, play peek-a-boo with the child, or lift baby with hand under baby's bottom or knees)

Tick-tock, tick-tock,
I'm a little cuckoo clock.
Tick-tock, tick-tock,
Now it's almost three o'clock.
Cuckoo! Cuckoo! Cuckoo!

Book: *Peekaboo Morning* by Rachel Isadora

Action rhyme: "The Grand Old Duke of York" ⓒ

(A bouncing rhyme or for marching in place or in a circle. Follow the words and lift child up and down or help child raise arms above head and so on)

Oh, the grand old Duke of York,
He had 10,000 men.
He marched them up to the top of the hill
And he marched them down again.
And when they were up, they were up.
And when they were down, they were down.

But when they were only halfway up *(Pause)*
They were neither up nor down!
They marched them to the left,
They marched them to the right,
They even marched them upside-down,
Now isn't that a sight!

Song: "The Wheels on the Bus" (Traditional)

The wheels on the bus go round and round, round and round, round and round. The wheels on the bus go round and round, all through the town.

> *(Move baby's hands around each other or move baby's legs as if on a bicycle)*

The wipers on the bus go swish, swish, swish, etc.

> *(Move baby's arms or legs side to side)*

The windows on the bus go up and down, etc.

> *(Move baby's arms or legs up and down)*

The doors on the bus go open and shut, etc.

> *(Do peek-a-boo or open arms wide bringing together with a clap)*

The horn on the bus goes beep, beep, beep, etc.

> *(Tap baby's tummy or nose)*

The wheels on the bus go round and round, round and round, round and round. The wheels on the bus go round and round, all through the town.

> *(Move baby's hands around each other or baby's legs as if on a bicycle)*

Rocking rhyme: "Acka Backa" ⊙

> *(Sitting with child on lap rock back and forth; for a livelier group use this rhyme as a bounce)*

Acka backa soda cracker, acka backa boo!
Acka backa soda cracker, I love you! *(Hug child)*
Acka backa soda cracker, acka backa boo!
Acka backa soda cracker, up goes you!
Acka backa soda cracker, acka backa boo!
Acka backa soda cracker, I love you! *(Hug child)*

Book: *I Love Animals* by Flora McDonnell

Song: "Head and Shoulders, Knees and Toes" ⊙

> *(To the tune of "London Bridge," touch each body part when named)*

Head and shoulders, knees and toes,
Knees and toes.
Head and shoulders, knees and toes,

Knees and toes.
And eyes, and ears, and mouth and nose.
Head and shoulders, knees and toes,
Knees and toes.

Music time: Bring out rhythm instruments for children to play along with music CD of children's songs, classical, or another style you prefer.

Closing song: "The More We Get Together" from *If You're Happy and You Know It, Sing Along with Bob #1* by Bob McGrath

Distribute handouts.

Program 2—Script

Introduction: Welcome to story time—Introduce yourself and then have each participant introduce self and child. Offer tips to make this a good time for all.

Welcome song: "Hello Everybody" (From *Sally's from Wibbleton to Wobbleton* video by Sally Jaeger)

Stretch rhyme: "Open, Shut Them" ⓒⒹ

(Move the baby's arms out to sides and back together, following directions in rhyme)

Open, shut them, open, shut them, give a little clap, clap, clap.
Open, shut them, open, shut them, put them in your lap, lap, lap.
Creep them, crawl them, creep them, crawl them, right up to your chin, chin, chin.

(Walk fingers up baby's chest to chin)

Open up your little mouth,

(Circle baby's mouth and pause)

But do not let them in!

(Tickle down chest)

Rocking rhyme: "Ride Baby Ride" ⓒⒹ on *Baby Record* by Bob McGrath and Katherine Smithrim

(Sitting: Rock back and forth or bounce on knee. Standing: bounce or walk around)

Ride baby ride—Ch, ch, ch, ch, ch, ch.
Ride that horsey ride—Ch, ch, ch, ch, ch, ch.
Ride baby ride—Ch, ch, ch, ch, ch, ch.
Ride that horsey ride—Ch, ch, ch, ch, ch, ch.
Whoa . . . ! *(Give baby a hug)*

Bouncing rhyme: "Acka Backa" ⓒⒹ

(Sitting with child on lap, rock back and forth; for a livelier group use this rhyme as a bounce)

Acka backa soda cracker, acka backa boo!
Acka backa soda cracker, I love you! *(Hug child)*
Acka backa soda cracker, acka backa boo!
Acka backa soda cracker, up goes you!
Acka backa soda cracker, acka backa boo!
Acka backa soda cracker, I love you! *(Hug child)*

Song: "The Wheels on the Bus" (Traditional)

The wheels on the bus go round and round, round and round, round and round. The wheels on the bus go round and round, all through the town.

(Move baby's hands around each other or move baby's legs as if on a bicycle)

The wipers on the bus go swish, swish, swish, etc.

(Move baby's arms or legs side to side)

The windows on the bus go up and down, etc.

(Move baby's arms or legs up and down)

The doors on the bus go open and shut, etc.

(Do peek-a-boo or open arms wide bringing together with a clap)

The horn on the bus goes beep, beep, beep, etc.

(Tap baby's tummy or nose)

The wheels on the bus go round and round, round and round, round and round. The wheels on the bus go round and round, all through the town.

(Move baby's hands around each other or move baby's legs as if on a bicycle)

Rocking rhyme: "Tick-Tock" ⓒ

(In a sitting position, hold baby and gently rock back and forth. On the word "cuckoo," play peek-a-boo or with hand under baby's bottom or knees, lift baby)

Tick-tock, tick-tock
I'm a little cuckoo clock.
Tick-tock, tick-tock,
Now it's almost three o'clock.
Cuckoo! Cuckoo! Cuckoo!

Action rhyme: "Roly-Poly" ⓒ

(Standing, move baby in the directions indicated; sitting, gently move baby's arms or hands around each other and in the directions indicated)

Roly-poly, roly-poly, up–up–up.
Roly-poly, roly-poly, down–down–down.
Roly-poly, roly-poly, out–out–out.
Roly-poly, roly-poly, in–in–in.

Circle activity: "Ring Around the Rosie" (Traditional)

Ring around the rosie,
A pocket full of posies,
Ashes, ashes,
We all fall down!

Cows are in the meadow,
Eating buttercups.
Lightening, thunder
We all stand up!

Bouncing rhyme: "Rooster Crows" ⓒⓓ

(Bounce baby on knees. Lift baby from one knee to the other or lift over head and spin around on "away he goes")

One, two, three—baby's on my knee
Rooster crows and away *(child's name)* goes!

Tickle rhyme: "'Round and 'Round the Garden" ⓒⓓ

'Round and 'round the garden goes the teddy bear.
   (Draw circles using fingers around baby's tummy, back, hand)
One step, two step, tickle *(child's name)* under there!
   (Walk fingers up baby's body and tickle under chin or arm)

Music time: Free dance time. Pick a CD (classical, folk, rock) and encourage movement to it.

Closing: Bring out board books or toy and distribute handouts.

Program 3—Script

Introduction: Welcome to story time—Introduce yourself and then have each participant introduce self and child. Offer tips to make this a good time for all.

Bouncing rhyme: "Rooster Crows" ⓒⓓ

(Bounce baby on knees. Lift baby from one knee to the other or lift up in the air over head and spin around on "away he goes")

One, two, three—baby's on my knee
Rooster crows and away *(child's name)* goes!

Tickle rhyme: "These Are Baby's Fingers"

These are *(baby's name)* fingers
These are *(baby's name)* toes
This is *(baby's name)* bellybutton
Around and around it goes!

(Tickle baby's fingers)
(Tickle baby's toes)
(Tickle baby's bellybutton)
(Make circle shape around baby's bellybutton)

Book: *Read to Your Bunny* by Rosemary Wells

Bouncing rhyme: "Cheek, Chin" (Reprinted with permission from *Hippety-Hop, Hippety-Hay,* by Opal Dunn and Sally Anne Lambert, published by Frances Lincoln Limited, copyright © 1999).

(Tap each body part while reciting this rhyme)
Cheek, chin, cheek, chin, cheek, chin, NOSE,
Cheek, chin, cheek, chin, cheek, chin, TOES,
Cheek, chin, cheek, chin, cheek, chin—UP baby goes!

(When diapering, lift baby's ankles up together and slip diaper underneath!)

Action rhyme: "Trot, Trot to Boston" 💿

Trot, trot to Boston,	*(Bounce baby on lap)*
Trot, trot to Lynn.	*(Bounce baby on lap)*
Look out little *(baby's name)* You might fall in!	*(Tip baby to one side)*
Trot, trot to Boston,	*(Bounce baby on lap)*
Trot, trot to town.	*(Bounce baby on lap)*
Look out little *(baby's name)* You might fall down!	*(Move your legs apart, hold baby firmly and drop though opening)*

Free dance: Put on a waltz and have participants move around the room in time to the music while holding baby.

Today's tip: Nursery rhymes and phonological awareness

Book: *All Fall Down* by Helen Oxenbury

Tickle rhyme: "Jeremiah, Blow the Fire" 💿
(Blow softly on baby's belly, getting stronger each time)

Jeremiah, blow the fire, puff, puff, puff.
First you blow it gently...
Then you blow it rough.

Action rhyme: "Here We Go Up–Up–Up!" 💿

Here we go up–up–up.	*(Lift baby up in the air)*
And here we go down–down–down.	*(Lower baby towards floor)*
And here we go back-and-forth, and back-and-forth.	*(Swing baby back and forth)*
And here we go around and around and around.	*(Turn around holding baby)*

Closing announcements: Let participants know of activities coming up that might interest them, such as an early literacy workshop.

Closing song: "Good-bye Song"

Good-bye babies!
Good-bye babies!
Good-bye babies, it's time to say bye-bye!

> *(Using the tune of "Good Night Ladies," wave bye-bye to group or say good-bye to each baby by name)*

Program 4—Script

Introduction: Welcome to story time—Introduce yourself and then have each participant introduce self and child. Offer tips to make this a good time for all.

Opening song: *(Your choice)*

Bouncing rhyme: "Rickety, Rickety Rocking Horse"

> *(Gently rock back and forth or gallop around holding baby, giving hug on last line)*

Rickety, rickety rocking horse,
Over the hills we go—oh!
Rickety, rickety rocking horse,
Giddy-up, giddy-up, whoa!

Tickle rhyme: "These Are Baby's Fingers"

These are *(baby's name)* fingers	*(Tickle baby's fingers)*
These are *(baby's name)* toes	*(Tickle baby's toes)*
This is *(baby's name)* bellybutton	*(Tickle baby's bellybutton)*
Around and around it goes!	*(Make circles around baby's bellybutton)*

Book: *Clap Hands* by Helen Oxenbury

Clapping rhyme: "Muffin Man"

> *(Clap hands in time with the words)*

Oh, do you know the muffin man,   Oh, yes, I know the muffin man,
The muffin man, the muffin man?   The muffin man, the muffin man.
Oh, do you know the muffin man?   Oh, yes, I know the muffin man,
Who lives on Drury Lane?   Who lives on Drury Lane!

Song: "The Wheels on the Bus" (Traditional)

The wheels on the bus go round and round, round and round, round and round. The wheels on the bus go round and round, all through the town.

> *(Move baby's hands around each other or move baby's legs as if on a bicycle)*

The wipers on the bus go swish, swish, swish, etc.

> *(Move baby's arms or legs side to side)*

The windows on the bus go up and down, etc.

> *(Move baby's arms or legs up and down)*

The doors on the bus go open and shut, etc.

> *(Do peek-a-boo or open arms wide bringing together with a clap)*

The horn on the bus goes beep, beep, beep, etc.

> *(Tap baby's tummy or nose)*

The wheels on the bus go round and round, round and round, round and round. The wheels on the bus go round and round, all through the town.

> *(Move baby's hands around each other or move baby's legs as if on a bicycle)*

Free dance: Folk music that provides a lively beat everyone can move to

Book: *Can I Have a Hug?* by Debi Gliori

Tickle rhyme: "Wiggle, Wiggle" ⓒⒹ

> *(Wiggle index finger around in baby's sight so baby can follow it visually. Dramatic pause before tickling "THERE!")*

Wiggle, wiggle little finger
Wiggle, wiggle in the air
Wiggle, wiggle little finger
And come down . . . THERE!

Action rhyme: "Trot, Trot to Boston" ⓒⒹ

Trot, trot to Boston,	*(Bounce baby on lap or hip)*
Trot, trot to Lynn.	*(Bounce baby on lap)*
Look out little *(baby's name)* You might fall in!	*(Tip baby to one side)*
Trot, trot to Boston,	*(Bounce baby on lap)*
Trot, trot to town.	*(Bounce baby on lap)*
Look out little *(baby's name)* You might fall down!	*(If sitting, move your knees apart, hold baby firmly and drop though opening; if standing, bend down)*

Closing announcements

Closing song: "Cuddle Up and Sing" from Tickle Tune Typhoon's recording *Baby Tickle Tunes: Patty-Cakes and Peek-A-Boos*

Program 5—Script

Introduction: Welcome to story time—Introduce yourself and then have each participant introduce self and child. Offer tips to make this a good time for all.

Opening song: *(Your choice)*

Clapping rhyme: "Patty-Cake, Patty-Cake" ⓒⒹ

> *(Baby is lying on back on floor or sitting on adult's lap. Do actions to the rhyme by manipulating baby's arms. Instead of "B," baby's name and initial may be used)*

Patty-cake, patty-cake, baker's man
Bake me a cake as fast as you can.
Roll it and pat it and mark it with a "B"
And put it in the oven for baby and me!

Tickle rhyme: "Eensy, Weensy Spider" ⓒⒹ

The eensy, weensy spider went up the water spout.
> *(Baby on tummy, walk/tickle fingers up baby's back)*

Down came the rain and washed the spider out!
> *(Slide fingers down baby's back from head to toes)*

Out came the sun and dried up all the rain,
> *(Rub baby's back)*

And the eensy, weensy spider went up the spout again.
> *(Baby on tummy, walk/tickle fingers up baby's back)*

Rocking rhyme: "Tick-Tock" ⓒⒹ

> *(In a sitting position, hold baby and gently rock back and forth. On the word "cuckoo," play peek-a-boo or with hand under baby's bottom or knees, lift baby)*

Tick-tock, tick-tock,
I'm a little cuckoo clock.
Tick-tock, tick-tock,
Now it's almost three o'clock.
Cuckoo! Cuckoo! Cuckoo!

Bouncing rhyme: "Mother and Father and Uncle John" ⓒⒹ

Mother and Father and Uncle John	*(Bounce baby on lap)*
Went to town, one by one.	*(Tip baby to one side)*
Mother fell off,	
And Father fell off,	*(Tip baby to other side)*
But Uncle John went on and on and on!	*(Bounce baby on lap)*

Action rhyme: "Roly-Poly" 🔘

(Standing in circle, move baby as indicated, moving toward center of circle and out; if sitting, gently move baby's arms as indicated)

Roly-poly, roly-poly, up–up–up.
Roly-poly, roly-poly, down–down–down.
Roly-poly, roly-poly, out–out–out.
Roly-poly, roly-poly, in–in–in.

Stretch rhyme: "Apple Tree" 🔘 *(Baby lies on back)*

Way up high in the apple tree	*(Raise arms above baby's head)*
Two little apples did I see.	*(Use index finger to massage around baby's eyes)*
So I shook that tree as hard as I could,	*(Jiggle baby's body)*
And d-o-w-n came the apples,	*(Tickle fingers down baby's body)*
Umm! They were good!	*(Give baby cuddles and kisses)*

Song: "The Wheels on the Bus" (Traditional)

The wheels on the bus go round and round, round and round, round and round. The wheels on the bus go round and round, all through the town.

(Move baby's hands around each other or move baby's legs as if on a bicycle)

The wipers on the bus go swish, swish, swish, etc.

(Move baby's arms or legs side to side)

The windows on the bus go up and down, etc.

(Move baby's arms or legs up and down)

The doors on the bus go open and shut, etc.

(Play peek-a-boo or open arms wide, bringing together with a clap)

The horn on the bus goes beep, beep, beep, etc.

(Tap baby's tummy or nose)

The wheels on the bus go round and round, round and round, round and round. The wheels on the bus go round and round, all through the town.

(Move baby's hands around each other or move baby's legs as if on a bicycle)

Bouncing rhyme: "To Market, to Market" 🔘

To market, to market to buy a fat pig,
Home again, home again jiggity jig.
To market, to market to buy a fat hog,
Home again, home again jiggity jog.

(Bounce baby on lap or hip if standing)

Closing song: "The More We Get Together" from *If You're Happy and You Know It, Sing Along with Bob #1* by Bob McGrath

Program 6—Script

Introduction: Welcome to story time—Introduce yourself and then have each participant introduce self and child. Offer tips to make this a good time for all.

Opening song: "Where Is Baby?"

(Tune is "Frere Jacques"; clap while singing)

Where is baby? Where is baby?
There you are! There you are!
We're so glad to see you. We're so glad to see you.
Yes we are! Yes we are!

Stretch rhyme: "Open, Shut Them" ⏺

(Move the baby's arms out to sides and back together, following directions in rhyme.)

Open, shut them, open, shut them, give a little clap, clap, clap.
Open, shut them, open, shut them, put them in your lap, lap, lap.
Creep them, crawl them, creep them, crawl them, right up to your chin, chin, chin.

(Walk fingers up baby's chest to chin)

Open up your mouth,   *(Circle baby's mouth and pause)*

But do not let them in!   *(Tickle down chest)*

Tickle rhyme: "These Are Baby's Fingers"

These are baby's fingers,
These are baby's toes.
This is baby's bellybutton, around and around it goes!

(Tickle body parts as indicated and insert baby's name when repeated)

Song: "Head and Shoulders, Knees and Toes" ⏺

(Touch each body part indicated)

Head and shoulders, knees and toes,knees and toes.
Head and shoulders, knees and toes, knees and toes.
Eyes and ears and mouth and nose.
Head and shoulders, knees and toes, knees and toes.

Clapping rhyme: "Pussy Cat, Pussy Cat" ⏺

(Clap hands to rhythm of rhyme or use as an exercise or stretch—touch baby's hands and feet to one another, first the same side, then opposite—right hand to left foot, left hand to right foot)

Pussycat, pussycat where have you been?
I've been to London to visit the queen.
Pussycat, pussycat what did you there?
I frightened a little mouse under her chair.

Tickle rhyme: "There Was a Little Man" ⏵

There was a little man,	*(Point to baby)*
He had a little crumb,	*(Tickle baby's cheek)*
And over the mountain he did run.	*(Run fingers over baby's head)*
With a belly full of fat	*(Jiggle baby's belly)*
And a big, tall hat,	*(Pat baby's head)*
And a pancake stuck to his bum, bum, bum.	*(Pat baby's bottom)*

Circle song: "Ring Around the Rosie"

(Individual adult holds baby and turns in circle or group walks around in a circle)

Ring around the rosie,
A pocket full of posies,
Ashes, ashes,
We all fall down!

Tickle rhyme: "Shoe a Little Horse" ⏵

Shoe a little horse.	*(Pat baby's foot)*
Shoe a little mare.	*(Pat baby's other foot)*
But let the little pony run bare, bare, bare.	*(Pat baby's bottom)*

Clapping rhyme: "Patty-Cake, Patty-Cake" ⏵

(Baby is lying on back on floor or sitting on adult's lap. Do actions to the rhyme by manipulating baby's arms. Instead of "B," baby's name and initial may be used)

Patty-cake, patty-cake, baker's man,
Bake me a cake as fast as you can!
Roll it and pat it and mark it with a "B"
And put it in the oven for baby and me!

Tickle rhyme: "'Round and 'Round the Garden" ⏵

Round and round the garden goes the teddy bear.	*(Draw circles on baby's hand, belly, back)*
One step,	*(Walk fingers up towards baby's head)*
Two step,	*(Walk fingers up towards baby's head)*
Tickle *(baby's name)* under there!	*(Tickle baby under chin or arm)*

Closing song: "Butterfly Kisses" from *'Round and 'Round the Garden: Music in My First Year* by John M. Feierabend and Luann Saunders

Programs for 12 to 24 Months

Program 7—Script

Introduction: Welcome to story time—Introduce yourself and include tips to make this a good time for all.

Opening song: "The More We Get Together"

Clapping rhyme: "Patty-Cake, Patty-Cake" 🆑

Patty-cake, patty-cake, baker's man,
Bake me a cake as fast as you can!
Roll it and pat it and mark it with a "B"
And put it in the oven for baby and me!

Stretch rhyme: "Apple Tree" 🆑

Way up high in the apple tree	*(Stretch arms above head)*
Two little apples did I see.	*(Point to eyes)*
So I shook that tree as hard as I could,	*(Wiggle and shake whole body)*
And d-o-w-n came the apples,	*(Bring arms down to sides)*
Umm! They were good!	*(Rub tummy)*

Rocking rhyme: "Tick-Tock" 🆑
   (Child sits on lap, or, if big enough, stands alone to rock sideways)

Tick-tock, tick-tock,
I'm a little cuckoo clock.
Tick-tock, tick-tock,
Now it's almost three o'clock.
   (Pause)
Cuckoo! Cuckoo! Cuckoo!
   (Play peek-a-boo or lift in air)

Book: *Brown Bear, Brown Bear, What Do You See?* by Bill Martin

Song: "Head and Shoulders, Knees and Toes" 🆑
   (Touch each body part when named)

Head and shoulders, knees and toes, knees and toes.
Head and shoulders, knees and toes, knees and toes.
Eyes and ears and mouth and nose.
Head and shoulders, knees and toes, knees and toes.

Action rhyme: "The Grand Old Duke of York" 🆑

(This works as a bouncing rhyme, marching in place or in a circle. Follow directions in rhyme such as lifting child up and down or help child raise arms up into the air above head)

Oh, the grand old Duke of York,
He had 10,000 men.
He marched them up to the top of the hill
And he marched them down again.
And when they were up, they were up.
And when they were down, they were down.
But when they were only halfway up *(Pause)*
They were neither up nor down!
They marched them to the left,
They marched them to the right,
They even marched them upside-down.
Now isn't that a sight!

Stretch rhyme: "Tall as a Tree"

Tall as a tree.	*(Standing, stretch arms above head)*
Wide as a house.	*(Stretch arms straight out to sides)*
Thin as a pin.	*(Put arms down to sides)*
Small as a mouse.	*(Crouch down to floor)*

Rhyme: "Cobbler, Cobbler" 🆑

(Pat shoe of child or have child pat adult's shoe)

Cobbler, cobbler, mend my shoe.
Give it one stitch, give it two.
Give it three, give it four,
And if it needs it, give it more!

Song: "The Wheels on the Bus"

The wheels on the bus go round and round, round and round, round and round. The wheels on the bus go round and round, all through the town.

(Move hands around each other)

The wipers on the bus go swish, swish, swish, etc.

(Move arms side to side)

The windows on the bus go up and down, etc.

(Move arms up and down)

The doors on the bus go open and shut, etc.

(Open arms wide bringing together with a clap)

The horn on the bus goes beep, beep, beep, etc.

(Tap tummy or nose)

The wheels on the bus go round and round, round and round, round and round. The wheels on the bus go round and round, all through the town.

(Move hands around each other)

Book: *The Bridge Is Up* by Babs Bell

Action rhyme: "Row, Row, Row Your Boat"

(Instruct children to get into their "boats" on the adults' laps and use a rowing action, moving the whole arm in a circular motion)

Row, row, row your boat gently down the stream.
Merrily, merrily, merrily, merrily life is but a dream.

Clapping rhyme: "1–2–3–4–5, I Caught a Fish Alive!"

1–2–3–4–5	*(Child on adult's lap, clap hands around child)*
I caught a fish alive!	*(Give child a hug)*
6–7–8–9–10	*(Clap hands around child)*
I let him go again!	*(Tickle your fingers up the child's body from feet to head)*

Music time: "Clap Your Hands" from *Circle Around* by Tickle Tune Typhoon

Closing song: "The More We Get Together" from *If You're Happy and You Know It, Sing Along with Bob #1* by Bob McGrath

Program 8—Script

Introduction: Welcome to story time—Introduce yourself and include tips to make this a good time for all.

Opening: "Hello Toes!" from *Hello Toes! Movement Games for Children* by Anne Leif Barlin

(Start with the feet but add hands, face, and other body parts as desired)

Hello toes!	*(Flex toes up toward body or wiggle feet)*
Goodbye toes!	*(Point toes away from body)*
Hello toes!	*(Flex toes up towards body or wiggle feet)*
Goodbye toes!	*(Point toes away from body)*
My toes are feeling shy today...	*(Turn feet inward and gently alternate placing one on top of the other)*
But, now they are feeling better!	*(Wiggle feet happily)*

(Repeat using hands, fingers, face, etc.)

Clapping rhyme: "Patty-Cake, Patty-Cake" ⓒⒹ

Patty-cake, patty-cake, baker's man	*(Clap hands together)*
Bake me a cake as fast as you can!	*(Roll hands around each other,*
Roll it and pat it and mark it with a "B"	*then pat all over body)*
And put it in the oven for baby and me!	*(Clap hands together)*

Bouncing rhyme: "Mother and Father and Uncle John" ⓒⒹ

(Beware! Children will learn to anticipate the tilts in this rhyme so be ready!)

Mother and Father and Uncle John	*(Bounce child on knee)*
Went to town one by one.	*(Tip child to one side)*
Mother fell off,	
Father fell off,	*(Tip child to other side)*
But Uncle John went on and on	*(Bounce child on knee)*
and on and on and on!	

Book: *Brown Bear, Brown Bear, What Do You See?* by Bill Martin

Song: "Down by the Station" from *Wee Sing 25th Anniversary Celebration* by Pamela Conn Beall and Susan Hagen Nipp

Bouncing rhyme: "From Wibbleton to Wobbleton" ⓒⒹ

(Bounce child on lap)

From Wibbleton to Wobbleton is 15 miles.
From Wobbleton to Wibbleton is 15 miles.
From Wibbleton to Wobbleton, from Wobbleton to Wibbleton,
From Wibbleton to Wobbleton is 15 miles.

Book: *The Bus for Us* by Suzanne Bloom

Rhyme: "Riding on My Pony" ⓒⒹ

(Child can gallop around the room or, for a quieter ride, on adult's lap)

Riding on my pony, my pony, my pony.
Riding on my pony,
Trot, trot, trot!

Book: *Freight Train* by Donald Crews

Action Rhyme: "Choo-Choo Train" ⓒⒹ (Reprinted with permission from *Little Songs for Little Me*, written by Nancy Stewart, copyright 2007)

This is a choo-choo train	*(Standing, bend arms at elbows)*
Puffing down the track.	*(Move arms forward and back in rhythm)*

Now it's going forward,	*(Walk forward)*
Now it's going back.	*(Walk backward)*
Now the bell is ringing,	*(Pull cord with closed fist)*
Now the whistle blows.	*(Hold fist near mouth)*
What a lot of noise it makes	*(Cover ears)*
Everywhere it goes.	*(Stretch arms out)*

Closing song: "Goodbye" (tune of "Good Night Ladies")

(Insert a different child's name into the song until all the children have been named, waving goodbye to each one in turn)

Goodbye *(child's name)*
Goodbye *(different child's name)*
Goodbye *(different child's name)*
It's time for us to go!

Program 9—Script

Introduction: Welcome to story time—Introduce yourself and then have each participant introduce self and child. Tips to make this a good time for all.

Rhyme: "Two Little Blackbirds"

Two little blackbirds sitting on a hill	*(Hold both hands up in the air)*
One named Jack and the other named Jill	*(Raise one hand and then the other)*
Fly away Jack!	*(Put one hand behind back)*
Fly away Jill!	*(Put other hand behind back)*
Come back Jack!	*(Bring one hand back to front)*
Come back Jill.	*(Bring other hand back to front)*

Song: "Baa, Baa, Black Sheep" CD

(Clap to rhythm of song or use as flannel board story)

Baa, baa, black sheep, have you any wool?	
Yes sir, yes sir, three bags full.	*(Hold up three fingers)*
One for my master,	*(Hold up one finger)*
And one for my dame,	*(Hold up two fingers)*
And one for the little boy who lives down the lane.	*(Hold up three fingers)*

Book: *Caterpillar's Wish* by May Murphy

Stretch rhyme: "Apple Tree" 💿

Way up high in the apple tree	*(Stretch over head)*
Two little apples did I see.	*(Make fists)*
So I shook that tree as hard as I could,	*(Wiggle and shake body)*
And d-o-w-n came the apples,	*(Bring arms down to sides)*
Umm! They were good!	*(Rub tummy)*

Tickle rhyme: "Criss, Cross, Applesauce" 💿

Criss, cross, applesauce,	*(Make X on child's back)*
Spiders climbing up your back!	*(Walk fingers up back)*
Cool breeze, tight squeeze,	*(Blow hair, give hug)*
And now you've got the shivers!	*(Tickle)*

Action song: "Here We Go 'Round the Mulberry Bush" 💿

Book: *Little Robin Redbreast: A Mother Goose Rhyme* illustrated by Shari Halpern

Tickle rhyme: "Beehive" 💿

Here is the beehive,	*(Make fist with one hand)*
Where are the bees?	*(Shrug shoulders)*
Hidden inside where nobody sees.	*(Point to fist)*
Soon they'll come out, out of the hive,	*(Open fist and tickle child)*
One, two, three, four, five!	

Tickle rhyme: "Here Comes a Mouse" 💿

Here comes a mouse—mousie, mousie, mouse.
   (Wiggle finger towards child)
On tiny light feet, and a soft pink nose,
   (Tap nose)
Tickle, tickle, wherever he goes.
   (Tickle)
He'll run up your arm and under your chin!
   (Run fingers up child's arm to chin)
Don't open your mouth or the mouse will run in!
   (Use finger to circle around child's mouth)
Mousie, mousie, mouse!
   (Tap nose)

Closing: Blow bubbles while children dance to lively music on CD.

Program 10—Script

Introduction: Welcome to storytime—Introduce yourself and then have each participant introduce self and child. Offer tips to make this a good time for all.

Clapping rhyme: "Patty-Cake, Patty-Cake" 🆑

(Instead of "B," insert child's name and initial)

Patty-cake, patty-cake, baker's man,
Bake me a cake as fast as you can!
Roll it and pat it and mark it with a "B"
And put it in the oven for baby and me!

Stretch rhyme: "Open, Shut Them" 🆑

(Move arms out to sides and back together, follow directions in rhyme)

Open, shut them, open, shut them, give a little clap, clap, clap.
Open, shut them, open, shut them, put them in your lap, lap, lap.
Creep them, crawl them, creep them, crawl them, right up to your chin, chin, chin.

(Walk fingers up chest to chin)

Open up your little mouth,

(Circle mouth and pause)

But do not let them in!

(Tickle)

Song: "The Wheels on the Bus" (Traditional)

The wheels on the bus go round and round, round and round, round and round. The wheels on the bus go round and round, all through the town.

(Rotate hands around each other)

The wipers on the bus go swish, swish, swish, etc.

(Move arms side to side)

The windows on the bus go up and down, etc.

(Move arms up and down)

The doors on the bus go open and shut, etc.

(Open arms wide bringing together with a clap)

The horn on the bus goes beep, beep, beep, etc.

(Tap tummy or nose)

The wheels on the bus go round and round, round and round, round and round. The wheels on the bus go round and round, all through the town.

(Rotate hands around each other)

Book: *All You Need for a Snowman* by Alice Schertle

Action rhyme: "Snow Is Falling Down" ⊙

Snow is falling down,	*(Arms above head, wiggle fingers downward)*
Shhhhhh!	*(Touch pointer finger to lips to "Shhh")*
Snow is falling down,	*(Arms above head, wiggle fingers downward)*
Shhhhhh!	*(Touch pointer finger to lips to "Shhh")*
Slowly, slowly, very slowly,	*(Arms above head, wiggle fingers downward)*
Snow is falling down,	
Shhhhhh!	*(Touch pointer finger to lips to "Shhh")*

Song/Book: *If You're Happy and You Know It Clap Your Hands* by David Carter

Action rhyme: "Roly-Poly" ⊙

(Standing—Move arms or hands around each other as directions indicated)

Roly-poly, roly-poly, up–up–up.
Roly-poly, roly-poly, down–down–down.
Roly-poly, roly-poly, out–out–out.
Roly-poly, roly-poly, in–in–in.

Book: *Snowballs* by Lois Ehlert

Closing activity: Play "Waltz of the Snowflakes" from a recording of the *Nutcracker Ballet* (while participants try to keep tulle circles in the air).

Program 11—Script

Introduction: Welcome to story time—Introduce yourself and then have each participant introduce self and child. Offer tips to make this a good time for all.

Opening song: "Hello My Friends" from *Baby Rattle and Roll* by Nancy Stewart

Stretch rhyme: "Apple Tree" ⊙

Way up high in the apple tree	*(Stretch over head)*
Two little apples did I see.	*(Make fists)*
So I shook that tree as hard as I could,	*(Wiggle and shake body)*
And d-o-w-n came the apples,	*(Bring arms down to sides)*
Umm! They were good!	*(Rub tummy)*

Rocking rhyme: "Tick-Tock" ⊙

(Child on lap or, if big enough, can stand alone to rock sideways)

Tick-tock, tick-tock,
I'm a little cuckoo clock.

Tick-tock, tick-tock,
Now it's almost three o'clock.   *(Pause)*
Cuckoo! Cuckoo! Cuckoo!   *(Play peek-a-boo or raise child in air)*

Tickle rhyme: "This Little Piggy" 💿

   (Wiggle child's fingers or toes; wiggle arms and legs)

This little piggy went to market.
This little piggy stayed home.
This little piggy had roast beef.
And this little piggy had none.
And this little piggy ran wee, wee, wee all the way home.

   (Tickle all over)

Song: "When Cows Get Up in the Morning" from *Little Songs for Little Me* by
Nancy Stewart or "Old MacDonald Had a Farm" (Traditional)

Book: *Brown Bear, Brown Bear, What Do You See?* by Bill Martin

Song: "The Wheels on the Bus" (Traditional)

The wheels on the bus go round and round, round and round, round and
round. The wheels on the bus go round and round, all through the town.

   (Rotate hands around each other)

The wipers on the bus go swish, swish, swish, etc.

   (Move arms side to side)

The windows on the bus go up and down, etc.

   (Move arms up and down)

The doors on the bus go open and shut, etc.

   (Open arms wide bringing together with a clap)

The horn on the bus goes beep, beep, beep, etc.

   (Tap tummy or nose)

The wheels on the bus go round and round, round and round, round and
round. The wheels on the bus go round and round, all through the town.

   (Rotate hands around each other)

Tickle rhyme: "'Round and 'Round the Garden" 💿

'Round and 'round the garden goes the teddy bear.

   (Draw circles on hand, belly, or back)

One step,   *(Walk fingers up child's arm)*

Two step,   *(Walk fingers up towards head)*

Tickle *(child's name)* under there!   *(Tickle under chin or arm)*

Action rhyme: "Great Big Spider" ⓒⓓ or "Eensy, Weensy Spider" ⓒⓓ

(For infants use "Eensy, Weensy"; for children who can stand use "Great, Big")

The eensy, weensy (great big) spider went up the water spout.

(Baby on tummy, adult walks/tickles fingers up baby's back; older child stands and moves arms and legs as if climbing)

Down came the rain and washed the spider out.

(Slide fingers down baby's back from head to toes; bend at waist and touch ground)

Out came the sun and dried up all the rain,

(Rub baby's back; raise arms over head in form of circle)

And the eensy, weensy (great big) spider went up the spout again.

(Baby on tummy, adult walks/tickles fingers up baby's back; older child stands and moves arms and legs as if climbing)

Song: "Head and Shoulders, Knees and Toes" ⓒⓓ

(To the tune of "London Bridge," touch each body part when named)

Head and shoulders, knees and toes, knees and toes.
Head and shoulders, knees and toes, knees and toes.
Eyes and ears and mouth and nose.
Head and shoulders, knees and toes, knees and toes.

Book: *Down On the Farm* by Merrily Kutner

Bouncing rhyme: "To Market, to Market" ⓒⓓ

To market, to market to buy a fat pig,
Home again, home again jiggity jig.
To market, to market to buy a fat hog,
Home again, home again jiggity jog.

(Bounce baby on lap, or hip if standing)

Activity: Dance around to "Shake Your Sillies Out" from *Singable Songs for the Very Young* by Raffi.

Book: *Where Is the Green Sheep?* by Mem Fox

Closing song: "The More We Get Together" (Traditional)

Program 12—Script

(Developed and compiled by the Children's team at Launceston Library, Australia, 2004)

Welcome, introductions, and tips

Opening rhyme: "Open, Shut Them" ⊚

(Do actions with hands)

Open, shut them,
Open, shut them,
Give a little clap, clap, clap.
Open, shut them,
Open, shut them,
Lay them in your lap, lap, lap.

Creep them, crawl them,	*(Walk fingers up towards child's head)*
Creep them, crawl them,	*(Tap child's chin)*
Right up to your chin, chin, chin.	
Open up your little mouth,	*(Tickle child's mouth)*
But do not let them in!	*(Run fingers down)*

Stretch rhyme: "I Know a Giraffe"

I know a giraffe
With a neck that's so high
She stretches and stretches it
Up to the sky

(Stretch head high or raise arms above head)

She lives on the plains
With her family, too,
But you might see her
When you visit the zoo.

(Point to others)

Action rhyme: "Two Little Blackbirds"

Two little blackbirds	*(Wiggle both hands)*
Sitting on a hill.	
One named Jack,	*(Wiggle right hand)*
One named Jill.	*(Wiggle left hand)*
Fly away Jack,	*(Hide right hand behind back)*
Fly away Jill.	*(Hide left hand behind back)*
Come back Jack!	*(Bring right hand back)*
Come back Jill!	*(Bring left hand back)*

Song: "Wiggerly Woo," action song ten from www.babycareadvice.com. Click "Browse Our Articles" then "Play" to locate nursery rhymes.

Action rhyme: "Five Little Monkeys"

> *(Repeat until no monkeys left)*

Five little monkeys jumping on the bed	*(Swing hand, fingers pointing downward)*
One fell off and bumped his head.	*(Tap head)*
Mama called the doctor,	*(Hold hand to ear as if answering phone)*
And the doctor said, "No more monkeys jumping on the bed!"	*(Shake finger "NO!)*

Book: *Brassy Bird Band* by Calvin Irons

Action rhyme: "Giddyup Horsey"

Giddyup horsey, to the fair.

> *(Bounce baby or "gallop" in a circle)*

What will we buy when we get there?
A penny apple and a penny pear.
Giddyup horsey, to the fair.

> *(Lift baby at end)*

Tickle rhyme: "Little Cottage"

Little cottage in a wood,	*(Make roof with hands)*
Little man at a window stood,	*(Look through hands for window)*
Saw a rabbit running by,	*(Fingers run)*
Knocking at the door.	*(Knock in air)*
'Help me! Help me! Help!' he cried,	*(Hands up and down in air)*
'See the hunters on their way.' 'Little rabbit, come inside,	*(Point for hunters and beckon)*
You'll be safe with me.'	*(Stroke hand)*

Rhyme: "Bobby Shaftoe"

Bobby Shaftoe went to sea, Silver buckles on his knee. He'll come back and marry me, Pretty Bobby Shaftoe.	Bobby Shaftoe's fine and fair, Combing down his auburn hair. He's my friend for evermore, Pretty Bobby Shaftoe.

Book: Select a number story such as *Ten, Nine, Eight* by Molly Bang.

Action rhyme: "An Elephant Goes"

An elephant goes like this and that,	*(Stamp feet)*
He's terribly big,	*(Hands high)*
And terribly fat;	*(Hands wide)*
He has no fingers,	*(Wiggle fingers)*
And he has no toes,	*(Touch toes)*
But good gracious	*(Make a trunk out of arm)*
What a long nose!	

Song: "Hey Diddle, Diddle" 🅲🅳

Hey diddle, diddle,
The cat and the fiddle,
The cow jumped over the moon.
The little dog laughed
To see such fun,
And the dish ran away with the spoon.

Song: "Hickory, Dickory Dock" 🅲🅳

(Use rhythm instruments. Tap instrument on child's arm; older child can swing arms and clap to count)

Hickory, dickory dock,
The mouse ran up the clock.
The clock struck one, the mouse ran down!
Hickory, dickory dock!

Hickory, dickory dock,
The mouse ran up the clock.
The clock struck two, the mouse said BOO!
Hickory, dickory dock!

Hickory, dickory dock,
The mouse ran up the clock.
The clock struck three, the mouse said Wheeeee . . . . .
As he slid down the clock.

Book: *Maisy Loves You* by Lucy Cousins

Closing song: "Goodbye" (To the tune of "Mary Had a Little Lamb")

Goodbye everyone, goodbye everyone
(Wave goodbye)
Goodbye everyone
We're bound to leave you now

Merrily we roll along, roll along, roll along
Merrily we roll along, at toddler's rock and rhyme
Sweet dreams everyone, sweet dreams everyone

> *(Make sleeping action)*

Sweet dreams everyone
We're bound to leave you now

Program Outlines

These outlines are a format to which to add and subtract materials, depending on your own personal favorites and the length of the program. Books and rhymes that have been used successfully in programs for the very young can be found in Chapters 6 and 7 with suggested themes in Chapter 11.

Ages Newborn to 12 months

Program 1

Welcome to story time—Introduce yourself and then have each participant introduce self and child. Offer tips to make this a good time for all.

Welcome song: "The More We Get Together" from *If You're Happy and You Know It, Sing Along with Bob #1* by Bob McGrath

Clapping rhyme: "Patty-Cake, Patty Cake" ⓒⒹ

Cuddle rhyme: "Wash the Dishes" ⓒⒹ

Stretch rhyme: "Apple Tree" ⓒⒹ

Rocking rhyme: "Tick-Tock" ⓒⒹ

Book: *Peekaboo Morning* by Rachel Isadora

Action rhyme: "The Grand Old Duke of York" ⓒⒹ

Song: "The Wheels on the Bus" (Traditional)

Rocking rhyme: "Acka Backa" ⓒⒹ

Book: *I Love Animals* by Flora McDonnell

Song: "Head and Shoulders, Knees and Toes" ⓒⒹ

Music time: Rhythm instruments and CD of your choice

Closing song: "The More We Get Together"

Program 2

Welcome to story time—Introduce yourself and then have each participant introduce self and child. Offer tips to make this a good time for all.

Opening song: "Hello Everybody" (From *Sally's from Wibbleton to Wobbleton* video by Sally Jaeger)

Stretch rhyme: "Open, Shut Them" ⓒ⒟

Rocking rhyme: "Ride Baby Ride" ⓒ⒟

Bouncing rhyme: "Acka Backa" ⓒ⒟

Song: "The Wheels on the Bus"

Rocking rhyme: "Tick-Tock" ⓒ⒟

Action rhyme: "Roly-Poly" ⓒ⒟

Circle activity: "Ring Around the Rosie"

Bouncing rhyme: "Rooster Crows" ⓒ⒟

Tickle rhyme: "'Round and 'Round the Garden" ⓒ⒟

Music time: Free dance time—put on different kinds of music to dance/move around to.

Closing song: "Goodbye Babies"

Program 3

Welcome to story time—Introduce yourself and then have each participant introduce self and child. Offer tips to make this a good time for all.

Bouncing rhyme: "Rooster Crows" ⓒ⒟

Tickle rhyme: "These Are Baby's Fingers"

Book: *Read to Your Bunny* by Rosemary Wells

Bouncing rhyme: "Cheek, Chin" ⓒ⒟

Action rhyme: "Trot, Trot to Boston" ⓒ⒟

Free Dance: Free dance time—put on different kinds of music to dance/move around to.

Today's tip: Nursery rhymes and phonological awareness

Book: *All Fall Down* by Helen Oxenbury

Tickle rhyme: "Jeremiah, Blow the Fire" ⓒ⒟

Action rhyme: "Here We Go Up–Up–Up!" ⓒ⒟

Closing announcements

Closing song: "Good-bye Song"

Program 4

Welcome to story time—Introduce yourself and then have each participant introduce self and child. Offer tips to make this a good time for all.

Opening song: *(Your choice)*

Bouncing rhyme: "Rickety, Rickety Rocking Horse"

Tickle rhyme: "These Are Baby's Fingers"

Book: *Clap Hands* by Helen Oxenbury
Clapping rhyme: "Muffin Man"
Song: "The Wheels on the Bus"
Free dance
Book: *Can I Have a Hug?* by Debi Gliori
Tickle rhyme: "Wiggle, Wiggle" 🖸
Action rhyme: "Trot, Trot to Boston" 🖸
Closing announcements
Closing song: "Cuddle Up and Sing"

Program 5

Welcome to story time—Introduce yourself and then have each participant introduce self and child. Offer tips to make this a good time for all.

Opening song: *(Your choice)*
Clapping rhyme: "Patty-Cake, Patty-Cake" 🖸
Tickle rhyme: "Eensy, Weensy Spider" 🖸 *(Child on tummy)*
Rocking rhyme: "Tick-Tock" 🖸
Bouncing rhyme: "Mother and Father and Uncle John" 🖸
Standing action rhyme: "Roly-Poly" 🖸 *(Child standing)*
Stretch rhyme: "Apple Tree" 🖸
Song: "The Wheels on the Bus" (Traditional)
Bouncing rhyme: "To Market, to Market" 🖸
Closing song: "The More We Get Together"

Program 6

Welcome to story time—Introduce yourself and then have each participant introduce self and child. Offer tips to make this a good time for all.

Opening song: "Where Is Baby?"
Stretch rhyme: "Open, Shut Them" 🖸
Tickle rhyme: "These Are Baby's Fingers"
Song: "Head and Shoulders, Knees and Toes" 🖸 *(Touching body parts)*
Clapping rhyme: "Pussy Cat, Pussy Cat" 🖸
Tickle rhyme: "There Was a Little Man" 🖸
Circle song: "Ring Around the Rosie"
Tickle rhyme: "Shoe a Little Horse" 🖸
Clapping rhyme: "Patty-Cake, Patty-Cake" 🖸

Tickle rhyme: "'Round and 'Round the Garden"

Closing song: "Butterfly Kisses" from *'Round and 'Round the Garden: Music in My First Year* by John Feierabend and Luann Saunders

Ages 12 to 24 Months

Program 7

Welcome to story time—Introduce yourself and then have each participant introduce self and child. Offer tips to make this a good time for all.

Opening song: "The More We Get Together"

Clapping rhyme: "Patty-Cake, Patty-Cake" CD

Stretch rhyme: "Apple Tree" CD

Rocking rhyme: "Tick-Tock" CD

Book: *Brown Bear, Brown Bear, What Do You See?* by Bill Martin

Song: "Head and Shoulders, Knees and Toes" CD *(Touching body parts)*

Action rhyme: "The Grand Old Duke of York" CD

Stretch rhyme: "Tall as a Tree"

Rhyme: "Cobbler, Cobbler" CD

Song: "The Wheels on the Bus"

Book: *The Bridge Is Up* by Babs Bell

Action rhyme: "Row, Row, Row Your Boat"

Clapping rhyme: "1-2-3-4-5, I Caught a Fish Alive"

Music time: "Clap Your Hands" from *Circle Around* by Tickle Typhoon

Closing song: "The More We Get Together"

Program 8

Welcome to story time—Introduce yourself and then have each participant introduce self and child. Offer tips to make this a good time for all.

Opening song: "Hello Toes"

Clapping rhyme: "Patty-Cake, Patty-Cake" CD

Bouncing rhyme: "Mother and Father and Uncle John" CD

Book: *Brown Bear, Brown Bear, What Do You See?* by Bill Martin

Song: "Down by the Station"

Bouncing rhyme: "From Wibbleton to Wobbleton" CD

Book: *The Bus for Us* by Suzanne Bloom

Rhyme: "Riding on My Pony" CD

Book: *Freight Train* by Donald Crews
Action rhyme: "Choo-Choo Train" ⓒⅅ
Closing song: "Goodbye"

Program 9

Welcome to story time—Introduce yourself and then have each participant introduce self and child. Offer tips to make this a good time for all.

Rhyme: "Two Little Blackbirds"
Song: "Baa, Baa, Black Sheep" ⓒⅅ
Book: *Caterpillar's Wish* by May Murphy
Stretch rhyme: "Apple Tree" ⓒⅅ
Tickle rhyme: "Criss, Cross, Applesauce" ⓒⅅ
Action song: "Here We Go 'Round the Mulberry Bush" ⓒⅅ
Book: *Little Robin Redbreast: A Mother Goose Rhyme* illustrated by Shari Halpern
Tickle rhyme: "Beehive" ⓒⅅ
Tickle rhyme: "Here Comes a Mouse" ⓒⅅ
Closing: Blow bubbles while children dance to lively music on CD.

Program 10

Welcome to story time—Introduce yourself and then have each participant introduce self and child. Offer tips to make this a good time for all.

Clapping rhyme: "Patty-Cake, Patty-Cake" ⓒⅅ
Stretch rhyme: "Open, Shut Them" ⓒⅅ
Song: "The Wheels on the Bus"
Book: *All You Need for a Snowman* by Alice Shertle
Action rhyme: "Snow Is Falling Down" ⓒⅅ
Song/Book: *If You're Happy and You Know It Clap Your Hands* by David Carter
Action rhyme: "Roly-Poly" ⓒⅅ
Book: *Snowballs* by Lois Ehlert
Closing activity: Play "Waltz of the Snowflakes" from a recording of the *Nutcracker Ballet* (while participants try to keep tulle circles in the air).

Mixed Age Groups

Program 11

Welcome to story time—Introduce yourself and then have each participant introduce self and child. Offer tips to make this a good time for all.

Opening song: "Hello My Friends" from *Baby Rattle and Roll* by Nancy Stewart

Stretch rhyme: "Apple Tree" ⊚

Rocking rhyme: "Tick-Tock" ⊚

Tickle rhyme: "This Little Piggy" ⊚

Song: "When Cows Get Up in the Morning" from *Little Songs for Little Me* by Nancy Stewart or "Old MacDonald Had a Farm" (Traditional)

Book: *Brown Bear, Brown Bear, What Do You See?* by Bill Martin

Song: "The Wheels on the Bus" (Traditional)

Tickle rhyme: "'Round and 'Round the Garden" ⊚

Action rhyme: "Great Big Spider" ⊚ or "Eensy, Weensy Spider" ⊚

Song: "Head and Shoulders, Knees and Toes" ⊚ *(Touching body parts)*

Book: *Down on the Farm* by Merrily Kutner

Bouncing rhyme: "To Market, to Market" ⊚

Activity: Dance around to "Shake Your Sillies Out" from *Singable Songs for the Very Young* by Raffi.

Book: *Where Is the Green Sheep?* by Mem Fox

Closing song: "The More We Get Together" (Traditional)

Program 12

(Developed and compiled by the Children's team at Launceston Library, Australia, 2004)

Welcome to story time—Introduce yourself and then have each participant introduce self and child. Offer tips to make this a good time for all.

Opening rhyme: "Open, Shut Them" ⊚

Stretch rhyme: "I Know a Giraffe"

Action rhyme: "Two Little Blackbirds"

Song: "Wiggerly Woo"

Action rhyme: "Five Little Monkeys"

Book: *Brassy Bird Band* by Calvin Irons

Action rhyme: "Giddyup Horsey"

Tickle rhyme: "Little Cottage"

Rhyme: "Bobby Shaftoe"

Book: *Ten, Nine, Eight* by Molly Bang

Action rhyme: "An Elephant Goes"

Song: "Hey Diddle, Diddle" ⊚

Song: "Hickory, Dickory Dock" ⊚

Book: *Maisy Loves You* by Lucy Cousins
Closing song: "Goodbye"

Resources

Ready Made Programs

Cobb, Jane. 2007. *What'll I Do With the Baby-O? Nursery Rhymes, Songs, and Stories for Babies*. Vancouver, BC: Black Sheep Press.

Ernst, Linda. L. 1995. *Lapsit Services for the Very Young*. New York: Neal-Schuman.

_____. 2001. *Lapsit Services for the Very Young II*. New York: Neal-Schuman.

Herr, Judy, and Terri Swim. 2002. *Creative Resources for Infants and Toddlers*. 2nd ed. Albany, NY: Delmar Learning.

Maddigan, Beth. 2003. *The Big Book of Stories, Songs and Sing-Alongs: Programs for Babies, Toddlers and Families*. Westport, CT: Libraries Unlimited.

Marino, Jane. 2003. *Babies in the Library!* Lanham, MD: Scarecrow Press.

Marino, Jane, and Dorothy F. Houlihan. 1992. *Mother Goose Time: Library Programs for Babies and Their Caregivers*. Bronx, NY: H.W. Wilson.

Raines, Shirley, Karen Miller, and Leah Curry-Rood. 2002. *Story Stretchers for Infants, Toddlers, and Twos: Experiences, Activities, and Games for Popular Children's Books*. Beltsville, MD: Gryphon House.

Schiller, Pam. 2005. *The Complete Resource Book for Infants: Over 700 Experiences for Children from Birth to 18 Months*. Beltsville, MD: Gryphon House.

Web Sites for Programs and Materials

www.itg.uiuc.edu/people/mcdowell/laptime
Babies' Lap Time
> Kate McDowell, Children's Librarian at The Urbana Free Library, Illinois. Includes books and sample programs.

www.hclib.org/BirthTo6/Newsletter/newsletter.html
Hennepin County Library—Minnesota
> This site has booklists, early literacy information, fingerplays and songs, and you can also subscribe to their early literacy newsletter.

www.tsl.state.tx.us/ld/projects/trc/2005/manual/toddlers
The Library Development Division of the Texas State Library and Archives Commission
> Material from 2005 Texas State Reading Program manual

www.unc.edu/~sllamber/pathfinder/babybooks.html
Mother Goose Time—Library programs with books and babies.
> Created by Sylvia Leigh Lambert

www.prge.lib.md.us/LibraryCenter/ParentsBIB.html
Prince George's County Memorial Library System—Maryland
> A guide for librarians who wish to introduce parents and babies to the fun of sharing books.

11
More Programming Ideas

Many librarians prefer to create original programs. Even these individuals may need some help getting started or may want a shortcut when faced with a deadline. This chapter can be used to begin, develop, and expand programming for the very young child and his or her caregivers. It includes books from the annotated booklist arranged by theme and rhymes organized by type. Remember to use the resources at the end of Chapter 10 for more program ideas.

Books by Theme

Animals

Baby Signs for Animals by Linda Acredolo and Susan Goodwyn
Brown Bear, Brown Bear, What Do You See? by Bill Martin
Bunny and Me by Adele Aron
Bunny's First Snowflake by Monica Wellington
Can You Hop? by Lisa Lawston
Come Here, Cleo! by Caroline Mockford
Dads Are Such Fun! by Jakki Wood
Daisy's Day Out by Jane Simmons
Down on the Farm by Merrily Kutner
Duck in the Truck by Jez Alborough
Duckie's Rainbow by Frances Barry
Five Little Chicks by Nancy Tafuri
Fuzzy Fuzzy Fuzzy! by Sandra Boynton
Ha! Ha! by Guido Van Genechten
A Hat for Minerva Louise by Janet Stoeke
Hello! by Guido Van Genechten
Here a Chick, Where a Chick? by Suse MacDonald

How Kind! by Mary Murphy
I Like Books by Anthony Brown
I Love Animals by Flora McDonnell
It's My Birthday by Helen Oxenbury
Just Ducky by Kathy Mallat
Kiss Kiss! by Margaret Wild
Let's Be Animals by Ann Turner
Let's Go! by Tania Hurt-Newton
Little White Duck by Walt Whippo, illustrated by Joan Paley
Maisy Dresses Up by Lucy Cousins
Maisy Drives the Bus by Lucy Cousins
Maisy's Morning on the Farm by Lucy Cousins
Mama's Little Bears by Nancy Tafuri
Moo, Baa La, La, La by Sandra Boynton
Mouse's First Fall by Lauren Thompson
New House for Mouse by Petr Horacek
Number One, Tickle Your Tum by John Prater
One Little Duck by DK Publishing
One Red Rooster by Kathleen Sullivan Carroll
Overboard! by Sarah Weeks
Peek-A-Moo! by Marie Torres Cimarusti
Peek-A-Pet by Marie Torres Cimarusti
Peek-A-Zoo by Marie Torres Cimarusti
Pepo and Lolo and the Red Apple by Ana Martin Larranago
Pepo and Lolo Are Friends by Ana Martin Larranago
Sleepy Me! by Marni McGee
Snuggle Wuggle by Jonathan London
Ten Red Apples by Virginia Miller
The Bridge Is Up by Babs Bell
This Little Chick by John Lawrence
Three Little Kittens by Tanya Linch
Tickle Tum! by Nancy Van Laan
Too Loud! By Guido Van Genechten
Very Quiet Cricket by Eric Carle
We're Going on a Bear Hunt by Michael Rosen
What We Do by Reg Cartwright
Where Is the Green Sheep? by Mem Fox
Who Says Woof? by John Butler
Whose Nose and Toes? by John Butler

Apples

A New House for Mouse by Petr Horacek
Pepo and Lolo and the Red Apple by Ana Martin Larranago
Ten Red Apples by Virginia Miller

Babies

Baa, Baa, Black Sheep! by Annie Kubler
Baby Danced the Polka by Karen Beaumont
Baby Faces by Margaret Miller
Baby Goes Beep by Rebecca O'Connell
Baby Hearts and Baby Flowers by Remy Charlip
Baby Knows Best by Kathy Henderson
Counting Kisses by Karen Katz
Look at the Baby by Kelly Johnson
On Mother's Lap by Ann Scott
One Little Spoonful by Aliki
Peekaboo Morning by Rachel Isadora
Peek-A-Little Boo by Sheree Fitch
Show Me! by Tom Tracy
Star Baby by Margaret O'Hair
What's on My Head? by Margaret Miller
Where Is Baby's Belly Button? by Karen Katz

Baths

Bubbles, Bubbles by Kathi Appelt

Bears

Brown Bear, Brown Bear, What Do You See? by Bill Martin
Mama's Little Bears by Nancy Tafuri
Number One, Tickle Your Tum by John Prater
Ten Red Apples by Virginia Miller
We're Going on a Bear Hunt by Michael Rosen

Bedtime

Baby Danced the Polka by Karen Beaumont
Baby Hearts and Baby Flowers by Remy Charlip
Baby Signs for Bedtime by Linda Acredolo and Susan Goodwyn
Counting Kisses by Karen Katz
Hush, Little Baby by Maria Frazee
The Night the Moon Blew Kisses by Lynn Manuel
Sleepy Me! by Marni McGee
Time for Naps by Jane Yolen

Birds

Little Robin Redbreast: A Mother Goose Rhyme illustrated by Shari Halpern

Boats

Boats by Byron Barton
Ship by Chris Demarest

Body

Baby Faces by Margaret Miller
Busy Toes by C.W. Bowie
Do Your Ears Hang Low? by Caroline Jayne Church
Look at the Baby by Kelly Johnson
My Nose, Your Nose by Melanie Walsh
Show Me! by Tom Tracy
Star Baby by Margaret O'Hair
What's on My Head? by Margaret Miller
Where Is Baby's Belly Button? by Karen Katz

Bus

The Bus for Us by Suzanne Bloom
Maisy Drives the Bus by Lucy Cousins

Cars

Let's Go! by Tania Hurt-Newton
Red Light, Green Light by Anastasia Suen

Cats

Come Here, Cleo! by Caroline Mockford
Little Robin Redbreast: A Mother Goose Rhyme illustrated by Shari Halpern
Three Little Kittens by Tanya Linch

Chickens

Five Little Chicks by Nancy Tafuri
A Hat for Minerva Louise by Janet Stoeke
Here a Chick, Where a Chick? by Suse MacDonald

Clothing

A Hat for Minerva Louise by Janet Stoeke
Maisy Dresses Up by Lucy Cousins

Colors

Brown Bear, Brown Bear, What Do You See? by Bill Martin
Duckie's Rainbow by Frances Barry
Go Away, Big Green Monster! by Ed Emberley
One Red Rooster by Kathleen Sullivan Carroll

Concepts

My First Book of Opposites by Kim Deegan

Counting

Millions of Snowflakes by Mary McKenna Siddals
Number One, Tickle Your Tum by John Prater
Ten Red Apples by Virginia Miller

Daddy

Dads Are Such Fun! by Jakki Wood
Tickle, Tickle by Dakari Hru

Daily Life

The Baby Goes Beep by Rebecca O'Connell
Baby Knows Best by Kathy Henderson
Baby Signs for Bedtime by Linda Acredolo and Susan Goodwyn
Bubbles, Bubbles by Kathi Appelt
It's My Birthday by Helen Oxenbury
Let's Play by Leo Lionni
Mommy Hug by Karen Katz
Morning Star by Mary McKenna Siddals
One Little Spoonful by Aliki
On Mother's Lap by Ann Scott
Overboard! by Sarah Weeks
Peekaboo Morning by Rachel Isadora
Star Baby by Margaret O'Hair
Tom and Pippo and the Bicycle by Helen Oxenbury
Wake Up, Me! by Marni McGee
You Can Do It Too by Karen Baicker

Dance

Baby Danced the Polka by Karen Beaumont
Toddler Two-Step by Kathi Appelt

Ducks

Daisy's Day Out by Jane Simmons
Duck in a Truck by Jez Alborough
Duckie's Rainbow by Frances Barry
Just Ducky by Kathy Mallat
Little White Duck by Walt Whippo illustrated by Joan Paley
One Little Duck by DK Publishing

Fall

Maisy Dresses Up by Lucy Cousins
Mouse's First Fall by Lauren Thompson
Pepo and Lolo and the Red Apple by Ana Martin Larranago
Ten Red Apples by Virginia Miller

Families

Can I Have a Hug? by Debi Gliori
Dads Are Such Fun! by Jakki Wood
Daisy's Day Out by Jane Simmons
Kiss Kiss! by Margaret Wild
Mama's Little Bears by Nancy Tafuri
Mommy Hug by Karen Katz
The Night the Moon Blew Kisses by Lynn Manuel
On Mother's Lap by Ann Scott
Snowballs by Lois Ehlert
Snuggle Wuggle by Jonathan London
Tickle, Tickle by Dakari Hru
You Can Do It Too by Karen Baicker

Farms

Down on the Farm by Merrily Kutner
Five Little Chicks by Nancy Tafuri
A Hat for Minerva Louise by Janet Stoeke
Here a Chick, Where a Chick? by Suse MacDonald
How Kind! by Mary Murphy
I Love Animals by Flora McDonnell
Let's Be Animals by Ann Turner
Maisy's Morning on the Farm by Lucy Cousins
Moo, Baa, La, La, La by Sandra Boynton
One Red Rooster by Kathleen Sullivan Carroll
Peek-A-Moo by Marie Torres Cimarusti
Pepo and Lolo and the Red Apple by Ana Martin Larranago
Pepo and Lolo Are Friends by Ana Martin Larranago
This Little Chick by John Lawrence
Where Is the Green Sheep? by Mem Fox

Feelings

Baby Faces by Margaret Miller
Can I Have a Hug? by Debi Gliori
Counting Kisses by Karen Katz
Go Away, Big Green Monster! by Ed Emberley
How Kind! by Mary Murphy

Kiss Kiss! by Margaret Wild
Mommy Hug by Karen Katz
The Night the Moon Blew Kisses by Lynn Manuel
Pepo and Lolo Are Friends by Ana Martin Larranago
Snuggle Wuggle by Jonathan London

Flannel Board

The Bridge Is Up by Babs Bell
Brown Bear, Brown Bear, What Do You See? by Bill Martin
The Bus for Us by Suzanne Bloom
It's My Birthday by Helen Oxenbury
Millions of Snowflakes by Mary McKenna Siddals
Ten Red Apples by Virginia Miller

Food

It's My Birthday by Helen Oxenbury
One Little Spoonful by Aliki

Friends

Bunny and Me by Adele Aron
Caterpillar's Wish by Mary Murphy
It's My Birthday by Helen Oxenbury
Just Ducky by Kathy Mallat
Mouse's First Fall by Lauren Thompson
Pepo and Lolo and the Red Apple by Ana Martin Larranago
Pepo and Lolo Are Friends by Ana Martin Larranago
This Little Chick by John Lawrence
Tom and Pippo and the Bicycle by Helen Oxenbury

Games

Overboard! by Sarah Weeks
Peekaboo Morning by Rachel Isadora
Peek-A-Little Boo by Sheree Fitch
Show Me! by Tom Tracy
Wake Up, Me! by Marni McGee
We're Going on a Bear Hunt by Michael Rosen
Where Is Baby's Belly Button? by Karen Katz

Interactive

Do Your Ears Hang Low? by Caroline Jayne Church
Go Away, Big Green Monster! by Ed Emberley

Lift-the-Flap

Here a Chick, Where a Chick? by Suse MacDonald

Peek-A-Moo by Marie Torres Cimarusti
Peek-A-Pet by Marie Torres Cimarusti
Peek-A-Zoo by Marie Torres Cimarusti
Where Is Baby's Belly Button? by Karen Katz

Love

Can I Have a Hug? by Debi Gliori
Counting Kisses by Karen Katz
Kiss Kiss! by Margaret Wild
Mommy Hug by Karen Katz

Mice

Let's Play by Leo Lionni
Mouse's First Fall by Lauren Thompson
Maisy Dresses Up by Lucy Cousins
Maisy's Morning on the Farm by Lucy Cousins
A New House for Mouse by Petr Horacek

Mothers

Kiss Kiss! by Margaret Wild
Mama's Little Bears by Nancy Tafuri
Mommy Hug by Karen Katz
On Mother's Lap by Ann Scott
Snuggle Wuggle by Jonathan London

Movement

Baby Danced the Polka by Karen Beaumont
Can You Hop? by Lisa Lawston
Let's Be Animals by Ann Turner
Toddler Two-Step by Kathi Appelt
What We Do by Reg Cartwright

Multicultural

Baa, Baa, Black Sheep! by Annie Kubler
Baby Faces by Margaret Miller
My Nose, Your Nose by Melanie Walsh
Peekaboo Morning by Rachel Isadora
Peek-A-Little Boo by Sheree Fitch

Music

Baa, Baa, Black Sheep! by Annie Kubler
Baby Danced the Polka by Karen Beaumont
Charlie Parker Played Be Bop by Chris Raschka
Little White Duck by Walt Whippo

Night—*see* Bedtime

Numbers

Millions of Snowflakes by Mary McKenna Siddals
Number One, Tickle Your Tum by John Prater
Ten Red Apples by Virginia Miller

Nursery Rhymes

Little Robin Redbreast: A Mother Goose Rhyme illustrated by Shari Halpern
Three Little Kittens by Tanya Linch

Participation

Brown Bear, Brown Bear, What Do You See? by Bill Martin
We're Going on a Bear Hunt by Michael Rosen

Photographs

Baby Faces by Margaret Miller
Baby Signs for Animals by Linda Acredolo and Susan Goodwyn
Baby Signs for Bedtime by Linda Acredolo and Susan Goodwyn
Bunny & Me by Adele Aron Greenspun
Look at the Baby by Kelly Johnson
What's on My Head? by Margaret Miller

Planes—*see* Things That Go

Play

Chicky Chicky Chook Chook by Cathy MacLennan
Just Ducky by Kathy Mallat
Let's Play by Leo Lionni
Mouse's First Fall by Lauren Thompson
Overboard! by Sarah Weeks
Tickle, Tickle by Dakari Hru

Question and Answer Story

Here a Chick, Where a Chick? by Suse MacDonald
Mama's Little Bears by Nancy Tafuri
Where Is the Green Sheep? by Mem Fox
Who Says Woof? by John Butler
Whose Nose and Toes? by John Butler

Rabbits

Bunny's First Snowflake by Monica Wellington
Overboard! by Sarah Weeks
Tickle Tum! by Nancy Van Laan

Rain

Duckie's Rainbow by Frances Barry
Raindrop, Plop! by Wendy Cheyette Lewison
Rainsong/Snowsong by Philemon Sturges

Seasons

All You Need for a Snowman by Alice Schertle
Bunny's First Snowflake by Monica Wellington
Caterpillar's Wish by Mary Murphy
Frozen Noses by Jan Carr
The Happy Day by Ruth Krauss
A Hat for Minerva Louise by Janet Stoeke
Little Robin Redbreast: A Mother Goose Rhyme illustrated by Shari Halpern
Maisy Dresses Up by Lucy Cousins
Millions of Snowflakes by Mary McKenna Siddals
Mouse's First Fall by Lauren Thompson
The Night the Moon Blew Kisses by Lynn Manuel
Pepo and Lolo and the Red Apple by Ana Martin Larranago
Rainsong/Snowsong by Philemon Sturges
Snowballs by Lois Ehlert
Ten Red Apples by Virginia Miller
A Winter Day by Douglas Florian

Sign Language

Baa, Baa, Black Sheep! by Annie Kubler
Baby Signs for Animals by Linda Acredolo and Susan Goodwyn
Baby Signs for Bedtime by Linda Acredolo and Susan Goodwyn
Brown Bear, Brown Bear, What Do You See? by Bill Martin
Let's Play by Leo Lionni
Mama's Little Bears by Nancy Tafuri

Snow

All You Need for a Snowman by Alice Schertle
Rainsong/Snowsong by Philemon Sturges
Snowballs by Lois Ehlert

Song

Baa, Baa, Black Sheep! by Annie Kubler
Do Your Ears Hang Low? by Caroline Jayne Church
Hush, Little Baby by Maria Frazee
I Like Books by Anthony Brown
Little White Duck by Walt Whippo
One Little Duck by DK Publishing

Sounds

Baby Goes Beep by Rebecca O'Connell
Daisy's Day Out by Jane Simmons
Ha! Ha! by Guido Van Genechten
I Love Animals by Flora McDonnell
Moo, Baa, La, La, La by Sandra Boynton
One Red Rooster by Kathleen Sullivan Carroll
Peek-A-Moo by Marie Torres Cimarusti
This Little Chick by John Lawrence
Too Loud! by Guido Van Genechten
Very Quiet Cricket by Eric Carle
Who Says Woof? by John Butler

Spring

Caterpillar's Wish by Mary Murphy
Little Robin Redbreast: A Mother Goose Rhyme illustrated by Shari Halpern
Rainsong/Snowsong by Philemon Sturges

Stories in Rhyme

Baby Hearts and Baby Flowers by Remy Charlip
Brown Bear, Brown Bear, What Do You See? by Bill Martin
Busy Toes by C.W. Bowie
Can I Have a Hug? by Debi Gliori
Charlie Parker Played Be Bop by Chris Raschka
Chugga-Chugga, Choo-Choo by Kevin Lewis
Come Here, Cleo! by Caroline Mockford
Down on the Farm by Merrily Kutner
Frozen Noses by Jan Carr
Little Robin Redbreast: A Mother Goose Rhyme illustrated by Shari Halpern
Look at the Baby by Kelly Johnson
Moo, Baa, La, La, La by Sandra Boynton
Morning Star by Mary McKenna Siddals
My First Action Rhymes by Lynne Cravath
Number One, Tickle Your Tum by John Prater
One Red Rooster by Kathleen Sullivan Carroll
Raindrop, Plop! by Wendy Cheyette Lewison
Rainsong/Snowsong by Philemon Sturges
Red Light, Green Light by Anastasia Suen
Show Me! by Tom Tracy
Sleepy Me! by Marni McGee
Snowballs by Lois Ehlert
Star Baby by Margaret O'Hair
Three Little Kittens by Tanya Linch
Tickle Tum! by Nancy Van Laan

Wake Up, Me! by Marni McGee
A Winter Day by Douglas Florian

Things That Go

Boats by Byron Barton
The Bridge Is Up by Babs Bell
The Bus for Us by Suzanne Bloom
Chugga-Chugga, Choo-Choo by Kevin Lewis
Duck in a Truck by Jez Alborough
Five Trucks by Brian Floca
I Love Trains by Philemon Sturges
Let's Go! by Tania Hurt-Newton
Maisy Drives the Bus by Lucy Cousins
Red Light, Green Light by Anastasia Suen
Ship by Christ Demarest
Tom and Pippo and the Bicycle by Helen Oxenbury

Toys

Baby Knows Best by Kathy Henderson
Time for Naps by Jane Yolen
Tom and Pippo and the Bicycle by Helen Oxenbury

Trains

Chugga-Chugga, Choo-Choo by Kevin Lewis
I Love Trains by Philemon Sturges

Trucks

Duck in a Truck by Jez Alborough
Five Trucks by Brian Floca

Water—see Baths and/or Rain

Weather

Duckie's Rainbow by Frances Barry
Raindrop, Plop! by Wendy Cheyette Lewison

Winter

All You Need for a Snowman by Alice Schertle
Bunny's First Snowflake by Monica Wellington
Frozen Noses by Jan Carr
The Happy Day by Ruth Krauss
A Hat for Minerva Louise by Janet Stoeke
Millions of Snowflakes by Mary McKenna Siddals
The Night the Moon Blew Kisses by Lynn Manuel
Rainsong/Snowsong by Philemon Sturges

Snowballs by Lois Ehlert
A Winter Day by Douglas Florian

Zoo

Dads Are Such Fun! by Jakki Wood
Peek-A-Zoo by Marie Torres Cimarusti

Rhymes by Type

How to use a rhyme is very subjective. Different individuals may view the same rhyme as a tickle, a cuddle, a bounce, or even a marching game. A rhyme can change by simply varying its actions. The following list groups the rhymes in this book by type and may be used as a guideline. Create a file of index cards, each having a rhyme with its directions on it, to keep track of your favorites. Arrange them by title or by type, whatever works for you. (CD indicates audio versions on CD-ROM, unless otherwise specified.)

Bounces CD

"Acka Backa"
"Diddle Diddle Dumpling"
"From Wibbleton to Wobbleton"
"Hey Diddle, Diddle"
"Humpty Dumpty"
"Leg Over Leg"
"Mother and Father and Uncle John"
"My Pony Macaroni"
"Ride a Cock Horse" (text only on CD)
"Ride Baby Ride"
"Rooster Crows"
"This Is the Way the Ladies Ride"
"Trot, Trot to Boston"

Claps and Taps CD

"Baa, Baa, Black Sheep"
"Cheek, Chin" (text only on CD)
"Clap Your Hands"
"Cobbler, Cobbler"
"Head and Shoulders, Knees and Toes"
"Here's a Ball for Baby"
"Hey Diddle, Diddle"
"One, Two, Buckle My Shoe"
"Patty-Cake, Patty-Cake"
"Pease Porridge Hot"
"Pussycat, Pussycat"
"Shoe a Little Horse"

Cuddles ⊙

"Acka Backa"
"Here Is Baby"
"Ride Baby Ride"
"Wash the Dishes"

Marches/Walking ⊙

"Choo-Choo Train"
"The Grand Old Duke of York"
"Great Big Spider"
"Here We Go 'Round the Mulberry Bush"
"POP—Goes the Weasel"
"Ride Baby Ride"
"Riding on My Pony"
"Teddy Bear, Teddy Bear"
"To Market, to Market"

Massages ⊙

"Acka Backa"
"Great Big Spider"
"Wash the Dishes"

Rocking ⊙

"Gray Squirrel"
"Here Is Baby"
"Humpty Dumpty"
"Tick-Tock"

Stretches ⊙

"Apple Tree"
"Here's a Ball"
"One, Two, Buckle My Shoe"
"Open, Shut Them"
"Pussycat, Pussycat"
"Roly-Poly"

Tickles ⊙

"Beehive"
"Criss, Cross, Applesauce"
"Eensy, Weensy Spider"
"Here Comes a Mouse"
"Jeremiah, Blow the Fire"
"Rain Is Falling Down"

"'Round and 'Round the Garden"
"'Round the World"
"There Was a Little Man"
"This Little Piggy"
"Wiggle Your Fingers"

12

Handouts, Displays, and Signs

Often there is more information to share at a program than there is time available. Handouts, displays and signs are methods of conveying additional and supportive information to the participants. This extra material can also enable participants to recreate the literary experience on their own. Preparation time is needed to create or locate quality material. Investing this time has numerous benefits. Handouts, once created, can be reused at future programs or incorporated into other literacy events. They can supply participants with useful information, materials, or activities that can reinforce or expand on what was presented. Displays can highlight a theme or call attention to materials that support the program but might otherwise be overlooked. Signs can be directional and/or informative without taking time from the program. The effort of creating handouts, displays and having good signage allows the participants to become familiar with the facility, the program and possible services available to them.

Handouts

Everyone grabs for the handouts, but how many people actually read and use them? The best thing to keep in mind when creating handouts is simplicity. Quite often people can be overloaded with handouts or just overlook their importance. Handouts may also take time to create, time to locate, and time to purchase. They should serve a purpose rather than just be "something to take home." Handouts should be placed where they can be seen by the adults but out of reach of the youngest participants. A table at the back of the room or by the door is ideal. On occasion, handouts may need to be distributed by the presenter if additional explanation about them is necessary. There are basically three kinds of handouts: preexisting organization materials that can be used as handouts, those created for a specific program or purpose, and ready-made handouts.

177

Existing Handouts

This type of material can be made available for participants to pick up at every program. It can focus on one location or numerous locations, a special service or a variety of services. They can include but are not limited to:

- Brochure including the hours, address, and phone number of the organization
- List of services or special services available to this particular group (customized for parents, childcare providers, etc.)
- Library card applications
- Presenter's business card
- Organization's newsletter, monthly calendar or program flyer
- Free parenting newspapers or magazines that are distributed through the library
- Park district catalogs, community college offerings, "U-pick" farm guides, and so on

Created Handouts

These handouts are created to reflect a program's theme, focus on a specific topic of interest or meet a given need. They are often a single sheet of paper. For example, a handout of rhymes, songs, and activities about farms might be created in order to help the participants remember what went on in class and to re-create or expand upon the program activities outside the program location. Handouts can provide the participants with guidelines for participating in the program, resources on a topic of interest, or enable participants to remember program materials, such as the words to rhymes and songs, at home. When creating an original handout keep in mind the words you choose and placement on the paper. Use language that can be understood by participants but does not talk down to them. Filling the page to capacity may save paper but more than likely will make the material unreadable. In the appendix and on the CD-ROM, you will find examples and templates of different kinds of handouts that can be copied.

Another created handout is one in which rhymes, songs, resources, recommended books, etc., are compiled into a booklet format and given to all participants. These can range in length from a couple of pages to much longer. Booklets may take more time to create but once created they can simply be periodically updated. Zoe Lewis, of Adelaide Hills Council Library Service in Australia, created an exceptional booklet titled *Baby Bounce & Rhyme* that is an example of this. This 28-page booklet also includes information on the program schedule, places to take very young children, rhymes with directions and, of course, reasons to read to infants and toddlers. To view this booklet online go to the Adelaide Hills Council Web site at http://www.ahc.sa.gov.au/site/page.cfm?u=151 and click on "Download the *Baby Bounce & Rhyme* booklet." (Please be aware of and respect the copyright notice included in the booklet.)

Smaller booklets may be a single sheet folded in quarters with each page having a rhyme on it. Whatever its length, make sure the booklet meets your need to enhance your program.

Tips to Keep in Mind When Creating Handouts

- Simplicity—It is very easy to fill an entire page with rhymes, patterns, information, and so on. Try to arrange the material so that there is white space on the page. Handouts that are too wordy or use too small a font will more than likely not be read. If the handout is a guide for expectations of the class, consolidate them rather than making a lengthy list. An example of this could be the guidelines for the young toddler program (ages 12–24 months with adult) I conduct:

  1) I do not expect the children to sit still but I do expect their caregiver to keep them safe.
  2) It is not easy for children this age to share so encourage caregivers to put everything away and focus on the program.
  3) Big people take part—the more the adult participates, the more the child will want to as well.

  These simple directions can be made into a poster on a wall, a sign in an acrylic holder on the display table, or given to participants as part of a handout.

- Identify—Make sure the recipients know where the handouts came from. It is possible that the organization's policy may require the organization's name, address, phone number, or logo on the handout. Including the presenter's name and contact information can also prove useful. People with questions or concerns tend to find it easier to contact a specific individual especially if a relationship has been created.

- Citation—It may seem like a small thing to include where the information, idea, or pattern came from, but it may prove invaluable. If the master is lost or destroyed and needs to be replicated, finding it again will be much easier. Resources for ideas should be given credit and copyright laws need to be taken into account when using someone else's material.

- Attention Grabbers—Color, size, and pictures can all be used to draw attention to the handout. The paper color can reflect the season (gold for fall, green for spring), a program series (all young toddler materials the same color), or theme (blue for a theme of "Things That Are Wet!"). The copy paper size that is usually used to make handouts is 8.5" x 11" and works well in most cases. If the handout is to be more of a booklet or used repeatedly it might be advisable to shrink the size and use sturdier paper. For example, a booklet filled with rhymes that the parent can keep in the diaper bag could be created from half sheets of paper (5.5" x 8.5") and stapled in the middle. A heavier weight paper will increase its durability. If the program has a logo or you use the same clip art for every handout created for a series it will help identify them. Supplying a folder or a large envelope with the program name or logo on it will help participants keep the program's handouts together.

- Disclaimers—Investigate to see if any disclaimers need to be included on materials printed by the organization. For example, you may wish to request that those who have special needs contact the presenter prior to the program so that arrangements can be made, such as having a sign language interpreter for a child who is hearing impaired.
- Reason for Being—Does the handout enhance your program in some way? A handout that covers the rhymes and stories used for the program helps the adult learn the material. Including a brief statement/fact that relates or supports the importance of reading to the very young can not only validate the program, but reinforce the positive action of the adult participants. An evaluation handout can provide feedback from participants, support for such programming, and suggest ways to improve it.

Ready-Made Handouts

Ready-made handouts save time but may also be costly. They are available on the Internet, from conference programs that offer sample handouts, or through exchange amongst colleagues or libraries. Many handouts from experts in the field are offered online for purchase or even for free download. This is true especially in the area of child development and early literacy. Organizations such as the American Library Association, the National Association for the Education of Young Children, Talaris Research Institute, and Zero to Three offer a wide variety of brochures. With the increasing importance of early literacy, many libraries have developed programs and post the supporting materials on their Web sites. Multnomah County Library in Oregon, Hennepin County Library in Minnesota, King County Library System in Washington, and many other libraries share their handouts, booklists, and ideas though the Internet.

See the Resources section (Resources for Handouts) for sites that offer handout materials for purchase and/or free downloads.

Handouts should have a purpose and value to those they are being given to. It is possible to not only become overwhelmed receiving handouts but by creating them. When using handouts, whether original or preexisting, keep in mind the reason why they are being created. Are they informational? Are they an introduction or support for the program? Will they enhance the program? What will be the benefit of distributing them?

Displays

Displays can bring participants' attention to materials, services, and ideas of which they need to be made aware. Displays can be as simple as books upright on a table or can be elaborate creations with backdrop and props, depending on how much time you have to prepare them. Displays also add to the educational value of the program by making supplemental materials available to the group. An adult with a small child in hand will have limited time and ability to browse materials. If the display is located in the same area as the program the chances of it being seen are greater than if it is out in another area. Posting a "Check These Out!" sign (see page 195) on or near the display area will encourage participants to not only look at the material but check it out, as well as subtly reminding them not to just walk off with library materials. If the program is being conducted in a location outside the library itself, be sure to check prior to the program that location's policy regarding displays. When planning displays, keep in mind the following:

- Where will the display be located? Using a table, the top of bookcases, or a shelf will help keep materials out of reach of little hands. Place the display where it will cause the least amount of distraction during the program, preferably in the back of the room or by the entrance/exit door. If the display is outside the program area, make sure to mention its location or, if time allows, escort the group to it.
- What size should it be? It is not necessary to use a large, oversized table; a card-table size will do. If you use a large table, do not feel compelled to fill it up. Half of it could be used as display, the other half for handout distribution.
- How much time is needed to set up a display? In reality, not very much time at all. Displays are intended to be a sample, not everything available. Creating a display on a specific topic may necessitate collecting materials over a period of time but often a walk through the collection can garner significant display material.
- Should the display table be decorated? For safety reasons, the use of a tablecloth is not recommended because children learning to stand up or walk on their own may grab for it and pull everything down on top of them. Using puppets or props can increase a display's visibility but may also lead to upset children who want them now!

Ideas for Displays

1. Books on parenting: General parenting guides, adoption, discipline, the working parent, and communicating with children.
2. Books that support the adult: Things to do with young children, places to go in the area (such as park district information booklets), self-help books, arts and craft books, starting a play group, selecting a daycare or preschool, and so on.
3. Books on topics such as child development, the importance of play, language development, and brain development. Display materials from organizations that can assist and help the adult, on topics such as grandparents raising their grandchildren, for instance.
4. Magazines: Subscriptions can be costly and adults may find checking them out a great savings if they are on a limited budget. Since there are

so many magazines aimed at parenting and the very young child, having them available for preview is also a bonus. Suggested titles include, but are not limited to: *Parenting, Family Fun, Ladybug* and *Babybug.*

5. Special collections: Some libraries or organizations may circulate toys, puppets, and kits that have been created specifically with the very young in mind. King County Library System in Washington offers "Books to Grow On" kits, which are subject oriented and include board books, nonprint media, curriculum sheets, resource books for adults and puppet/toy/activity items that support the topic. (Check www.kcls.org for additional information.)

6. Books for the very young: The variety and quality of board books has increased over time. Displaying appropriate ones will help develop the adult's ability to recognize them and give them an opportunity to see, examine, and use the books. These books also create a colorful display!

7. Nursery rhymes: Nursery rhymes are no longer limited to Mother Goose but are available in many variations with all styles of illustrations. A display of traditional Mother Goose books, titles that cover rhymes and songs from other lands, and contemporary poetry for the very young can expand the adult's view of what types of rhymes are available.

8. Recommended or award books: Display titles that adults may recognize from their own childhood, titles that have earned an award for excellence, or additional titles that reflect the day's theme.

9. Books that can create a good home library: Adults may need to be reassured that board books, cloth or vinyl books, and books of lesser literary quality have a place in the home. Books that are worn and well loved have value also.

10. Various types of nonprint material: Quality recordings available in tape and CD format, recommended videos and DVDs for adult and child to view together, books on tape/CD, and the resources that help the adult select these materials will expand the world of language for all the participants. Having a tape/CD/VHS/DVD player enables the materials to be previewed. This will not only enhance the circulation of the nonprint material but also allow the participants to examine recordings prior to purchase.

Displays are a great way to inform and educate the participants, in addition to making browsing easier. They are not absolutely necessary but are one way to show that additional effort has been made to make this language experience the best possible one for all involved.

Signs

Use signs to identify, direct, and inform. With the use of computer software, such as Microsoft Word and Microsoft Publisher, creating signs has become much easier. Most software offers a variety of templates as well as colors, fonts, and pictures. The resulting signs are more professional looking than handwritten signs. Most signs for this type of program can fit on an 8.5" x 11" sheet of paper either in portrait or landscape orientation. Samples of signage are included in this chapter and on the CD-ROM.

To increase the life span of a sign, laminate it or insert it into a page protector. Cold laminating machines can be purchased from office supply or craft stores. These machines vary as to what size paper they laminate. In most cases, one that is wide enough to fit an 11-inch wide sheet across works fine. Plastic page protectors can be found in office supply, craft, department, and stationary stores. They can be used multiple times and make a nice place to store numerous signs in one location. Simply place the necessary sign so it is visible when posted with the others under it. When using a computer to create signs, remember to save them since with some alteration most signs can be used for other programs. Save them either to a folder just for signs or in the folder named for the program for which it is used, for instance, save a sign indicating "Story Time Has Started" to a "Story Time" folder.

Directional signs help remind adults where things are located, things that need to be done (e.g., check books out before leaving), and where the program is to take place. Informational signs can include the words to a new rhyme introduced at the program, a tip or fact that would be of interest to the adult participants, and information about upcoming programs. Offering information beyond what is available in the program helps increase the educational value of the program. Use a sign to inform the adults about a fact of early literacy you want to highlight, reasons why something in the program is important (such as rocking an infant while singing), or even to reassure the participants that they are doing a good job.

Investing time to create handouts, displays, and signs will payoff in the long run. They can increase the visibility of the program, elicit a positive response from the participants, assist in the understanding of the program, and allow more time for presenter and participants to interact and enjoy the program itself. If participants find value in handouts, displays, and signage, the program's value will increase, too.

Info Bites

Here are few quotes that can be incorporated into informational handouts or displays. For more, see the electronic resources that follow.

> "Although many experiences are said to contribute to early literacy, no other single activity is regarded as important as the shared book experience between caregivers and children."—Susan B. Neuman. 1999. "Books Make a Difference: A Study of Access to Literacy." *Reading Research Quarterly* (July-Sept): 286–311.

"The relationship between the skills with which children enter a school and their later academic performance is strikingly stable. For instance, research has shown that there is nearly a 90 percent probability that a child will remain a poor reader at the end of the fourth grade if the child is a poor reader at the end of the first grade. Further, knowledge of alphabet letters at entry into kindergarten is a strong predictor of reading ability in 10th grade."—Ernest L. Boyer. 1991. *Ready to Learn: A Mandate for the Nation.* San Francisco: Carnegie Foundation for the Advancement of Testing.

"The single most significant factor influencing a child's early educational success is an introduction to books and being read to at home prior to beginning school."—Richard C. Anderson, et al. 1985. *Becoming a Nation of Readers: The Report of the National Commission on Reading.* Chicago: University of Illinois.

"Children who are read to three or more times a week are nearly twice as likely as other children to show three or more skills associated with emerging literacy."—Christine W. Nord, et al. 1999. "Home Literacy Activities and Signs of Children's Emerging Literacy, 1993 and 1999." *Statistics in Brief* series. Washington DC: National Center for Education Statistics.

"By age three the children in professional families would have heard more than 30 million words, the children in working-class families 20 million, and the children in welfare families 10 million. To equalize the cumulative experience of the welfare children at age three to that of the working-class children in the number of words said to them would require the addition of 12 million words. That is one year's worth of words heard by a child in a professional family, and one and a half year's worth of words for a child in a working-class family."—Betty Hart and Todd R. Risley. 1995. *Meaningful Differences in the Everyday Experience of Young American Children.* Baltimore, MD: Brookes Publishing.

"When you read with your children, you show them that reading is important, but you also show them they're important—that they are so important to you that you will spend 20 minutes a day with your arm around them."—Laura Bush at the Moscow Children's Book Festival. 2003. Reported in *Library and Information Update*, November 2003.

"The acquisition of a first language is the most complex skill anyone ever learns. And this task needs to be virtually complete by the time a child reaches school age."—David Crystal. 1997. *Cambridge Encyclopedia of Languages.* Cambridge: Cambridge University Press.

Resources for More "Info Bites"

Clearinghouse on Early Education and Parenting
    The Clearinghouse on Early Education and Parenting (CEEP) is part of the Early Childhood and Parenting (ECAP) Collaborative at the University of Illinois at

Urbana–Champaign. CEEP provides publications and information to the world-wide early childhood and parenting communities.

http://ceep.crc.uiuc.edu/eecearchive

Institute for Learning & Brain Sciences

"The Institute for Learning and Brain Sciences is an interdisciplinary center dedicated to discovering the fundamental principles of human learning that will enable all children to achieve their full potential. Our goal is to become the world's foremost research generator on early learning and development. We will translate and disseminate cutting-edge research discoveries to global constituents in order to help unify the science of learning and the practice of learning." (I-LABS Web site) From the homepage click on "News & Information," then "Media Coverage" for reports and articles.

http://ilabs.washington.edu/index.html

Jim Trelease

Jim Trelease, author of *The Read-Aloud Handbook*, which is now in its sixth edition, offers facts and data from various research studies that support reading aloud to children of all ages. It is a site that will direct you to additional authoritative data.

http://www.trelease-on-reading.com

Institute of Educational Sciences, US Department of Education National Center for Education Statistics.

http://www.nces.ed.gov/ecls/index.asp

Reading Is Fundamental

The largest children's literacy organization in the United States offers facts, tips, and links for educators and parents, in addition to RIF coordinators on early literacy development for children birth through age eight.

http://rif.org

Talaris Institute

This organization provides information from research papers, offers downloadable handouts, a free newsletter, and more that will "advance knowledge of early learning and the importance of parenting in the first years of life." (Talaris Web site)

Http://telaris.org

Resources

Resources for Handouts

Adelaide Hills Council—Library Services—*Baby Bounce & Rhyme* booklet
http://www.ahc.sa.gov.au/site/page.cfm?u=151
American Library Association—*Raise a Reader/Born to Read/Every Child Ready to Read @ Your Library*
ala.org
ala.org/ala/alsc/ECRR/ECRRHomePage.htm

Hennepin County Library, Minnesota
  www.hclib.org
King County Library System, Washington
  www.kcls.org
Multnomah County Library, Oregon
  www.multcolib.org
National Association for the Education of Young Children
  naeyc.org
Reading Rockets—Offers hundreds of articles that provide research-based and best-practice information for educators, parents, and others concerned about reading achievement.
  readingrockets.org/atoz
Talaris Research Institute—Seattle, WA
  talaris.org
Talk to Your Baby—Great Britain—A campaign run by the National Literacy Trust to encourage parents and childcare providers to talk more to children from birth to three.
  www.talktoyourbaby.org.uk
Zero to Three—National headquarters in Washington, DC and western office in California.
  zerotothree.org

Resources for Facts and Tips

Print

Hart, Betty and Todd R. Risley. 1995. *Meaningful Differences in the Everyday Experience of Young American Children.* Baltimore, MD: Paul H. Brookes.
Shonkoff, Jack P. and Deborah A. Phillips, ed. 2000. *From Neurons to Neighborhoods: The Science of Early Childhood Development.* Washington, DC: National Academy Press.
Zigler, Edward F., Dorothy G. Singer, and Sandra J. Bishop-Josef. 2004. *Children's Play: The Roots of Reading.* Washington, DC: Zero to Three Press.

Web Sites

www.ala.org/ala/alsc/ECRR/researcha/Research.htm
Every Child Ready To Read @ Your Library
  American Library Association

www.naeyc.org
National Association for the Education of Young Children

www.nces.ed.gov
National Center for Education Statistics

Resources for Clip Art, Stickers, Stamps, Borders, etc.

Dover Publications, Inc.
   31 E. 2nd St.
   Mineola, NY 11501

Ellison Educational Equipment
   PO Box 8309
   Newport Beach, CA 92658-8209
   800-253-2238
   www.ellison.com

Highsmith/Upstart
   W5527 State Rd. 106
   PO Box 800
   Fort Atkinson, WI 53538-0800
   800-448-4887
   www.highsmith.com

Kidstamps
   PO Box 18699
   Cleveland Heights, OH 44118
   800-727-5437
   www.kidstamps.com

APPENDIX

SAMPLE PROGRAM HANDOUTS

Handouts and Templates on CD

Babies and Language

Acredolo, Linda P. 2002. *Baby Signs: How to Talk to Your Baby Before Your Baby Can Talk.* New York: Contemporary Books.

Apel, Kenn. 2001. *Beyond Baby Talk: A Parent's Complete Guide to Language Development.* Roseville, CA: Prima.

Doughterty, Dorothy P. 1999. *How to Talk to Your Baby.* Garden City Park, NY: Avery.

Garcia, Joseph. 2001. *Sign with Your Baby.* Seattle, WA: Northlight, and Stratton-Kehl.

Glinkoff, Roberta M. 2000. *How Babies Talk: The Magic and Mystery of Language in the First Three Years of Life.* New York: Plume.

Hogg, Tracy. 2001. *Secrets of the Baby Whisperer: How to Calm, Connect, and Communicate with Your Baby.* New York: Ballantine Books.

Segal, Marilyn M. 1998. *Your Child at Play. Birth to One Year: Discovering the Senses and Learning About the World.* New York: Newmarket Press.

Shore, Penny A. 2002. *How Your Baby and Child Learns.* Toronto: Parent Kit.

Silberg, Jackie. 1999. *125 Brain Games for Babies: Simple Games to Promote Early Brain Development.* Beltsville, MD: Gryphon House.

Main Street Library

Bibs 'n' Books

A program of rhymes and stories
for children under 2
(and their caregivers)

INFORMATION AND LIBRARY SERVICES

(Bibs 'n' Books continues on pages 192 and 193.)

Bibs 'n' Books

Welcome to Main Street Library
Service's Bibs 'n' Books program.

These sessions are aimed at children who are a little
young for our regular story time.
Of course, big brothers and sisters and grandparents are
always very welcome to come along and take part.

Bibs 'n' Books is more than just a story time
session aimed at younger children. It is a
literacy-based program and a great way for
parents and caregivers to share songs,
rhymes, books, laughter, and fun with their
children.

We hope that both you and your child enjoy this
special bonding time in the library.

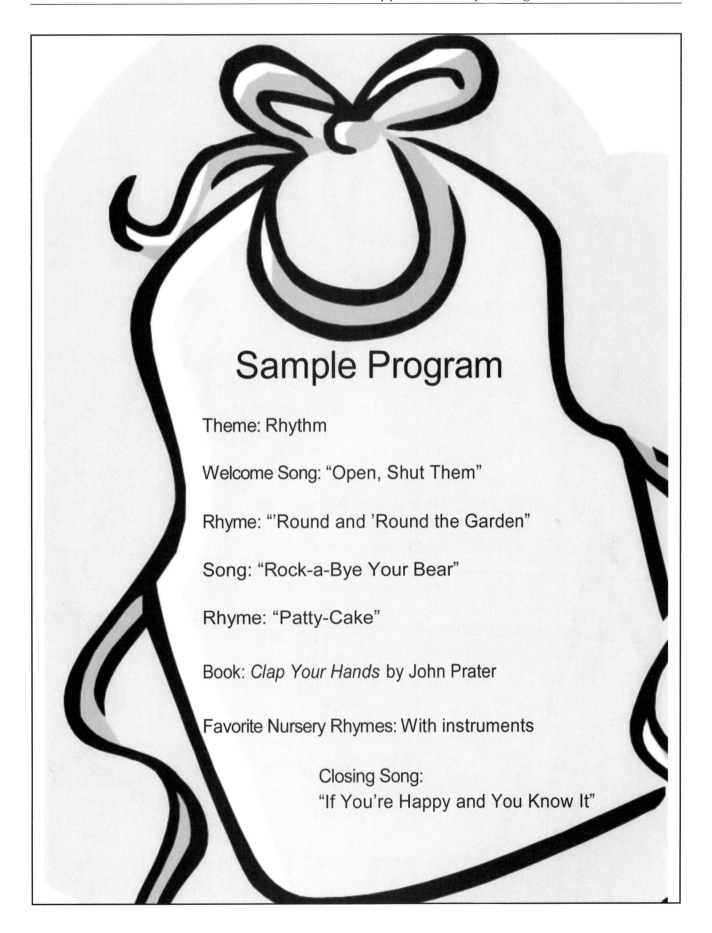

Sample Program

Theme: Rhythm

Welcome Song: "Open, Shut Them"

Rhyme: "'Round and 'Round the Garden"

Song: "Rock-a-Bye Your Bear"

Rhyme: "Patty-Cake"

Book: *Clap Your Hands* by John Prater

Favorite Nursery Rhymes: With instruments

Closing Song:
"If You're Happy and You Know It"

Main Street City Library
Presents

Bibs 'n' Books

A program of rhymes and stories for
children under 2
(and their caregivers)

When: Thursdays (school term only)
Time: 10:30 a.m.
Where: Children's area
              Main Street City Library

Program Preview and Launch
February 22, 200_
With talk on:
"Benefits of Books for Babies"

Program Starting February 22, 200_

No bookings required
For further information,
Contact the library at:
555-5555

INFORMATION AND LIBRARY SERVICES

Fold here to display as sign on bookshelf or table.

CHECK THESE OUT!

Fold here to display as sign on bookshelf or table.

**Sorry
Story time has started
Please wait.**

Check

these

out!

*Insert picture or
clip art here*

Early Literacy Ideas
From Baby Story Time Training
April 6, 2006

King County Library System Children's Librarians were assigned to brainstorm ways to apply the six early literacy skills, based on the Every Child Ready to Read @ Your Library program, to children under two years of age. The ideas could be used in story time, or could be tips to give parents and caregivers.

Print Motivation

- Keep books in child's bed, so child wakes up to them!
- Treat books as toys—keep them in the toy box.
- Let children choose the books at the library, bookstore, etc.—in story time, too!
- Let children see you read—model reading behavior!
- Read with enthusiasm!
- Pay attention to children's cues and moods-shorten a story, insert movement activities, or just move on! Keep it positive.
- Read/choose books that YOU like, too. Children will pick up on your feelings!

Vocabulary

- Identify pictures in books.
- Elaborate on a picture—for example: when you see a picture of a dog, identify the type of dog as well (e.g., Dalmatian dog).
- Ask children what they see, both in books and in daily life.
- Use props.
- Use simple rhymes.
- Name body parts in song or rhyme ("Head, Shoulders, Knees and Toes," for example).
- Be aware that children's books use more rare words than speech.
- Understand that children generally have a higher listening comprehension than oral ability, so read, read, read!

Narrative Skills

- Narrate daily tasks, such as preparing meals.
- Let baby babble back. Ask questions, and wait for answers, whether they are oral or facial expressions.

- Narrate while in the car.
- Tell family stories.
- Use felt board stories.
- Use puppets or toys to tell stories or explain things.
- Use dialogic reading.
- Read books!

Phonological Awareness

- Include rhyming words and alliterative rhymes in songs, rhymes, books, and flannel board stories (e.g., *Brown Bear, Brown Bear* has both rhyming and alliteration).
- Use rhyming with toys, such as blocks ("blocks rhymes with socks!") or ball rolling (each time you or baby rolls the ball, say another word that rhymes with "ball").
- Teach parents rhyming games, such as "Willaby Wallaby Woo," using children's names.
- Make animal sounds.
- Use bubbles as props for bubble songs.

Letter Knowledge

- After doing "Patty Cake" once with the letter "B" for baby, do it again, but have adults use their child's name.
- Trace letters.
- Let children play with foam letters.
- Let children play with die-cut letters.
- Use play dough, or other methods of sensory learning to create letters.
- Sing the alphabet song.
- Work on sound–letter connections.

Print Awareness

- Point to letters/words as you read to children.
- Read signs: "That says . . ."
- Turn books upside-down or backwards, and have children correct you.
- Let children play with books to learn to turn pages.
- Put labels on familiar objects.
- Spell child's name with magnetic letters, blocks, etc.

(Name of Program)
Presenter: (Name)
(Dates)

Evaluation

Please take a moment to fill this out. Your information will help us plan and develop programs that serve our community best. Thank you!

1. Were the stories and rhymes presented during this program suitable for your child?

   Always   Usually   Sometimes   Never

2. Did you and your child enjoy this program?

   Always   Usually   Sometimes   Never

3. Was the time of the program convenient for you and your child?

   Yes   No   If not, why?_____

4. What was your child's response to the program?

   Very positive   Positive   Negative   Very Negative   No Response

5. Did you take any of the materials used for the program home to use?

   Always   Usually   Sometimes   Never

6. Did you borrow books from the library for your child before attending this program?

   Yes   No

7. Did you check out books that you learned about from this program?

   Yes   No

8. Will you continue to borrow materials for your child from the library?

   Yes   No

9. What was the best thing about this program?

10. What was the least favorite thing about this program?

11. Any other comments or suggestions?

(Name of Program)
Presenter: (Name)
(Dates)

Evaluation

Please take a moment to fill this out. Your information will help us plan and develop programs that serve our community best. Thank you!

1. How old is your child? _____

2. How did you find out about this program? _____

3. How many classes did you attend? _____

4. Have you attended similar programs here or at other locations?   Yes   No

5. Were the materials used suitable for the age range?   Yes   No

6. Name one new thing you have learned. _____

7. Have you used any of the ideas and materials presented at home?   Yes   No

8. Have you added anything from this class to your daily activities?   Yes   No

   If so, what? _____

9. Did you find handout sheets helpful?   Yes   No

10. Did you read the information sent home?   Yes   No

11. Has your interaction with your child changed since being in the class? Yes No

12. What did you like best about the program? _____

13. What did you like least about the program? _____

14. Was the time relatively convenient?   Yes   No

15. Did this program meet your expectations?   Yes   No

16. If offered again, would you attend this class?   Yes   No

17. Please tell us how can we improve this program for you and your child:

(Name of Program)
Presenter: (Name)
(Dates)

Evaluation

Please take a moment to fill this out. Your information will help us plan and develop programs that serve our community best. Thank you!

1. I found the information in this program to be:

   Very interesting   Interesting   Not helpful   What information?

2. My understanding of the importance of reading to my child has:

   Increased greatly   Improved   Not changed   Still have no idea
                                                             why it's important

3. The handout sheets were:

   Very informative   Informative   Not very   What sheets?
                                           informative

4. Our number of library visits has:

   Increased   Stayed the   Decreased
                    same

5. We use the program materials in our family's routine:

   Daily   Weekly   Occasionally

6. The presenter was:

   Amazing   Very good   Okay   Lacking

7. The best thing about the program was:

8. The program would have been better if:

Baby Rhyming Time— Rhymes and Directions

Open, Shut Them

*(Do hand motions with baby's hands and arms.
Tap or circle child's mouth on appropriate line.)*

Open, shut them. Open, shut them.
Give a little clap, clap, clap!
Open, shut them. Open, shut them.
Put them in your lap, lap, lap.
Creep them, creep them, creep them,
Creep them right up to your chin, chin, chin.
Open up your tiny mouth . . .
But do not let them in!

Humpty Dumpty

*(Bounce child gently on lap or sit on floor with child on raised knees.
Part legs or straighten them so child slides down when Humpty Dumpty falls.)*

Humpty Dumpty sat on a wall.
Humpty Dumpty had a great fall!
All the King's horses and all the King's men,
Couldn't put Humpty together again.

Tick-Tock

*(Rock back and forth until the "Cuckoo" line. Then for each "Cuckoo"
you can play peek-a-boo or tip child forward on your lap.)*

Tick-tock, tick-tock, I'm a little cuckoo clock.
Tick-tock, tick-tock, Now it's almost three o'clock-
Cuckoo! Cuckoo! Cuckoo!

Wash the Dishes

*(Stroke child's body from right shoulder to left hip and then left shoulder to right hip [repeat 2x].
On "Ding" tap child's nose. Repeat strokes 2x and then kiss each cheek and belly.)*

Wash the dishes
Wipe the dishes
Ring the bell for tea . . . DING!
Three good wishes
Three good kisses
I will give to thee.
One . . . Two . . . Three!

How You Can Help Your Child **GROW**!

Key Facts about Early Brain Development:

Get Active! Children learn by doing.

Relationships Matter! Children learn best in a relationship with a caring adult.

Over and over! Children learn through repetition.

Windows of Opportunity! The early years are essential for language development.

KING
COUNTY
LIBRARY
SYSTEM

Young Toddler

Story Time

Ages 12-24 Months

with Adults

Please enter quietly

Thank you!

Remember:

Get involved with what we are doing.

Snacks and toys away for now.

Time for sharing after the program.

Have fun!

This is the

9:45 a.m.

Baby Rhyming Time

For Newborn to 12 months

with Adult

Next Class is at 10:45 a.m.

Please Wait

Thank You

Tiny Tales

Mondays
July 11, 18, and 25
10:30 a.m.

For ages 18 months and younger, with adult.

Story time designed with the very young child and caregiver in mind.

Newport Way Library
425-747-2390
kcls.org

Reasonable accommodation for individuals with disabilities is available; please contact the library prior to the event should you require such accommodation.

Story Time at the (Name of Library)

You and your child will soon participate in the calculated expression of joy we call story time! The stories, games, finger plays, and activities used in story time are designed to:

- Foster a love of language and books.
- Introduce standard works of literature for young children.
- Provide your child with an early group experience.
- Encourage an increased attention span.
- Demonstrate new activities for you to enjoy with your child at home.
- Provide a pleasant introductory experience to the library.

To help ensure the fullest enjoyment of the program, here are a few guidelines:

- Please arrive on time. The room will be open five minutes before class starts so you can get settled and ready for fun. Young children are easily distracted and latecomers become the focus of attention.
- If your child is exceptionally restless during a session, feel free to leave the room and join us later or return the following week. This will minimize the distraction for everyone. It is okay to leave—we understand!
- Help your child participate by being attentive and active yourself. Gently focus your child's attention on each story or activity.

Story time is a special time to meet new friends—in books and in person!
During our story times we open the doors to the world of language and literature.
Thanks for coming on the adventure with us!

After story time, we encourage you and your child to explore the children's area in the main library. You can then share with your child the "public library experience." To make the most of this experience, remember to stay with your child, for without a caring adult they may "get lost." You can also model behavior for being in the library. Remember:

- Please use quiet "inside" voices.
- For safety reasons, do not allow your child to run around.
- Stay with your child in order to share this language experience.

Feel free to call us if you have any questions or concerns!

Presenter's Name
Children's Librarians
Library Name
Phone Number

Some Songs and Rhymes We Shared Today—
Try Them at Home!

Songs We Sang Today
"Hello Everybody" from *Sally's from Wibbleton to Wobbleton* video
"Ring Around the Rosy" (Traditional)
"Wheels on the Bus" from *Sing Along with Bob #1* by Bob McGrath

Ride Baby Ride
(Fun for bouncing baby on your knee or galloping around)
Ride baby ride—Ch, ch, ch, ch, ch, ch.
Ride that horsey ride—Ch, ch, ch, ch, ch, ch.
Ride baby ride—Ch, ch, ch, ch, ch, ch.
Ride that horsey ride—Ch, ch, ch, ch, ch, ch.
Whoa…! *(Give baby a hug)*

Acka Backa
(With baby on your lap, rock back and forth, or bounce on knee)
Acka backa soda cracker, acka backa boo!
Acka backa soda cracker, I love you! *(Hug child)*
Acka backa soda cracker, acka backa boo!
Acka backa soda cracker, up goes you! *(Lift child upwards)*
Acka backa soda cracker, acka backa boo!
Acka backa soda cracker, I love you! *(Hug child)*

'Round & 'Round the Garden
'Round and 'round the garden goes the teddy bear.
(Draw circles on baby's tummy, back, and hand with your finger)
One step, two step, tickle *(child's name)* under there!
(Walk your fingers up baby's arm or chest, ending with a tickle under chin or arm)

"The single most important activity for building the knowledge required for eventual success in reading is reading aloud to children."
Becoming a Nation of Readers, 1985

Some Books and Rhymes We Shared Today— Try Them at Home!

Books We Read Today

All Fall Down by Helen Oxenbury
Read to Your Bunny by Rosemary Wells

One, Two, Three

One, two, three, baby's on my knee
(Bounce baby on your knee)
Rooster crows and away he goes!
*(If sitting, lift baby from one knee to the other;
if standing, lift baby in the air and spin around)*

Cheek, Chin

(Reprinted with permission from *Hippety-Hop, Hippety-Hay*, by Opal Dunn and Sally
Anne Lambert, published by Frances Lincoln Limited, copyright © 1999)
(Tap each body part while reciting this rhyme)
Cheek, chin, cheek, chin, cheek, chin, NOSE,
Cheek, chin, cheek, chin, cheek, chin, TOES,
Cheek, chin, cheek, chin, cheek chin—
UP baby goes!
(When diapering baby, hold baby's ankles together, lift up and slip diaper underneath)

Jeremiah, Blow the Fire

(Blow on baby's belly starting softly and getting stronger each time)
Jeremiah, blow the fire, puff, puff, puff.
First you blow it gently...
Then you blow it rough.

Here We Go Up–Up–Up

Here we go up–up–up
(Lift baby up in the air)
Here we go down–down–down
(Lower baby towards floor)
Here we go back-and-forth, back-and-forth
(Swing baby back and forth)
And here we go around and around and around
(Turn around holding baby)

Things to remember:
Have fun! Talk to your baby about the book! Read aloud! Read often!

Some of the Books and Rhymes We Shared Today—
Try Them at Home!

Books We Read Today

Clap Hands by Helen Oxenbury
Can I Have a Hug? by Debi Gliori

Bouncing Rhyme: "Rickety, Rickety Rocking Horse"

Rickety, rickety rocking horse,
Over the fields we go!
Rickety, rickety rocking horse,
Giddy up! Giddy up! Whoa! *(Lean back on "Whoa")*

Tickle Rhyme: "These Are Baby's Fingers"
(Touch appropriate body part on baby)

These are baby's fingers,
These are baby's toes.
This is baby's bellybutton,
Around and around it goes!

Bouncing Rhyme: "Trot, Trot to Boston"

Trot, trot to Boston,
Trot, trot to Lynn.
Look out little baby, you might fall in! *(Dip baby on "fall in")*

Trot, trot to Boston,
Trot, trot to Dover.
Look out little baby, you might fall over! *(Tip baby to side on "fall over")*

Trot, trot to Boston,
Trot, trot to town.
Look out little baby, you might fall down! *(Dip baby on "fall down")*

TIP:
Using rhymes and songs is a great way to help your child learn the names of different body parts! "Head and shoulders, knees and toes" is a fun song to use!

Some Rhymes and Books We Shared Today— Try Them at Home!

Patty-Cake, Patty-Cake

(Holding baby's hands gently clap them together and follow the directions. Instead of using the letter "B," use your own baby's name and initial.)

Patty-cake, patty-cake, baker's man
Bake me a cake as fast as you can.
Roll it and pat it and mark it with a "B"
And put it in the oven for baby and me!

Eensy, Weensy Spider

The eensy, weensy spider
went up the water spout.
(Walk/tickle your fingers up your baby's back or arm)
Down came the rain
and washed the spider out.
(Slide your fingers down from head to toes)
Out came the sun
and dried up all the rain,
(Rub your baby's back)
And the eensy, weensy spider
went up the spout again.
(Walk/tickle your fingers up your baby's back or arm)

Roly-Poly

(Gently move baby's arms as indicated. You can also hold your baby while standing in front of a mirror. This way your baby can see the movement.)

Roly-poly, roly-poly, up–up–up.
Roly-poly, roly-poly, down–down–down.
Roly-poly, roly-poly, out–out–out.
Roly-poly, roly-poly, in–in–in.

Tick-Tock

(Holding baby in lap, gently rock back and forth. When saying "cuckoo" play peek-a-boo, or with your hand behind baby's knees, tip baby upwards.)

Tick-tock, tick-tock,
I'm a little cuckoo clock.
Tick-tock, tick-tock,
Now it's almost three o'clock.
Cuckoo! Cuckoo! Cuckoo!

Mother and Father and Uncle John

Mother and Father and Uncle John
went to town, one by one.
(Bounce your baby on your lap)
Mother fell off,
(Tip your baby to one side)
And Father fell off,
(Tip your baby to other side)
But Uncle John went on
and on and on!
(Bounce your baby on your lap)

Apple Tree

Way up high in the apple tree
(Raise your baby's arms above baby's head)
Two little apples did I see.
(Use your index finger to massage around baby's eyes)
So I shook that tree as hard as I could,
(Jiggle your baby's body)
And d-o-w-n came the apples,
(Tickle your fingers down baby's body)
Umm! They were good!
(Give lots of cuddles and kisses)

To Market, to Market

(Bounce your baby on your lap or hip)
To market, to market to buy a fat pig,
Home again, home again jiggity jig.
To market, to market to buy a fat hog,
Home again, home again jiggity jog.

Songs
"The Wheels on the Bus" from
If You're Happy and You Know It, Sing Along with Bob #1
by Bob McGrath

"The More We Get Together" from
If You're Happy and You Know It, Sing Along with Bob #1
by Bob McGrath

Take your child on a visit to the library and see what you find!

(Insert library information or "info bite" here.)

Some Rhymes, Books, and Songs We Shared Today— Try Them at Home!

The Grand Old Duke of York
(This is a fun bouncing rhyme or march)
Oh, the grand old Duke of York,
He had 10,000 men.
He marched them up
To the top of the hill
And he marched them down again.
And when they were up, they were up.
And when they were down, they were down.
But when they were only halfway up
They were neither up nor down!
They marched them to the left,
They marched them to the right.
They even marched them upside-down,
Now isn't that a sight!

1-2-3-4-5, I Caught a Fish Alive
*(Holding your child, clap your hands
around him or her,
then catch on "alive," and tickle on
"again")*
1-2-3-4-5
I caught a fish alive!
6-7-8-9-10
I let him go again!

Tall as a Tree
Tall as a tree.
(Standing, stretch arms above head)
Wide as a house.
(Stretch your arms straight out from sides)
Thin as a pin.
(Put arms down at sides)
Small as a mouse.
(Crouch down to floor)

Cobbler, Cobbler
*(Pat shoe of child or have child pat adult's
shoe)*
Cobbler, cobbler, mend my shoe.
Give it one stitch, give it two.
Give it three, give it four.
And if it needs it, give it more!

Books We Read Today
Brown Bear, Brown Bear by Bill Martin
The Bridge Is Up by Babs Bell

Songs We Sang Today
"Head and Shoulders, Knees and Toes," "The More We Get Together," and "The Wheels on the Bus" from *If You're Happy and You Know It, Sing Along with Bob #1*
by Bob McGrath
"Clap Your Hands" from *Circle Around* by Tickle Tune Typhoon
"Row, Row, Row Your Boat" from *Songs & Games for Toddlers* featuring Bob McGrath and Katherine Smithrim

"By age three, children from privileged families have heard 30 million more words than children from poor families. By kindergarten the gap is even greater.
The consequences are catastrophic."

Betty Hart and Todd R. Risley
"The Early Catastrophe: The 30-Million Word Gap"
American Educator, Spring 2003
(www.aft.org/pubs-reports/american_educator/spring2003/index.html)

Resources

Print Resources

Acredolo, Linda and Susan Goodwyn. 2000. *Baby Minds: Brain-Building Games Your Baby Will Love*. New York: Bantam Books.

_____. 2005. *Baby Hearts: A Guide to Giving Your Child an Emotional Head Start*. New York: Bantam Books.

_____. 2002. *Baby Signs: How to Talk with Your Baby Before Your Baby Can Talk*. New York: Contemporary Books.

Ada, Alma Flor and F. Isabel Campoy. 2003. *Pio Peep! Traditional Spanish Nursery Rhymes*. New York: HarperCollins.

Albrecht, Kay and Linda G. Miller. 2000. *The Comprehensive Infant Curriculum: A Complete, Interactive Curriculum for Infants from Birth to 18 Months*. Beltsville, MD: Gryphon House.

Anderson, Richard C., Elfrieda H. Hiebert, Judith A. Scott, and Ian A.G. Wilkinson. 1985. *Becoming a Nation of Readers: The Report of the Commission on Reading*. Urbana–Champaign, IL: Center for the Study of Reading.

Anderson-Wright, Judith, Robert Berg, and Joseph Garcia. 2003. *Pick Me Up! Fun Songs for Learning Signs*. Seattle: Sign2me/Northlight Communications.

Apel, Kenn and Julie J. Masterson. 2001. *Beyond Baby Talk: From Sounds to Sentences—A Parent's Complete Guide to Language Development*. Roseville, CA: Prima Publishing.

Arnold, Renea and Nell Colburn. 2006. "Really Good Research: Some Persuasive Evidence to Share with Those Who Serve Young Children." *School Library Journal* 52 (November): 31.

Arnold, Renea and Nell Colburn. 2006. "Howdy, Partner: Community Alliances Can Help You Reach the Next Generation of Readers." *School Library Journal* 52 (May): 35.

_____. 2006. "The Perfect Partner: Head Start is an Ideal Ally for Promoting Early Literacy." *School Library Journal* 52 (March): 37.

_____. 2007. "Read to Me! Summer Reading for Preschoolers." *School Library Journal* 52 (July) 37.

Bailey, Becky A. 2000. *I Love You Rituals*. New York: Quill.

Bang, Molly. 1983. *Ten, Nine, Eight*. New York: Greenwillow Books.

Barlin, Anne Leif. 1989. *Hello Toes! Movement Games for Children*. Pennington, NJ: Princeton Books.

Bell, Babs. 2004. *The Bridge Is Up!* New York: HarperCollins.

Bloom, Suzanne. 2001. *The Bus for Us*. Honesdale, PA: Caroline Press.

Brazelton, T. Berry. 1992. *Touchpoints Birth to 3: Your Child's Emotional and Behavioral Development*. Reading, MA: Perseus Publishing.

Butler, Dorothy. 1998. *Babies Need Books*. rev. ed. Portsmouth, NH: Heinemann.

Carlson, Ann and Mary Carlson. 1999. *Flannelboard Stories for Infants and Toddlers*. Chicago: American Library Association.

_____. 2005. *Flannelboard Stories for Infants and Toddlers, Bilingual Edition*. Chicago: American Library Association.

Carlson, Frances M. 2006. *Essential Touch: Meeting the Needs of Young Children*. Washington, DC: National Association for the Education of Young Children.

Carter, David. 1997. *If You're Happy and You Know It Clap Your Hands*. New York: Cartwheel Books.

Cass-Beggs, Barbara. 1978. *Your Baby Needs Music*. New York: St. Martin's Press.

Cobb, Jane. 2007. *What'll I Do With the Baby-O? Nursery Rhymes, Songs, and Stories for Babies*. Vancouver, BC: Black Sheep Press.

Cole, Joanna. 1991. *The Eentsy, Weentsy Spider: Fingerplays and Action Rhymes*. New York: Mulberry Books.

Conkling, Winifred. 2001. *Smart-Wiring Your Baby's Brain: What You Can Do to Stimulate Your Child During the Critical First Three Years*. New York: Quill/HarperCollins.

Conners, C. Keith. 1989. *Feeding the Brain: How Foods Affect Children*. New York: Plenum Press.

Cousins, Lucy. 2003. *Maisy Loves You*. Cambridge, MA: Candlewick Press.

Crews, Donald. 1978. *Freight Train*. New York: Greenwillow Press.

DeJong, Lorraine. 2003. "Using Erikson to Work More Effectively with Teenage Parents." *Young Children* 58 (March): 87–95.

Dennison, Paul E. and Gail E. Dennison. 1986. *Brain Gym: Simple Activities for Whole Brain Learning*. Ventura, CA: Edu-Kinesthetics.

Diamond, Marian and Janet Hopson. 1998. *Magic Trees of the Mind: How to Nurture Your Child's Intelligence, Creativity and Healthy Emotions from Birth Through Adolescence*. New York: Dutton.

Dunn, Opal. 1999. *Hippety-Hop Hippety-Hay: Growing with Rhymes from Birth to Age Three*. New York: Henry Holt.

_____. 2001. *Hippety-Hop, Hippety-Hay: Growing with Rhymes from Birth to Age Three*. Frances Lincoln Childrens Books.

Ehlert, Lois. 1995. *Snowballs*. San Diego: Harcourt Brace.

Eliot, Lisa. 1999. *What's Going On in There? How the Brain and Mind Develop in the First Years of Life*. New York: Bantam Books.

Ernst, Linda. L. 1995. *Lapsit Services for the Very Young*. New York: Neal-Schuman.

_____. 2001. *Lapsit Services for the Very Young II*. New York: Neal-Schuman.

Feierabend, John M. 2000. *The Book of Simple Songs & Circles*. Chicago: GIA First Steps.

_____. 2000. *The Book of Bounces: Wonderful Songs and Rhymes Passed Down from Generation to Generation for Infants & Toddlers*. Chicago: GIA First Steps.

_____. 2000. *The Book of Tapping & Clapping: Wonderful Songs and Rhymes Passed Down from Generation to Generation for Infants & Toddlers*. Chicago: GIA First Steps.

_____. 2000. *The Book of Wiggles & Tickles: Wonderful Songs and Rhymes Passed Down from Generation to Generation for Infants & Toddlers*. Chicago: GIA First Steps.

Feinberg, Sandra, Joan F. Kuchner, and Sari Feldman. 1998. *Learning Environments for Young Children: Rethinking Library Spaces and Services*. Chicago: American Library Association.

Feinberg, Sandra, and Sari Feldman. 1996. *Serving Families and Children Through Partnerships*. New York: Neal-Schuman.

Flint Public Library. 2000. *Ring a Ring o' Roses: Stories, Games and Fingerplays for Pre-School Children*. 11th ed. Flint, MI: Flint Public Library.

Fox, Mem. 2001. *Reading Magic: Why Reading Aloud to Our Children Will Change Their Lives Forever*. New York: Harcourt.

_____. 2004. *Where Is the Green Sheep?* New York: Harcourt.

Garcia, Joseph. 2001. *Sign With Your Baby: How to Communicate With Infants Before They Can Speak*. Bellingham, WA: Stratton-Kehl Publications.

Garvey, Catherine. 1991. *Play*. 2nd rev. ed. London: Fontana.

Ghoting, Safoj Nadkarni, and Pamela Martin-Diaz. 2006. *Early Literacy Storytimes @ Your Library*. Chicago: American Library Association.

Gliori, Debi. 2002. *Can I Have a Hug?* New York: Scholastic.

Go, Joanne, Janet Pozmantier, and Laurie Segal Robinson. 2001. *The First Years: A Parent and Caregiver's Guide to Helping Children Learn*. New York: DK Publishing.

Golinkoff, Roberta, and Kathy Hirsh-Pasek. 1999. *How Babies Talk: The Magic and Mystery of Language in the First Three Years of Life*. New York: Dutton.

Gopnik, Alison, Andrew Meltzoff, and Patricia Kuhl. 1999. *The Scientist in the Crib: Minds, Brains, and How Children Learn*. New York: William Morrow.

Hall, Mary, and Susan Howlett. 2003. *Getting Funded: The Complete Guide to Writing Grant Proposals*. 4th ed. Portland, OR: Portland State University, Continuing Education Press.

Halpern, Shari, illus. 1994. *Little Robin Redbreast: A Mother Goose Rhyme*. New York: North-South Books.

Hannaford, Carla. 1995. *Smart Moves: Why Learning Is Not All in Your Head*. Alexander, NC: Great Ocean Publishers.

Hart, Betty, and Todd Risley. 1996. *Meaningful Differences in the Everyday Experience of Young American Children*. Baltimore, MD: Brookes Publishing.

Heath, Alan, and Nicki Bainbridge. 2004. *Baby Massage: The Calming Power of Touch*. New York: DK Publishing.

Herr, Judy, and Terri Swim. 2002. *Creative Resources for Infants and Toddlers*, 2nd ed. Clifton Park, NY: Thomson Delmar Learning.

_____. 2003. *Making Sounds, Making Music, and Many Other Activities for Infants: 7 to 12 Months.* Clifton Park, NY: Thomson Delmar Learning.

_____. 2003. *Rattle Time, Face to Face, and Many Other Activities for Infants: Birth to 6 Months.* Clifton Park, NY: Thomson Delmar Learning.

_____. 2002. *Sorting Shapes, Show Me, and Many Other Activities for Toddlers: 13 to 24 Months.* Clifton Park, NY: Thomson Delmar Learning.

Hewitt, Karen. 2001. "Blocks as a Tool for Learning: A Historical and Contemporary Perspective." *Journal of the National Association for the Education of Young Children* 56 (January): 6-13.

Hirsh-Pasek, Kathy, and Roberta Michnick Golinkoff, with Danie Eyer. 2003. *Einstein Never Used Flash Cards: How Our Children Really Learn—and Why They Need to Play More and Memorize Less.* Emmaus, PA: Rodale.

Humpal, Marcia Earl, and Jan Wolf. 2003. "Music in the Inclusive Environment." *Young Children* 58 (March): 103–07.

Isadora, Rachel. 2002. *Peekaboo Morning.* New York: G.P. Putnam's Sons.

Isbell, Rebecca, and Betty Exelby. 2001. *Early Learning Environments That Work.* Beltsville, MD: Gryphon House.

Katz, Laurie, and Teris K. Schery. 2006. "Including Children with Hearing Loss in Early Childhood Programs." *Young Children* 61 (January): 86–95.

Koralek, Derry, ed. 2004. *Spotlight on Young Children and Play.* Washington, DC: National Association for the Education of Young Children.

Kutner, Merrily. 2004. *Down on the Farm.* New York: Holiday House.

Leiderman, Roni Cohen, and Wendy S. Masi, eds. 2001. *Baby Play: 100 Fun-Filled Activities to Maximize Your Baby's Potential.* San Francisco: Creative Publishing International.

Levine-Gelb Comunications, Claire Lerner, and Lynette A. Ciervo. 2002. *Getting in Tune: The Powerful Influence of Music on Young Children's Development.* Washington, DC: Zero to Three.

Madden, Lee. 2006. "Taking It All In." *Children and Libraries* 4, no. 3 (Spring): 15–16.

Maddigan, Beth. 2003. *The Big Book of Stories, Songs and Sing Alongs: Programs for Babies, Toddlers and Families.* Westport, CT: Libraries Unlimited.

Marino, Jane. 2003. *Babies in the Library!* Lanham, MD: Scarecrow Press.

_____. 1992. *Mother Goose Time: Library Programs for Babies and Their Caregivers.* New York: H.W. Wilson.

Martin, Bill. 1967. *Brown Bear, Brown Bear, What Do You See?* New York: Henry Holt.

McClure, Vimala. 2000. *Infant Massage: A Handbook for Loving Parents.* New York: Bantam Books.

McDonnell, Flora. 1994. *I Love Animals.* Cambridge, MA: Candlewick Press.

McGuinness, Diane. 2004. *Growing a Reader from Birth: Your Child's Path from Language to Literacy.* New York: W.W. Norton & Co.

McKechnie, Lynn. 2004. "The Young Child/Adult Caregiver Storytime Program as Information Ground." Paper presented at Library Research Seminar III, Kansas City, MO, October.

Miller, Anne Meeker. 2007. *Baby Sing & Sign. Communicate Early with Your Baby: Learning Signs the Fun Way through Music & Play.* New York: Marlowe.

Miller, Karen. 1999. *Simple Steps: Developmental Activities for Infants, Toddlers, and Two Year Olds.* Beltsville, MD: Gryphon House.

Murphy, Mary. 1966. *Caterpillar's Wish.* New York: DK Publishing.

Odean, Kathleen. 2003. *Great Books for Babies and Toddlers: More Than 500 Recommended Books For Your Child's First Three Years.* New York: Ballantine Books.

Orozco, Jose-Luis. 1997. *Diez Deditos: Ten Little Fingers & Other Play Rhymes and Action Songs from Latin America.* New York: Puffin Books.

Oxenbury, Helen. 1999. *All Fall Down.* New York: Little Simon.

_____. 1999. *Clap Hands.* New York: Little Simon.

Preschool Services and Parent Education Committee/Association for Library Services to Children. 2000. *How to Learn and Grow with Music: A Selective Audio List for Infants and Toddlers.* Chicago: American Library Association.

Raines, Shirley, Karen Miller, and Leah Curry-Rood. 2002. *Story S-t-r-e-t-c-h-e-r-s for Infants, Toddlers, and Twos: Experiences, Activities and Games for Popular Children's Books.* Beltsville, MD: Gryphon House.

Schertle, Alice. 2002. *All You Need for a Snowman.* San Diego: Harcourt.

Schickedanz, Judith A. 1999. *Much More than the ABCs: The Early Stages of Reading and Writing.* Washington, DC: National Association for the Education of Young Children.

Schiller, Pam. 2005. *The Complete Resource Book for Infants: Over 700 Experiences for Children from Birth to 18 Months.* Beltsville, MD: Gryphon House.

Schiller, Pam, Rafael Lara-Alecio, and Beverly J. Irby. 2004. *The Bilingual Book of Rhymes, Songs, Stories, and Fingerplays.* El Libro Bilingue de Rimas, Canciones, Cuentos y Juegos. Beltsville, MD: Gryphon House.

Shonkoff, Jack P., and Deborah A. Phillips, ed. 2000. *From Neurons to Neighborhoods: The Science of Early Childhood Development.* Washington, DC: National Academy Press.

Shore, Rebecca. 2002. *Baby Teacher: Nurturing Neural Networks from Birth to Age Five.* Lanham, MD: ScarecrowEducation Book.

Shore, Rebecca, and Janis Strasser. 2006. "Music for Their Minds." *Young Children* 61 (March): 62–67.

Sierra, Judy. 1997. *The Flannel Board Storytelling Book.* New York: Wilson.

Silberg, Jackie. 1998. *I Can't Sing Book for Grownups Who Can't Carry a Tune in a Paper Bag . . . But Want to Do Music with Young Children.* Beltsville, MD: Gryphon House.

_____. 1999. *125 Brain Games for Babies.* Beltsville, MD: Gryphon House.

_____. 2001. *Games to Play with Babies*, 3rd ed. Beltsville, MD: Gryphon House.

_____. 2002. *Games to Play with Toddlers*, rev. ed. Beltsville, MD: Gryphon House.

Silberg, Jackie, and Pam Schiller. 2003. *The Complete Book of Rhymes, Songs, Poems, Fingerplays, and Chants.* Beltsville, MD: Gryphon House.

Sousa, Edward. 2005. *How the Brain Learns to Read.* Thousand Oaks, CA: Corwin Press.

Stetson, Emily, and Vicky Stetson. 2001. *Little Hands Fingerplays and Action Songs.* Charlotte, VT: Williamson Publishing.

Stokes, Beverly. 2002. *Amazing Babies: Essential Movement for Your Baby in the First Year.* Toronto, ON: Move Alive Media.

Trelease, Jim. 2001. *The Read-Aloud Handbook.* New York: Penguin.

Walter, Virginia. 2001. *Children and Libraries: Getting It Right.* Chicago: American Library Association.

Watkins, Jan. 2006. "Grandparents Raising Grandchildren: The Growing Task Facing a New Generation." *Children and Libraries* 4 (Spring): 13–14.

Waycie, Linda. 2006. "Groups for Grandparents Raising Grandchildren." *Children and Libraries* 4 (Spring): 17–18.

Wells, Rosemary. 1997. *Read to Your Bunny.* New York: Scholastic.

Willner, Isabel. 2000. *The Baby's Game Book.* New York: Greenwillow.

Wilmes, Liz, and Dick Wilmes. 1994. *Felt Board Fun.* Elgin, IL: Building Blocks.

————. 1985. *Parachute Play.* Elgin, IL: Building Blocks.

Woodfield, Julia. 2004. *Healing Massage for Babies and Toddlers.* Edinburgh, UK: Floris Books.

Yolen, Jane. 2006. *This Little Piggy: Lap Songs, Finger Plays, Clapping Games, and Pantomime Rhymes.* Cambridge, MA: Candlewick.

Young Children, the Journal of the National Association for the Education of Young Children. 61 (July 2006), section focusing on early childhood development, 12–56.

Zigler, Edward F., Dorothy G. Singer, and Sandra J. Bishop-Josef. 2004. *Children's Play: The Roots of Reading.* Washington, DC: Zero to Three.

Zuravicky, Orli. 2005. *Baby Faces.* New York: Rosen Publishing Group.

Electronic Resources

Adelaide Hills Council—Library Services—*Baby Bounce & Rhyme* booklet
www.ahc.sa.gov.au/site/page.cfm?u=151

American Association of Retired People.
http://aarp.org

American Library Association. *Every Child Ready to Read @ Your Library.*
www.ala.org/ala/pla/plaissues/earlylit/earlyliteracy.htm

ALSC. *Born to Read: How to Raise a Reader.*
www.ala.org/ala/alsc/alscresources/borntoread/bornread.htm

American Sign Language Web.
http://commtechlab.msu.edu/sites/aslweb/browser.htm

Brooklyn Public Library. Brooklyn Reads to Babies.
www.brooklynpubliclibrary.org/first5years/pdf/BRTBALA2007.pdf

Clearinghouse on Early Education and Parenting.
http://ceep.crc.uiuc.edu/eecearchive

Family Place @ Middle Country Public Library.
www.mcpl.lib.ny.us/familyplace

First Book.
   www.firstbook.org
Gayle's Preschool Rainbow.
   www.preschoolrainbow.org/preschool-rhymes.htm
HandSpeak.
   www.handspeak.com
Head Start.
   www.acf.hhs.gov/programs/hsb
Hennepin County Library.
   www.hclib.org/BirthTo6/Newsletter/newsletter.html
Institute for Learning & Brain Sciences.
   http://ilabs.washington.edu/index.html
Kidzsing Garden of Song.
   www.gardenofsong.com
King County Library System.
   www.kcls.org
Kirchoefer, Kathy. Babies Into Books.
   www.prge.lib.md.us/Bks-Info/ParentsBIB.html
Lambert, Sylvia Leigh. Mother Goose Time Pathfinder: Library Programs with
   Books and Babies.
   www.unc.edu/~sllamber/pathfinder/mothergooseindex.html
Lessen-Firestone, Joan. *Building Children's Brains.*
   www.mi-aimh.msu.edu/publications/JoanFirestone.pdf
The Library Development Division of the Texas State Library and Archives Commission.
   www.tsl.state.tx.us/ld/projects/trc/2005/manual/toddlers
Library of Congress. Center for the Book.
   www.loc.gov/loc/cfbook
Martin-Diaz, Pamela, Sharon Deeds, and Deb Nobble. 2006. "Leave No Pre-Schooler
   or Toddler Behind: Summer Reading Programs and Our Youngest Patrons."
   Public Library Association Conference.
   http://www.placonference.org/2006/handouts_audiotapes.cfm
McDowell, Kate. Babies' Lap Time.
   www.itg.uiuc.edu/people/mcdowell/laptime/index.html. The Urbana Free Library.
Montgomery County Public Libraries.
   www.montgomerycountymd.gov/content/libraries
Mother Goose Pages.
   www.personal.umich.edu/%7Epfa/dreamhouse/nursery/rhymes.html
Multnomah County Library.
   www.multcolib.org
National Association for the Education of Young Children.
   www.naeyc.org
National Literacy Trust. Talk To Your Baby.
   www.talktoyourbaby.org.uk

National Center for Education Statistics.
  www.nces.ed.gov
National Center for Early Development & Learning (NCEDL).
  www.fpg.unc.edu/~ncedl/PAGES/research.cfm
National Institutes of Health.
  www.niehs.nih.gov/kids/musicchild.htm
National Center for Family Literacy.
  www.famlit.org
National Early Childhood Technical Assistance Center.
  www.nectac.org/
Pikes Peak Library District. Grandparents Raising Grandchildren.
  http://library.ppld.org/Kids?ForParentsAndTeachers/LinkPicks.asp
Prince George's County Memorial Library System.
  www.prge.lib.md.us/LibraryCenter/ParentsBIB.html
Public Library Association/Association for Library Services to Children. 2005. *Every Child Ready to Read @ Your Library*. Chicago: PLA/ALSC.
  www.ala.org/ala/alsc/ECRR/ECRRHomePage.htm
Public Library of Charlotte and Mecklenburg County. Read to Me, Charlotte!
  http://plcmc.org/readtomecharlotte/default.asp
Reach Out and Read.
  http://www.reachoutandread.org
Reading is Fundamental.
  http://rif.org
Read To Me Program, Inc.
  www.readtomeprogram.org/
Reading Rockets.
  www.readingrockets.org/atoz
Stewart, Nancy.
  www.nancymusic.com
Talaris Research Institute.
  www.talaris.org
Texas State Library/El Día de Los Niños: El Día de Los Libros.
  www.tsl.state.tx.us/ld/projects/ninos/index.html
Trelease, Jim.
  www.trelease-on-reading.com
Tufts University Child and Family Web Guide.
  www.cfw.tufts.edu/topic/4/76.htm
Washington State Department of Social and Health Services. BrainNet.
  www.brainnet.wa.gov
Washington State Department of Health—Child Profile.
  www.childprofile.org/hpmats/materials.html
Zero to Three.
  www.zerotothree.org

Distributors and Suppliers

AccuCut
www.accucut.com
1035 E. Dodge St.
Fremont, NE 68025
800-288-1670

Amazon
www.amazon.com

Baby Signs
www.babysigns.com
871 Cotting Ct., Suite I
Vacaville, CA 95688
800-995-0226

Badge-A-Minit
www.badgeaminit.com
345 North Lewis Ave.
Oglesby, IL 61348
800-223-4103
Fax: 815-883-9696

Beyond Play: Early Intervention Products for Young Children with Special Needs
www.beyondplay.com
1442A Walunut St. #52
Berkeley, CA 94709
877-428-1244

Bound-to-Stay-Bound
www.btsb.com

Childcraft
www.childcrafteducation.com
PO Box 3239
Lancaster, PA 17604
888-532-4453

ChildWood
8873 Woodbank Dr.
Bainbridge Island, WA 98110
800-362-9825

Community Playthings
www.communityplaythings.com
359 Gibson Hill Rd.
Chester, NY 10918-2321
800-777-4244

DEMCO
www.demco.com
PO Box 7488
Madison, WI 53707-7488
800-962-4463

Dover Publications, Inc.
31 E. 2nd St.
Mineola, NY 11501

Ellison Educational Equipment
www.ellison.com
PO Box 8309
Newport Beach, CA 92658-8209
800-253-2238

Environments, Inc.
www.environments@eichild.com
PO Box 1348
Beaufort, SC 29901-1348
800-EI-CHILD (800-342-4453)

Folkmanis
www.folkmanis.com
510-658-7677

Gaylord
PO Box 4901
Syracuse, NY 13221-4901
800-448-6160

Highsmith/Upstart
www.highsmith.com
W5527 State Rd. 106
PO Box 800
Fort Atkinson, WI 53538-0800
800-448-4887

International Playthings, Inc.
www.intplay.com
75D Lackawanna Ave.
Parsippany, NJ 07054
800-445-8347

Kidstamps
www.kidstamps.com
PO Box 18699
Cleveland Heights, OH 44118
800-727-5437

Kimbo Educational: the Children's Music Company
www.kimboed.com
PO Box 477M
Long Branch, NJ 07740-0477
800-631-2187

Lakeshore Learning
www.lakeshorelearning.com
2695 E. Dominguez St.
Carson, CA 90895
800-778-4456

Learning Resources
www.learningresources.com
380 N. Fairway Dr.
Vernon Hills, IL 60061
800-333-8281

Miss Jackie Music Company
jsilberg@interserv.com
5000 West 112th St.
Leawood, KS 66211

Music for Little People
www.mflp.com
POBox 757
Greenland, NH 03840
800-409-2457

Nurturing Pathways
www.nurturingpathways.com
18429 12th Ave. W.
Lynnwood, WA 98037
425-280-3805

Oriental Trading Company
www.orientaltrading.com
800-875-8480

Playsongs Publications Limited
www.playsongs.co.uk
Wimbish Lower Green
Saffron Walden, Essex
CB10 2XH
UK
Phone: 01799 599 054

Preschool Express
www.preschoolexpress.com

Ravenna Ventures, Inc.
www.ravennaventures.com
4756 Universtiy Village Pl. NE #117
Seattle, WA 98105
206-528-7556

Scholastic (in the Teachers Store)
http://shop.scholastic.com

Sign2me
www.sign2me.com
12125 Harbour Reach Dr., Ste. D
Mukilteo, WA 98275
877-744-6263

Sisters-in-Stitches
www.sisters-in-stitches.com
2423 Virginia
Everett, WA 98201
866-259-4140

SmileMakers
www.smilemakers.com
PO Box 2543
Spartanburg, SC 29304
800-825-8085
Fax: 800-825-6358

Canada
91 Station St. Unit 4
Ajax, ON L1S 3H2
800-667-5000
Fax: 800-223-2058

Rhyme, Fingerplay, and Song Title Index

Picture Book Title Index

225

Picture Book Author Index

Picture book titles by theme can be found in Chapter 11, pp. 161–173.

General Index

About the Author

Linda L. Ernst has been a children's librarian for the past 30 years. Actively serving very young children and their caregivers has been an important part of her job and one of the most enjoyable ones. Just as parents are encouraged to keep it simple and start early to expose their children to the world of language and literature, Ernst offers assistance in applying this knowledge to the areas of library service and programming for very young children. She has given training workshops for the King County Library, Seattle Public Library, Everett Public Library, and the Sno-Isle Library System in Washington. She has also given workshops in Kentucky, Michigan, San Francisco, and Scottsdale, Arizona. Conference programs include the Pennsylvania Library Association and the Washington Library Association. She has guided and encouraged adults to discover, develop, and to share the early literacy experience with very young children.

The Children's and Young Adult Services Interest Group of the Washington Library Association awarded Ernst the 2004 CAYAS Award for Visionary Library Service to Youth. Ernst has served as chair of the Early Childhood Programs and Services Committee for the Association for Library Service to Children and was a member of the 2007 Caldecott Award committee. She is currently employed by the King County Library System in Washington. This is her third book on the topic of libraries and very young children.